THE FAMINE IRISH

THE FAMINE IRISH

EMIGRATION AND THE GREAT HUNGER

EDITED BY CIARÁN REILLY

First published 2016

The History Press Ireland
50 City Quay
Dublin 2
Ireland
www.thehistorypress.ie

The History Press Ireland is a member of Publishing Ireland, the Irish book publishers' association.

British Library Cataloguing in Publication Data.
A catalogue record for this book is available from the British Library.

ISBN 978 1 84588 890 9

Typesetting and origination by The History Press

Printed and bound by TJ International Ltd

Contents

Acknowledgements

This collection of essays emanates from the Third Annual International Famine Conference, which was held at the Irish National Famine Museum at Strokestown Park House, County Roscommon in July 2013. Fittingly, to mark the year-long celebration, 'The Gathering', the theme of the conference examined 'The Famine Irish' and their experience of emigration during the 1840s and after. Bringing researchers together with a network of international experts, the conference approached the theme from the broadest possible historical perspective. Over the course of two days, the conference heard thoughtful and wide-ranging analysis of emigration and the diaspora during and after the Great Irish Famine. The quality of the papers delivered highlighted that the proceedings added significantly to the growing corpus of Famine and diaspora studies. The essays included in this volume demonstrate that where once distance may have hindered the study of Irish Famine emigrants, a new generation of scholars are making use of the wide availability of sources online and elsewhere. Indeed, the use of sources is particularly noteworthy, opening up as it does the individual experience of Irish Famine emigrants. Using these myriad of 'new' sources, the essays challenge long-held assumptions about the Famine Irish and provide a remarkable insight into the personal and family circumstances of some of those who were scattered across the globe. Moreover, they also lay the foundation for similar studies of the Irish émigré in locations not covered in the present volume.

A number of people are owed thanks for facilitating the conference in 2013 and for ensuring the completion of this collection of essays. Firstly, my sincere thanks to the contributors for their patience, expertise and diligence in the preparation of their essays. Likewise, thanks is owed to Professor Marian Lyons and Professor Terence Dooley of the Department of History, Maynooth University; Tim O'Connor, chairman of The Gathering Ireland 2013; Nollaig Feeney, Roscommon Heritage Officer; Michael Blanch, Committee for the Commemoration of the Irish Famine Victims and Pat McCarrick, Botháir. At Strokestown, the efforts of Jim Callery, Patrick Kenny, Caroilin Callery and Declan Jones have contributed immeasurably to the various conferences that have been held there annually since 2011. Likewise, John O'Driscoll, curator and general manager at Strokestown Park House, deserves special mention and thanks for his assistance in organising the Annual Famine Conference and other events. I am very grateful to Ronan Colgan, Beth Amphlett and the staff of The History Press Ireland for their dedication and willingness to publish this volume of essays. Lastly, the continued support of my family is greatly appreciated and in particular a special mention to Tara, Donnacha and Odhrán.

In his opening remarks to the conference in July 2013, and which follow, Tim O'Connor, chairman of The Gathering, complimented the speakers for their efforts, reminding them that their scholarship was a means of connecting with the thousands who left Ireland in the 1840s and after. It is in that spirit, then, that this book is offered.

Ciarán Reilly

Notes on Contributors

FIDELMA BYRNE is an Irish Research Council Postgraduate Scholar. Her research interests include nineteenth- and twentieth-century social history, landed estates and assisted emigration. She is currently completing her doctoral thesis entitled 'Estate management practices on the Wentworth-Fitzwilliam estates in Yorkshire and Ireland: a comparative study, 1815–65' at Maynooth University.

REGINA DONLON graduated with a PhD from Maynooth University in 2014. She is currently working as an Irish Research Council Postdoctoral Research Fellow at the National University of Ireland, Galway where her work examines assisted emigration from the west of Ireland to the American Midwest during the period from 1880 to 1930. Her research interests include Irish and European diasporas, American history in the Reconstruction era and transnationalism.

MARY LEE DUNN MA, whose Roscommon ancestors came from Kilglass parish and Elphin, is an independent scholar, former journalist, and a founder of the Ballykilcline Society. She is author of *Ballykilcline Rising: From Famine Ireland to Immigrant America* (2008) and continues her Irish research. She lives in Maine.

JAMES M. FARRELL is a Professor of Rhetoric and Chairperson in the Department of Communication at the University of New Hampshire, where he teaches classes in argumentation, propaganda, rhetorical theory, rhetorical criticism, and American public address. He received his PhD from the University of Wisconsin-Madison in 1988, and has published numerous critical and historical studies of eighteenth- and nineteenth-century American discourse.

LAWRENCE W. KENNEDY is a professor of history at the University of Scranton where he has taught since 1992. He earned his undergraduate and graduate degrees at Boston College and is the author of *Planning the City upon a Hill: Boston since 1630* (1992) and co-author of *Boston: A Topographical History* 3rd edition (2000). He has also written *Bricklayer Bill and the Workingman's Boston Marathon* with his son Patrick L. Kennedy (anticipated publication 2017) and is working on another book, *Patrick A. Collins: Irish Emigrant and American Politician, 1844-1905*.

CHRISTINE KINEALY has published extensively on nineteenth-century Irish history, particularly on the Famine era. Her publications include, *Charity and the Great Hunger: The Kindness of Strangers* (Bloomsbury, 2013) and *Repeal and Revolution: 1848 in Ireland* (Manchester University Press, 2009). She is founding Director of Ireland's Great Hunger institute at Quinnipiac University.

JASON KING is an Irish Research Council Postdoctoral Researcher in the Moore Institute at the National University of Ireland, Galway. He was previously a lecturer at the University of Limerick, Maynooth University, and an Assistant Professor of Canadian Irish Studies at Concordia University. His research specialises in Irish Famine memory and migration in past and present literary representations and performance. He is the curator of the digital Irish Famine Archive: http://faminearchive.nuigalway.ie.

PERRY MCINTYRE is an Adjunct Lecturer at the University of New South Wales and has worked as a genealogist, freelance historian and archivist for over twenty years. She has served on the committees of the History Council of New South Wales, the Society of Australian Genealogists, the Royal Australian Historical Society, the Australian Catholic Historical Society and the Great Irish Famine Commemoration Committee (chair 2012–15). She has published and spoken extensively on immigration and family history in Australia and Ireland. Her PhD on convict family reunion was published in 2010 by IAP as *Free Passage: The Reunion of Irish Convicts and their Families in Australia, 1788–1852*. She is a director of Anchor Books, Australia, formed to publish history, particularly relating to colonial Australia.

GERARD MORAN is Co-ordinator of History at the European School, Lacken, Brussels and has been a lecturer in the Department of History at NUI Galway and Maynooth University, where he established and was the Director of its MA in Irish History programme. His research interests include the Irish diaspora, the Great Famine and landlord and tenant relations in Ireland. He is the author of *Sending out Ireland's Poor: Assisted Emigration from Ireland in the Nineteenth Century* (2004), and joint editor of *Galway: History and Society* (1996) and *Mayo: History and Society* (2014).

BLÁTHNAID NOLAN graduated with a PhD from the School of Social Justice, UCD in 2013. Her thesis was titled *Power, Punishment and Penance: An Archival Analysis of the Transportation of Women from Grangegorman in Dublin to Hobart Town in Van Diemen's Land (Tasmania) 1844–1853*. She is an Honorary Associate of the University of Tasmania and has presented papers nationally and internationally. Her research interests include convict transportation, social history, history of criminology, penal history, colonial history, the British Empire, prosopography, and nineteenth-century history.

TIM O'CONNOR runs his own advisory business providing strategic advice and support to companies and organisations. His clients cover a range of sectors from financial services to renewable energy. He has also held several voluntary positions, including Chairmanship of the Advisory Board of The Gathering Ireland 2013. He worked in the Irish public service from 1972 to early 2010, most recently as Secretary General (Chief of Staff) to the President of Ireland. His career also includes almost thirty years in the Irish diplomatic service, in the Department of Foreign Affairs. A large portion of his career was spent working on the Northern Ireland Peace Process, including the Good Friday Agreement. He was the inaugural joint secretary of the North/South Ministerial Council (based in Armagh, Northern Ireland), established under the Agreement. He has also served terms as Director of the Africa Unit and of the Human Rights Unit in the Department of Foreign Affairs. His foreign postings included the embassies of Ireland in Bonn and Washington DC and most recently, from 2005–2007, he was Consul General of Ireland in New York, USA, with the rank of ambassador. From Killeedy in West Limerick, and educated at St Munchin's College, Limerick, Tim was awarded honorary doctorates from Maynooth University, the University of Ulster and Quinnipiac University (Connecticut, USA).

MICHAEL QUIGLEY is editor of the Canadian Association for Irish Studies Newsletter, formerly historian for Action Grosse Île, author of numerous essays on Grosse Île and the Great Hunger, and on local history subjects in Hamilton, Ontario. He holds a doctorate from McMaster University.

RICHARD REID is a graduate of Trinity College, Dublin and emigrated from Ireland to Australia in 1972. Until retirement in 2013 he worked as a high school teacher, museum education officer, exhibition curator and as a senior historian for an Australian federal government department. He gained his doctorate from the Australian National University in 1992 for a study of Irish assisted emigration to New South Wales from 1848 to 1870. Between 2007 and 2011 he was the National Museum of Australia's Senior Curator for the major exhibition – 'Not Just Ned: A True History of the Irish in Australia, 1788 to the present'. He is currently working, with others, on projects relating to Irish emigration to nineteenth-century Australia including the story of the 4,114 Famine orphans sent to that country from Irish workhouses between 1848 and 1850.

CIARÁN REILLY is a Postdoctoral Research Fellow at the Centre for the Study of Historic Irish Houses & Estates, Maynooth University. His publications include *The Irish Land Agent, 1830–1860: The case of King's County* (2014); *Strokestown and the Great Irish Famine* (2014) and *John Plunket Joly and the Great Famine in King's County* (2012).

DAMIAN SHIELS is an archaeologist and historian. Formerly one of the curators of the 'Soldiers & Chiefs' Military History Exhibition at the National Museum of Ireland, he is currently a Director with Rubicon Heritage Services Ltd and author of *The Irish in the American Civil War* (2013). In addition, he hosts a website on the Irish experience of that conflict at www.irishamericancivilwar.com.

Abbreviations

AOH	Ancient Order of Hibernians
CLEC	Colonial Land and Emigration Commissioners
CRF	Convict Reference File
NLI	National Library of Ireland
NAI	National Archives of Ireland
NARA	National Archives Records Administration
NYPL	New York Public Library
NSW	New South Wales
SA	Sheffield Archives
SRNSW	State Records New South Wales

NOTE ON MONEY

£ pounds
s shillings
d pence

Preface

Opening remarks by Tim O'Connor, chairman of The Gathering and former Irish Consul General in New York, at the Third Annual International Famine Conference at Strokestown Park House, 19 July 2013

I am delighted and honoured to open this timely and important conference which is taking place this year as part of our Gathering Ireland 2013 Initiative, which I have the privilege to chair. My thanks to Dr Ciarán Reilly for inviting me to make the opening remarks and to Ciarán and his colleagues at Maynooth University, particularly Professor Marian Lyons and Professor Terence Dooley, for their great support for The Gathering project generally. In the beautiful environs of Strokestown Park House, I must also make honourable mention of the Callery family, in particular Jim and Adeline, and to Caroilin for the fantastic work she has done in organising the overall Strokestown Gathering, which also begins today, and in which this Conference plays a key part. Could I also pay tribute to the great work of all involved in the Strokestown Famine Museum, a tremendous national asset, where our conference is taking place – General Manager John O'Driscoll and also Declan Jones and Patrick Kenny from the Westward Group, who have put so much into giving us this wonderful facility. I call the conference timely and important because it is both; timely because it sits right in the middle of The Gathering year, in which there is higher focus than ever before on the relationship between Ireland and its global family, and important because the subject matter of your deliberations shines a light right at the heart of that episode in Irish history which more than any other contributed to the reality that the Irish became an emigrant people, the Great Famine.

Firstly, however, a quick word about The Gathering Ireland 2013 initiative itself. A major feature of its origins was the need for a boost to our tourism industry. And it is certainly doing that. The Gathering, which is a government initiative and enjoys the strong support of the Taoiseach and the Tánaiste, was formally unveiled as a project by the Minister for Transport, Tourism and Sport, Leo Varadkar in October 2011. A project team was established in Fáilte Ireland, and Roscommon's own Jim Miley, the project director, and his team have been doing a great job getting the project up and out there, under the overall political direction, and with the strong personal support of Minister Varadkar and Minister of State at the Department of Tourism, the West's own Michael Ring. The overseas promotion and marketing for The Gathering is being expertly done by Tourism Ireland. I have the honour to serve in a voluntary capacity as the chairman of the Project Advisory Board. This is a group of people drawn from government, industry, academia, local government and the arts, and our role is to provide support and counsel to the project. It also includes Frank Dawson, the esteemed Roscommon County Manager and I want to take this opportunity to thank Frank for his wisdom and support. A word also about the great contribution being made by Frank's colleagues in the city and county councils, local development networks and Ireland Reaching Out in the roll-out of the project around the country, and indeed that of the insurance company Irish Public Bodies, who put €1 million into a community fund, which the government matched, and which has helped greatly also in terms of supporting that community engagement.

However, the real heroes of the project are the people of Ireland who have embraced The Gathering in their thousands. As we speak, we have 4,200 Gatherings registered on our website. These are drawn from parishes, communities, groups, clubs, educational, cultural and sporting organisations, companies and families, all around the country – all stepping up to the plate to do their bit, to make their contribution – and extending an invitation to our people around the world to return and gather with us sometime during 2013. And as I keep reminding people, 4,200 Gatherings isn't just 4,200 events and weekends. No, like this one in Strokestown, it is 4,200 committees meeting for months on end, planning, preparing, organising, thinking through, worrying, caring, inviting. The Gathering has been an enormous exercise in community engagement and endeavour, with big implications for the future. And the diaspora has responded. In their tens of thousands. As matters stand, visitor numbers are up over 6 per cent for the first five months of the year and over 15 per cent from North America, which is a great achievement at a time when tourism out of America as a whole is down 3 per cent. This is all very encouraging in tourism terms, and at The Gathering we are delighted about that. The tourism sector is a vital part of our economy, employing over 200,000 people and contributing 4 per cent to our national GNP. Of course, The Gathering goes beyond tourism, important as that sector is. In its essence it is about the enduring nature of the bond and connection that exist between those of us who stayed and those who left Ireland.

Having been part of The Gathering project for three years now, I have enjoyed a particular vantage point in terms of being able to observe it all close up and to reflect on the new insights about the nature of our relationship with the diaspora that are emerging as a result of the project. In doing so, I stress that I am not an academic scholar and these observations are personal ones of my own. Think of them as findings from the field, some of which may have validity in your eyes and some which may not – I will leave that to your own good judgement as scholars of the area. The other point I would make is that this is an evolving story and our understanding of its essence is changing as we learn more. What I do know for sure is that The Gathering has injected a significant new dynamic into the diaspora space in the Ireland context and I think it is only right that those of us who care about the relationship between us and our scattered kith should try to draw as much as we can from what it is telling us.

One obvious feature that The Gathering has served to shine a particular light on is the question of why 70 million people around the world regard their identity as Irish – what is such a sense of connection by so many people, including after several generations, all about? I suppose one of the thoughts that I have had on this as the year has progressed is that it may perhaps have to do with the DNA of the Irish. I asked a scholar friend of mine to put a number on the length of time Irish had been the spoken language of the people of the island of Ireland until its decline and loss in the nineteenth century. He said about 2,500 years. So the case can be made that the Irish – and I know there can be a big debate about that term, but let's at least say 'the people living on this island' – were a communal, clan-centred, cohesive, close-knit society with our own language for over two and a half millennia. And then, less than 200 years ago, two seismic events intervened to change everything – the dramatic decline in the use of Irish as a spoken language, and the Great Famine, which resulted in a huge portion of our people either dying or emigrating. As we know, that process of emigration has continued apace in the 170 years or so since then, accelerating in the decades after independence in 1922. As a result, there are now multiple times more people of Irish identity living overseas than there are in Ireland itself, a remarkable reality.

A thought occurred to me from all of that – it could be argued that the 170 years or so since the Famine is actually a very brief block of time in the context of two and half millennia and not enough to alter the fundamental DNA of the Irish in terms of being a people of community and kinship. And that therefore, whether we are aware of it or not, that context has meant that the process of separation involved in emigration over the generations has resulted in a sense of, can I call it, psychic loss, for both sides – both for those who left and for those who stayed. A bit like the sensation for twins who are separated at an early stage in life and experience during their subsequent lives apart a sense of not being quite fully whole.

Before I'm taken to task by the scholars, let me fully acknowledge that there is a further dimension of course in the Ireland story in the form of the relationship with England and the consequences of that, including through the plantations of the northern part of the island during the seventeenth century. The story of the Ulster Scots in the Ireland narrative and the significant numbers of that community who emigrated during the eighteenth and nineteenth century, particularly to North America, is an important piece of our demographic and diaspora jigsaw in its own right and deserving of a full study of its own. However, I don't believe it takes from the basic point I'm making above about what I would call the indigenous Irish.

I have two other interesting fragments from the field to share with you, both taken from *The Irish Times*. Firstly, in an interesting article on emigration on 21 March 2013 in *The Irish Times*, Irial Glynn from University College Cork included a quote from a great Maynooth professor of my era, Fr Liam Ryan, and it went like this: 'Emigration is a mirror in which the Irish nation can always see its true face'. A fascinating observation by a great scholar. Secondly, on 29 June 2013, *The Irish Times* reported on the Kennedy Gathering in Wexford the previous day. This involved the visit by over thirty members of the Kennedy clan commemorating the visit to Ireland fifty years ago of President Kennedy. The report quoted two comments from one of the Kennedy delegation, Douglas Kennedy, the youngest son of Bobby. He said that those four days of the visit to Ireland were the happiest days in the life of JFK – a pretty remarkable statement given the context. And secondly and even more profoundly, Douglas Kennedy observed that during those four days, JFK 'came to himself'. A remarkable claim and, if true, what an amazing insight – and certainly one for the scholars to ponder!

I wanted to make an attempt to add a thought of my own to Douglas Kennedy's great insight: if JFK came to himself during the four days of that iconic visit, then perhaps so did we, the people of Ireland. Four decades after independence, with little to show for it in terms of progress, and coming out of a further episode of mass and brutal emigration in the 1950s, with a real question mark about whether we could make it as an independent country, there came into our midst this extraordinary man, the most powerful person in the world – and he was one of us. The national lift was palpable. In the face of one who had left we saw the potential of our own possibility. That is why I say perhaps in those four days we also came to ourselves. Reading Douglas Kennedy's comment certainly put Liam Ryan's great insight into a new context. Perhaps that mirror Liam Ryan talked about was on full display in that farmyard in Wexford in June 1963.

However, I suppose my biggest learning in the course of The Gathering was about our role here at home. My biggest exposure to the diaspora issue was during my two years as Consul General of Ireland in New York from 2005 to 2007. I was frankly astonished by the scale of Irish America – their impact in the US, the way they shaped New York and still do today, exemplified by how the city becomes demonstrably Irish on St Patrick's Day, not as a sop to the Irish but as a true reflection of the centrality of our people to the place. Truly amazing. I left New York to return to Ireland in 2007 with a huge sense of the possibility of the diaspora space for Ireland. But the big shift for me as a result of The Gathering was the dawning of the realisation over the last year or so that the centre of gravity of the relationship does not lie out there but rather here at home. And that if the relationship between Ireland and its diaspora is to go to another level, the onus of first mover rests with us, the people living here in Ireland. Why? Because we are the custodians of the shared home place, the place where all the journeys began, theirs and ours. It is we, the people living here today, not those who left, who get to decide the wording of the notice on the gate of the home place – whether 'Keep Out', 'Don't Care' or 'Welcome Home'.

By the generous way they have embraced The Gathering, the people of Ireland have given their emphatic answer to that question and to what that notice should say. They have demonstrated in a powerful and moving way that they are willing and indeed eager to take up that role of custodian of the shared home place and extend the hand of authentic welcome to their kith around the world. The response of the diaspora has been tremendous, as the number of visitors shows. Even more profound has been the kind of engagement that has been happening at The Gatherings, when those who stayed come together with those who left. In a new way, what we are doing through The Gathering is assuming, this time in a very conscious and thoughtful way, our role on behalf of those who left as 'custodians of the shared home place', taking responsibility for doing the inviting and saying to the scattered: 'We welcome you back home, tell us your story and we celebrate you'. The result, as I say, has been moving and powerful and I have experienced several examples of this myself over the past weeks and months.

As we enter the decade of centenaries, and move towards Ireland at 100, I'm excited, therefore, about the new era which could be opening up in the relationship between Ireland and our remarkable diaspora. Despite the distances of geography and generation, the reality is that we remain *muintir* to each other and that is something of potentially huge value for both sides. What is now available is the possibility of a new understanding in the relationship between those who stayed and those who left, which could have major implications for both of us. We who live in Ireland have the opportunity to offer ourselves in a very particular way, as I have just suggested, as the 'custodians of the shared home place' of the heritage we share with the diaspora and their children – and indeed as custodians of the graves of the ancestors of those who left. They in their turn could serve as our pathfinders and support in a complex and globalised world, something that could have huge implications in terms of investment in Ireland, support for Irish companies and tourism.

Speaking of a globalised world, could I mention one other very important group in all of this, in my view – the 17 per cent of the population of Ireland who today are foreign-born; the New Irish, as they are called. The story of these people, also emigrants, who have come from other lands and chosen Ireland as their new home, is an exact parallel of the narrative of our people making theirs in other worlds. They bring with them the same energy and ambition and will to prevail that our people did to their adopted lands and thereby enrich our country just as our people enriched their new worlds. They are also very committed to Ireland and their future among us. I feel strongly that our discourse on and vision of diaspora should include them also in light of the powerful and rich contribution they have to make to our country.

So there we have it. It is over to you now, the scholars and practitioners in this fascinating world. As I said at the beginning, your role is central. For any dimension of the human journey, it makes sense that we understand it as fully as we can, both for its own sake but also so that we can decide on the wisest possible basis what to do with that knowledge. In relation to diaspora, as to any other issue of the human journey, good understanding is the pre-requisite of good action. Historically, emigration has sat in the Irish psyche as a major negative. And, without question, many of its dimensions in the Irish context have been deeply tragic for reasons we all know well. But now, almost 200 years after it began on the enormous scale that we know only too well, this is a timely moment, in the year of The Gathering and in the first year of the decade of centenaries, to take further stock of what the issue means in all its dimensions and in particular to further unpack what I think we all agree is the epicentre of the scattering, the Great Famine. One of the most moving dimensions of the Strokestown Gathering for instance is the visit of Richard Tye from Canada, a direct descendant of young Daniel Tighe, who emigrated from here during the Famine in 1847.

In that regard, I pay great tribute to you, the scholars. I see that work as a kind of 'CSI' on the linkage between the Famine and emigration. I think the work you are doing in following the stories and journeys of the Famine Irish is particularly fascinating, including in the way the threads of those stories and journeys continue all the way down to the present day, as exemplified by the Richard Tye story. If you combine that work with what is unfolding here in Ireland during The Gathering, perhaps we are moving towards an understanding that while the narratives of those who left were and are different to those who stayed, there is also a way in which they remain connected throughout in one overarching narrative as well – back to Liam Ryan's mirror.

1

'Shovelling out the paupers': The Irish Poor Law and assisted emigration during the Great Famine

Gerard Moran

Irish emigration in the nineteenth century was not a homogeneous experience for the estimated 8 million Irish people who left the country in search of a new life abroad. While the broad push and pull factors are used to indicate why the people departed, their emigrant experiences are as numerous as the numbers who left. The magnitude of the exodus was such that until recently historians have not categorised and examined the regional variations of those who emigrated. As David Fitzpatrick points out, the sheer scale of the exodus in the second half of the nineteenth century discouraged historians from standing back in order to appreciate the complexity and diversity of the emigration.[1] In recent years this apprehension has dissipated and historians have begun to examine the various subgroups that comprised this massive exodus, taking on board their background, the voyages to foreign destinations and what became of them after they reached the new lands they travelled to. This has led to a more diverse emigration experience being uncovered between those who had the finances to fund their exodus, such as migrants from Ulster and the surrounding counties in the 1815–1845 period, to those who were assisted by landlords, philanthropists, the government and the Poor Law guardians.[2]

In the nineteenth century nearly 500,000 were assisted by official bodies to emigrate from Ireland, with over 67,000 being aided by the

Poor Law.[3] In 1838 the Irish Poor Law came into existence, based on the system introduced into England four years previously. It was the first attempt to provide a structure in Ireland to deal with local poverty and destitution. While its principle function was to cater for the needs of the destitute population, mainly through the workhouse system, it was also empowered to deal with issues such as assisting people to emigrate, as had been suggested by various parliamentary commissions and select committees in the 1820s and 1830s. In the decades prior to the Great Famine opinion was divided as to the merits of assisting the Irish poor to emigrate. As early as 1817 Col. Robert Torrens had advocated emigration as a solution to the problem of poverty and destitution in Ireland, and by the 1820s other prominent economists such as Thomas Malthus had accepted the principle of sending Ireland's surplus population to the colonies, but only if it was part of an overall package to promote a social 'transition in Ireland'. On the other side George Strickland, a Yorkshire landowner, rejected assisted emigration as the panacea for Irish pauperism, stating that it would only create a vacuum that would be quickly filled up.[4] George Nicholls, the architect of the Irish Poor Law, recommended that some form of assisted emigration be incorporated into the Poor Law with the expense being shared between central government and the Poor Law unions. It was argued the government should contribute its share because the empire would benefit by having a surplus population settle in those colonies with population deficiencies, and individual landowners who assisted their poorer tenants to leave should be given financial assistance through the Poor Law.[5] However, this was rejected by the government because of cost and the only emigration provision that became part of the Poor Law was a clause permitting the boards of guardians, subject to the sanction of a special meeting of the ratepayers, to levy an emigration rate. This could only assist people who had been workhouse inmates for at least three months to settle in a British colony.[6]

There was much disappointment that the Poor Law was not enabled to provide large-scale pauper emigration. Some Poor Law unions bent the rules in order to facilitate emigration, as in Cork where the guardians were prepared to assist destitute paupers in the early 1840s to leave. Their involvement was probably due to a tradition in the city whereby paupers were helped by public and private charity, as in 1835 when 150 girls from the parish of St Mary's, Shandon, were sent to New South Wales. In March 1841 the Cork guardians were in the process of sending 191 paupers to various destinations when they were forced by the Poor Law Commissioners to cancel the plan because of opposition from local ratepayers, who stated that the guardians were exceeding their authority.[7]

In August 1843 the rule relating to Poor Law involvement in assisted emigration was modified, and under section eighteen, if two thirds of the guardians of a union agreed, they could assist people who had been pauper inmates for three months to emigrate to a British colony with the expense being charged to the union or the electoral division where the pauper had originally resided.[8] While this amendment made emigration easier, most unions were still reluctant to participate for financial reasons. Between 1844 and 1846 only 304 people were assisted, 184 leaving in 1846, involving sixteen unions: eight in Ulster (which sent out 244 paupers), four in Leinster, three in Munster and Manorhamilton in Connacht. Many of these were female orphans and single young mothers with children who were sent to Canada. Some received better treatment than others, getting landing money and assistance upon their arrival. Few of the workhouses along the western seaboard participated, the exceptions being Kanturk, Manorhamilton and Kilrush.[9] Most unions were reluctant to become involved in the emigration process because of the increased expenditure, especially those along the western seaboard, many of whom had only recently opened and incurred major debts, and who were seeking ways of cutting funding and were resisting further financial burdens being placed on them. It was also argued that providing assistance would make the workhouses more attractive to every person who wanted to leave, leading to a breakdown in the efficiency of the Poor Law. As one witness, Col. W.A. Clarke, the Poor Law Inspector for Killarney and Kenmare, told the Select Committee of the House of Lords Inquiry into the Poor Law in April 1849, '… every man would conceal his means and come into the workhouse, because he would say, "It gives me title to a free passage"'.[10] Where emigration was introduced it was often at the urgings of Poor Law Inspectors, as in the case of Captain Kennedy in Kilrush, or from local landowners as with Robert Small of Newmarket and Major Ball of Fortfergus. The Poor Law Extension Act of 1847 extended the assisted emigration provisions to all paupers, including those receiving relief outside of the workhouse, but few unions availed of it and the take-up was least in those areas where it was most needed, in particular along the west coast. As Alfred Power, the Assistant Poor Law Commissioner, stated in March 1849, money would have to be made available from outside funds rather than from the resources of the most distressed unions.[11] In some unions there was an ignorance of the emigration provisions, in particular where unelected vice-guardians were in charge. It had to be pointed out to the Galway vice-guardians in November 1848 by Revd Peter Daly and Thomas Birmingham that provision could be made for the ninety-three people that had been evicted in the Kinvara region, with the union at large paying one-third of the cost and the rest coming from the electoral divisions to which the individuals belonged.[12] However, it was virtually impossible for most Poor Law unions to engage in large-scale emigration programmes before 1849 as they were restricted by a cap of 6*d* in the £ for emigration purposes. The amount raised was negligible as it was pointed out it would only result in £100 being available for the Cappaghmore Electoral Division in the Limerick Poor Law Union.[13]

The onset of the Famine in 1845 and 1846 did result in the adoption by the Poor Law of schemes to help people to leave, but the overall figure was negligible. In August 1846, the Sligo guardians selected fifty-six paupers for emigration to Canada at a cost of £4 each, but it is unclear if the plan proceeded for they do not appear on the returns for 1844–6.[14] At this stage the Poor Law guardians throughout the country were looking for increased funding for assisted emigration as a way of dealing with the rapid rise in destitution and their inability to cope with the massive increase in pauper inmate numbers. By late 1846 many unions were experiencing massive financial difficulties, due to the upsurge in the numbers seeking admission to the workhouses and their inability to collect the rates. By this stage many unions were insolvent and over the coming months nearly one quarter had to be replaced by paid vice-guardians.[15]

It was during this period that assisted emigration was given serious consideration as a solution to the problem of over population, destitution and famine. In March 1847, John Robert Godley, the son of a landowner with estates in counties Leitrim and Meath, presented the Prime Minister, Lord John Russell, with a memorial signed by eighty-three noblemen, gentlemen and landed proprietors, which favoured the implementation of assisted emigration to Canada. A number of prominent individuals signed the memorial, including the Church of Ireland Archbishop of Dublin, Richard Whatley; the Earl of

Clanricarde; the Marquis of Sligo; and the Earl of Ormonde. This led to a major debate as to the merits of assisted emigration, and the government was forced to establish the Select Committee on Colonization from Ireland, which was chaired by Lord Monteagle, a strong advocate of emigration to the colonies. While the committee amassed an enormous amount of evidence and statements in favour of assisted emigration, the government was not prepared to fund a large-scale emigration programme because of the cost, and it was against the political economic theory of the day – that of *laissez-faire*. Nevertheless, it did open up the debate as to ways of assisting the poor to leave.[16]

By this stage the Poor Law guardians were examining every avenue to get rid of their long-term pauper inmates, especially females and children and over the next twelve years assisted emigration was one of the major approaches that were used to reduce the number of inmates and cut expenditure. In 1849, Denis O'Connor, the clerk of Limerick Union, said there was no other way of dealing with the large number of servants boys and girls in the workhouse, otherwise they would remain a permanent burden on the rates, while John Walsh, a Poor Law guardian from Kilkenny, argued that it would be better for the workhouse inmate and the economic well-being of the local community if the female pauper inmate was assisted to emigrate as it was costing £5 per year for her upkeep and better use of this money could be made by helping her to leave.[17] The financial argument was also put forward by Mr Minnitt, a Poor Law guardian in Nenagh, when he stated in October 1851 that if the union assisted 1,000 inmates they could recoup the money over two years and in the long term the union would save £3,000 annually.[18] John Vandeleur Stewart, chairman of the Letterkenny Board of Guardians, stated the annual cost of keeping a pauper in the workhouse was £6 1*s*, while the cost of sending that inmate to North America would be £4 10*s*, including provisions and clothing, 'and therefore a pauper family might be placed in a position in the colonies in which he might earn an independent livelihood at a cost which would little exceed his maintenance in the workhouse'.[19]

The people that caused the authorities most concern were the women and children as they were the largest groups within the workhouses with little short-term prospect of leaving the institutions. By February 1847 there were 63,000 young children in the workhouses and by mid-1849 there were 90,000; in Ulster they comprised 52 per cent of the total inmate population.[20] In May 1850 one-third of the adult inmates in Gort were women, and another 973 were girls aged between 9 and 15 years. In Galway, females represented 34 per cent of the total pauper population, and another 18 per cent were girls aged between 9 and 15.[21] Many children entered the workhouses because they were orphaned, but others were abandoned. Between March 1848 and August 1850, 31 per cent of the children in Cork workhouse were classified as having been deserted by their parents.[22] Ellen Griffin deserted her five children, placed them in Kilmallock workhouse and was on her way to North America when she was apprehended and brought before the guardians. She abandoned the children because she was unable to bring the whole family with her.[23] Parents left their children in the workhouses in the hope that they would be provided for, not realising that they could succumb to disease and death; for example, in Ballinrobe workhouse between February and March 1849 there were 428 deaths, including members of the Reed family from Castlebar. After the death of the husband, Lord Lucan evicted the family and the mother decided to go to England, but did not have the passage fares for the three children, who were sent to the workhouse. One of the children died shortly after entering the workhouse.[24] Many parents deserted their children, hoping that at some stage in the future they would be in a position to send back the fares for the children to join them, but such intentions did not always work out, as the parents died on the crossing to North America or at the quarantine stations such as Grosse Île.[25] With no other sanctuary, many children ended up in the workhouses, but this created its own problems as their long-term prospects were bleak and the authorities feared they would remain a permanent burden on the ratepayers. These orphaned and deserted children were regarded as a 'dead weight' by the authorities as it was believed their future prospects were poor.[26]

Women were the other group that caused most concern. Women were more likely than men to have to resort to the safety net of the workhouse in times of need, and their stay tended to be longer. Men could emigrate in search of work and leave their wives to look after the children. Even before the full impact of the potato failure was realised, the number of female inmates greatly outnumbered those of males. Throughout 1846 women comprised about 75 per cent of the adult inmate population in the Cork workhouse and they continued to be the main group over the next five years, while by March 1847 three quarters of the adult inmates in Nenagh workhouse were women.[27] However, the figures for widows in the workhouses are sometimes distorted, as many women entered the workhouse on the basis that their husbands had died, even though they had not. Women also became inmates claiming that they had been deserted by husbands leaving for the USA. According to the Poor Law Inspector, Col. W.A. Clarke:

> … they are not heard of for months, and a great many when they are out there marry again; they forget that they have wives and families at home, and their wives and families remain as permanent paupers in the workhouse.[28]

An examination of alleged desertion indicates that necessity drove many women into the workhouses when their husbands left for Britain or North America or stayed outside, hoping to secure employment. The workhouse thus became the safety net for women in the struggle for survival. For example, Thomas Nestor's wife told Tuam Petty Sessions that her husband had always supported her when he was able to, but in recent times he had been unable to. Edward Grady also appeared before Tuam Petty Sessions on the charge of desertion and not having supported his family for the previous twelve months. Grady told the court his wife had to seek refuge in the workhouse as he was unable to provide for himself, let alone his family, and he would support them if he had employment. He was sentenced to one month's imprisonment.[29] Likewise, Anne Grady applied for admittance to Parsonstown workhouse for herself and her family, stating her husband had deserted her and gone to England.[30] While many females can be legitimately classified as abandoned, others claimed so to gain admittance into the workhouses, but believed their husbands would come for them when their circumstances improved. Thus it was not surprising that a majority of the inmate population were women, comprising 59.5 per cent of the workhouse population in 1851.[31]

This vast female pauper population created problems for the authorities. The unions attempted to keep the women occupied, but given the numbers this was difficult to achieve. In June 1849, the Galway vice-guardians, on the matron's suggestion, employed some of the female inmates making fishing nets.[32] In March 1852 the master of the union called the board's attention 'to the evils likely to arise from the idleness of so many of the adult females'.[33] The absence of work created problems with the female inmates being disorderly and insubordinate and engaging in rioting in a number of workhouses. In December 1848, the paupers in Parsonstown workhouse, led by the women, rioted when the daily rations were reduced, and ransacked the stores. The constabulary were brought in to restore order. Disturbances were also reported in Carrickmacross, Nenagh, Enniscorthy, Castlebar and Tullamore workhouses when the inmates, mainly women, rioted.[34] In 1848, young females were so disruptive in the South Dublin Union that it was decided that the matron could use solitary confinement as a punishment.[35] While the issues that brought this disorder to a head were changes in diet or a reduction in the daily rations, it was also believed that the underlying causes were boredom and the feeling of hopelessness that the women had about their future. Limited employment opportunities were available for the workhouse paupers, and the idleness of the majority only 'increased the sense of desolation, uselessness and shame they experienced'.[36] Some who sought admission to the workhouses were so shocked by the conditions they witnessed that they left immediately. The employment of the female paupers and keeping them occupied within the workhouses was to remain a major concern for the authorities throughout the 1850s. While education and training were provided within the workhouses for children aged up to 13 years, it was felt that those between 13 and 19 had little to gain and the longer they remained as inmates the more their prospects of being rehabilitated outside the workhouse diminished. The plight of women who were long-term inmates was summed up by George P. Place, a witness before the 1861 Select Committee on the Poor Law, when he said, 'I think six or seven months' residence in a workhouse would be enough to demoralise the angels'.[37] It was thus not surprising that the Poor Law unions throughout the country sought a solution to the large number of long-term female inmates, as they would otherwise remain a permanent burden on the unions' finances, and posed a threat to the peace and order of the day-to-day running of the workhouses. For them emigration became the panacea to their problems. However, the impetus for emigration came not from within the Poor Law unions, but from the colonies.

With the workhouses full to capacity with a largely redundant population and an increasing demand for labour in the colonies, it seemed only natural that the problem of the population imbalance could be ameliorated by transferring the surplus population out of Ireland to Canada and Australia. That much of this surplus population was female only added to the solution as the colonies needed women. Throughout the 1820s and 1830s it was frequently suggested that Ireland's surplus population should be sent to the colonies to address their problems: in Australia the ratio was eight men for every woman. In 1833 the Chief Emigration Agent for Upper Canada, James Buchanan, told Lord Monteagle that the problem of overpopulation in Ireland was such that 'parents are daily constrained to say to their children, "we can no longer support you in idleness, go to America and earn your bread"'.[38]

Buchanan asked if the imperial parliament could help these people to go to Upper Canada, as depots could be established for the integration of the paupers in the colony. He suggested that if such a scheme was sanctioned, the people could be moved on a county or parish basis by the following autumn.[39] Similar views were also expressed by Lt Col. Edward MacArthur, a witness before the Select Committee of the House of Lords on Colonization from Ireland in 1847, when he said that any system which allowed large numbers of women to come to Australia would be a great advantage to the colonies and the colonial authorities were prepared to fund the transport of girls from Britain and Ireland.[40]

There were those who saw the infrastructural development in the colonies as a way of employing the workhouse male population, by sending them to those areas where there was a demand for labour. One such scheme was the Halifax to Quebec Railway in Canada, which was under construction in the late 1840s, and John Stewart suggested that the able-bodied paupers be sent there.[41] With the exception of the Peter Robinson emigration project from the Blackwater region of north Munster to Peterborough, Ontario between 1823 and 1825 none of these suggestions ever came to fruition, largely because of inadequate funding.[42] This changed in 1848 when the colonial authorities in Australia decided to provide the finances to bring female paupers from the workhouses to the colony. While the Australians were initially reluctant to accept female workhouse inmates, they eventually relented due to government pressure and the failure to attract pauper inmates from England and Wales to the colony. Between 1848 and 1850, 4,114 girls were sent from 118 workhouses in Ireland, with the first group of 185 girls leaving on the *Earl Grey* on 3 June 1848 from ten unions in

Ulster. While there was some hostility in Australia to the bringing-out of Irish paupers, which was the reason for the termination of the schemes in 1850, the overall outcome was positive as the girls met the demands for the much-needed female domestic labour and the demand for wives for the colonists. At the same time the workhouses were getting rid of a section of the inmate population who were regarded as a long-term burden on the unions' resources.[43]

The importance of the Female Orphan Schemes was that structures and procedures were put in place that were adopted for the other emigration schemes which involved Poor Law unions. The girls were to be between 14 and 18 years, preferably between 16 and 18 years, be free of any mental or bodily defects likely to impair their usefulness as settlers, their character for industry be satisfactory, be able to read and write and have some experience in domestic service as housemaids or nurses. Unlike the groups sent out from the workhouses and other institutions prior to 1848, the Australian authorities had complete control as to the candidates that came to the colony. While the Poor Law union officials drew up a list of suitable candidates the final decision rested with the Emigration Commissioners' Agent in Dublin, Lieutenant Henry, after he visited the workhouses and interviewed the candidates.

The Female Orphan Scheme to Australia was attractive to both the Poor Law unions and the female inmates. While most boards of guardians had been reluctant to engage with emigration prior to this the unions now saw it as an opportunity to get rid of a section of the young female inmate population at little expense to the ratepayers. As the Australian authorities paid the passage fares from Plymouth, the only expense for the Poor Law unions was to provide the emigrants with new clothing and their travel costs to the port of embarkation. The cost of sending the thirty-one girls from Killarney workhouse to Plymouth in April 1848, who were orphans and aged between 14 and 18 years, was £4 15*s* whereas it would have cost £155 to keep them in the workhouse for a year.[44] The positive attitude by the unions towards the schemes can be seen in that by May 1848, when the schemes came into force, eighty-six unions had forwarded lists of suitable girls for consideration, with each union using different criteria as to who should be selected: the Naas guardians chose forty of the healthiest workhouse orphans, Killarney initially wanted to send both male and female inmates, while Parsonstown selected those who were most likely to get a husband.[45] Government officials also had their own views as to who should be sent, with Thomas Reddington stating that only young female orphans who had been resident in the workhouses for a long period should be assisted.[46]

The enthusiasm for the emigration schemes amongst the female inmate population can be seen by the demand for assistances. When the scheme to Australia was first announced in February 1848 it resulted in large numbers of workhouse girls, as in the case of Nenagh, applying to be sent to the colony. When it was temporarily suspended later that year the guardians in most unions were inundated by the female inmates who wanted to leave, and this was a major factor in the Russell administration pressurising the Australian authorities to reopen the scheme. There is evidence that in the 1840s and early 1850s women were more receptive to emigration, especially when they had few prospects in Ireland. Some of the landlord emigration schemes of the 1840s were initiated by women who appealed directly to the landlord or his agent to be sent to North America.[47] Free emigration to the colonies was attractive to those with no future prospects. Even those who were not inmates sought admission to the workhouses so they could be assisted. For example, Jane Lane made repeated attempts to be admitted to Limerick workhouse so that she could be considered for assistance to North America, while in January 1850 a number of females entered Naas workhouse hoping they would be assisted to emigrate.[48] When the Ennis guardians decided in 1851 to send out pauper females from the workhouse, a number of girls left their employment in the town and sought admission in the workhouse so they could be included in an emigration scheme, while in the same year girls entered the Kilrush workhouse so that they could be eligible to be sent to North America.[49]

The success of the Female Orphan Scheme to Australia resulted in a more pragmatic approach being taken in relation to emigration from the workhouses. Under the 1843 and 1847 legislation the paupers had to be sent to the colonies, and no assistance could be provided to other destinations. This was in line with the view in the 1830s that the emigrants who went to such locations adopted anti-English sentiments. In 1849 two new measures were introduced which made emigration more attractive to the Poor Law unions and intending emigrants. The Poor Law unions were now allowed to extend the assisted emigration schemes to the USA. As it was a more attractive destination than the colonies, it was hoped that more of the pauper inmates would travel to that country. In his evidence to the Select Committee on the Poor Laws, the Earl of Clancarty had argued that the boards of guardians should be allowed to send paupers to destinations outside of the colonies.[50] In May 1849 the Prime Minister, Lord John Russell, came to an agreement with William Monsell, the MP for County Limerick, whereby boards of guardians were permitted to borrow money for emigration purposes. Aubrey de Vere, a Limerick landowner, had told the Select Committee on the Poor Law that the provisions under the existing legislation were inadequate and especially in those areas where there was great poverty, as the guardians were unable to collect money to fund the maintenance of the poor, and there was little enthusiasm among ratepayers to pay an additional tax for emigration.[51] However, under the new legislation a provision was inserted which increased the residency requirement in the workhouse from three months to one year. This was to ensure that the workhouses did not become emigration depots for the poor to use up their time before leaving for North America.

With more favourable regulations most Poor Law unions increasingly looked to emigration as a way of easing overcrowding in the workhouses and of reducing their financial liabilities. The economic benefits were outlined by William Monsell in January 1850, when he pointed out that the forty-two pauper girls sent from the Limerick workhouse on the *James Drake* from Liverpool would have cost the union £189 per year, but their passage was £226.[52] By this stage the inmate population was at an all-time high, and the long-term prognosis for reducing the numbers was not good because of the large-scale evictions that were taking place. The attempts to reduce the workhouse population through emigration in the 1849–50 period had little overall impact. While the Limerick guardians had assisted 102 people to leave between December 1849 and January 1850 the numbers entering the workhouse continued to rise, and by February 1850 stood at 6,500 and twelve months later reached 7,000.[53] Nevertheless, the guardians in most unions availed of every opportunity to send what they regarded as their 'permanent deadweight' to foreign destinations. On 1 November 1850 the Ennistymon guardians passed a resolution which said: 'It is the particular duty of the boards of guardians to provide for the present and future welfare of pauper orphans and that such cannot be carried efficiently in workhouses.'[54]

Opportunities were also considered outside of the colonies and the USA. In March 1850 the Poor Law Commissioners wrote to the guardians in most unions enclosing information about the advantages of sending paupers to Argentina where landed proprietors were prepared to provide employment and to pay for their travel. Members of Nenagh Board of Guardians were so taken with this opportunity that it was suggested that £3,000 be borrowed to progress the emigration.[55] This offer does not appear to have been taken up, probably because of the issue of language, and for most guardians and paupers Argentina was a largely unknown destination. Other locations that were considered by the guardians included South Africa. Between February 1849 and February 1850, the Wexford guardians sent three groups of female orphans to the Cape of Good Hope, the final selection comprising twenty paupers aged between 16 and 18 years. Among the group was 18-year-old Mary Lennard from Taghmon who prior to their departure read an address expressing the gratitude of the girls to the guardians.[56]

Not all of the boards of guardians were enthusiastic about sending out their pauper inmates. Some were reluctant participants, seeing it as an inevitable choice, while others adopted an approach that was at best nebulous. When the issue was debated by the Thurles Board of Guardians some members regretted that the best and strongest were forced to leave because of 'the visitations which it has pleased God to inflict upon their unfortunate country'.[57]

Some unions had a greater involvement in the emigration process than others. A number of reasons were responsible for this. First, those who had been actively involved in the Female Orphan Schemes to Australia from an early stage continued their involvement in sending out their paupers for most of the 1850s. Nenagh guardians had sent eighty-four girls under the 1848–50 schemes, and another 753 inmates between 1849 and 1860.[58] Second, those with a large inmate pauper population, and in particular with high numbers of women and children, saw emigration as the only way of reducing the group of 'permanent deadweights'. Scariff, Kilrush and Ennis unions each assisted over 400 people in 1851, while 800 paupers were sent from the Cork workhouse between 1852 and 1854. A pattern that emerged was that when there was an increase in the number of inmates the guardians resorted to emigration to reduce the number of paupers. In 1851 Ennis guardians assisted over 400 girls to leave for Canada, reflecting the large inmate population, and again in 1863 another twenty-five girls were sent to the North American colony.[59]

Often the inspiration behind the engagement in the assisted emigration schemes came from an energetic guardian, such as Francis S. Walker in Newcastle Union or Mr Minnitt in Nenagh Union, or forward-looking Poor Law union officials, such as Edward Senior in the north-west or R.A. Duncan who looked after the south-west. While the motive was in the main economic, they saw that the retention of the female paupers in the workhouses would have long-term negative consequences, and it was in the best interests of both the girls and the union that the girls be sent to the colonies. However, there was a realisation that there needed to be close co-operation between the unions and the colonial authorities. This had been advocated by Stephen de Vere in 1847 when he stated that for emigration to Canada to be successful it needed to be conducted in a manner that was beneficial to both sides. It would have to be properly co-ordinated and not just dumping the emigrants in Canada and letting the State look after them, as had been the case with the landlord emigration schemes.[60] R.A. Duncan realised the importance of a close co-operation between the Poor Law unions and the Canadian authorities. In April 1852 he informed A.C. Buchanan, the Chief Emigration Agent in Quebec, that a number of unions under his charge were contemplating sending up to 1,000 single girls to Quebec provided there were sufficient employment opportunities in the colony and he also wished to know if widows with a significant number of children of a working age would be accepted.[61] This correspondence resulted in advice being provided as to the structures that should be put in place in relation to the workhouse paupers: the emigrants should arrive in early summer when employment opportunities were at their best and landing money be forwarded to the emigration agent in Quebec which would be used to transfer the girls to their final destinations in the colony. On 9 June 1852, 280 inmates, nearly all single girls, but also a small number of widows with children, were sent from the Newcastle workhouse to Quebec on the *Roderick Dhu*, followed three weeks later by another 160 girls from Newcastle and 200 from Rathkeale. In August further groups from Newcastle, Listowel and Macroom followed.[62] Most unions adopted the strategies and procedures that were agreed between Buchanan and Duncan, and which were circulated to all the boards of guardians by the Poor Law Commissioners. These included the fifty-four single girls and a family comprising a widow and her two children from the Strokestown workhouse, and the eighty-five female orphans sent out by the Roscommon Union on the *Alert* from Sligo in July 1852.[63]

Canada was chosen as the prime destination for the workhouse emigrants for a number of reasons. The cost of transporting the emigrants to the North American colony was considerably lower than to Australia or South Africa: while the fare to Australia was £14, to Canada it could be secured for under £5. There was a great demand for female labour in Canada, especially domestic servants. In February 1852 A.B. Hawke, the Chief Emigration Agent in Toronto, stated he had immediate employment for up to 1,500 girls from the workhouses.[64] In the early 1850s emigrants were not drawn to the colony in the same numbers as up to 1850. The USA was now the main destination for the Irish emigrant, so the Canadian authorities began to correspond directly with emigration agents in Ireland, highlighting the employment opportunities and wages that were available in the colony. In February 1853 A.C. Buchanan wrote to the agents in Ireland urging them to persuade Irish emigrants to consider Canada as a destination for settlement and pointed out, 'Canada never presented a more favourable opening for the reception of all classes of emigrant than at the present'.[65] At the same time Buchanan was sending positive reports back to those Poor Law unions about the female paupers that had been sent to the jurisdiction. He reported that the 700 workhouse girls who were sent by the unions in 1851 were employed within two weeks of their arrival in Canada, and in his letter to the Kilrush guardians stated that all of the 362 girls had been provided for and each was in comfortable employment.[66]

Buchanan's positive reports to the boards of guardians inevitably resulted in the unions sending more of their female paupers to the colony. In writing to the Thurles Board of Guardians on 3 June 1854 he stated that the females who had arrived in Quebec on the *Energy* were doing well: twenty-three were sent to Bytown because of the high demand for female servants, and a committee had been established to look after them; three went to Upper Canada, five travelled to the USA, while Judy Cormack had decided to stay in Quebec.[67] Canada had other advantages as a destination for the pauper emigrants. The level of religious bigotry towards the Catholic pauper female inmates was not as great as in Australia. One of the main reasons for ending the Female Orphan Scheme to Australia in 1850 was the objections to the influx of poor workhouse Catholic girls with the colonists demanding that only Protestant girls be sent out.[68] Canada, with its large Catholic population, was not as hostile to the influx of Catholics from the Irish workhouses for, as Dympna McLoughlin shows, the Poor Law guardians' main concern was with the burden of pauperism within their institutions and the fate of the girls in Canada was secondary.[69]

While the Poor Law guardians adopted the general structures and procedures of the Australian schemes, there were also major differences between the two destinations. The guardians were intent on ensuring that the girls arrived in the colonies looking well and in a healthy state. The provision of new clothing had to be undertaken for a number of reasons. First, many of the girls had been long-term pauper inmates and on entering the workhouse had exchanged their clothes, often rags, for the institution's uniform. Often their clothes were burnt or could no longer be found. There was no alternative but to provide them with alternative clothing when they left for the colonies. Second, it was important that the girls arrive in the colonies properly clothed in order that they would be quickly employed. The colonial authorities also had to be impressed so that future shipments of workhouse inmates would be allowed to travel. Third, the workhouse authorities had learned from the experiences of the of the landlord assisted emigration schemes of the late 1840s, when the arrival of emigrants from the Palmerston, Lansdowne and Wandesforde estates had been condemned by the Canadian authorities because of their appearance and their poor attire.[70] First impressions were important, and in most cases the Quebec officials commented favourably on the emigrants' experiences who were sent in the 1850s. The fifty-four girls assisted by the South Dublin Union in 1854 were provided with two gowns, a shift of gingham, a flannel petticoat, a still petticoat, two calico shifts, three pairs of stockings, one pair of shoes, one warm cloak, one pair of stays, two caps, one neck kerchief, one bonnet, a coarse and a fine comb, and a bag to accommodate all their belongings.[71] The girls were also medically examined before their departure to ensure they were fit to travel and a medical superintendent was appointed to accompany the group on the voyage. A chaperone was also employed to travel to ensure their safety. In May 1854 the South Dublin Union advertised for a matron to travel with the emigrants on the *Colombus*, offering remuneration of £5 and a free passage to the colony, while the Limerick paupers who left on the *Theron* were accompanied by the matron Mary Flanagan.[72] Great care was taken that there was no criticism of the girls when they arrived in the North American colony.

However, the structures and procedures recommended by the Canadian authorities were not always adhered to by the guardians. While A.C. Buchanan and the Poor Law Commissioners stated that 'landing money' should be provided so that the girls could be forwarded to their final destinations and that it be sent to the emigration agent in Quebec, not all unions followed these instructions. The 160 paupers sent out from the Carlow workhouse on the *Anaadale* from Liverpool in September 1852 were given the money when they boarded the ship, and much of the money was spent on the passage. After they arrived in Quebec the Canadian authorities had to provide funds for them to travel to their final destinations.[73] The group from Waterford workhouse who arrived in July 1851 received nothing, although they had been promised 15s each when they arrived in Canada.[74] The recommendations in relation to when the paupers should be sent were not always adhered to by many unions, and the girls did not arrive in the colony until September and October, creating problems for the authorities in securing positions for them.

The schemes to Australia were better co-ordinated and planned than those to British North America. All of the girls sent to Australia went to one port, Plymouth, allowing the authorities to be in total control of the operation. Those going to Canada left from several ports, such as Cork, Limerick, New Ross, Sligo and Galway, so it was difficult to monitor the ships and ensure they adhered to the regulations as to provisions and the number of passengers they could carry. Whereas the Australians chartered the boats that left from Plymouth, the Poor Law unions engaged the boats that left for North America, usually as a result of a tendering process. While the guardians were instructed that only young single females should be sent to Canada, there were occasions where the unions saw it as an opportunity to dispose of their long-term troublesome inmates. The view was taken that once they arrived in the North American colony they became the responsibility of the Canadian authorities. In October 1850, eighty paupers were sent from the Cork workhouse to New Brunswick on the *Susan*, including two who were blind, a number who had problems with alcohol and fifteen who were over 40 years, the eldest being Tomas Leary who was 76 years old.[75]

Groups were also assisted who were described as 'refractory girls' and the authorities were glad to send them to Canada.[76] Some unions sent out widows and their children who had little hope of looking after themselves, as with groups sent out from the Gorey and New Ross workhouses in 1858 and 1859.[77]

The Canadian authorities did not have an input in the selection of the emigrants and as a result had no control over who landed on their shores. While there was a demand for labour in Canada the authorities never contributed financially to the emigration of the female paupers, and inevitably had to accept those who arrived even though they were unsuitable. A large number of women in 1858 had entered the workhouses in the hope of being sent to Canada, as in Enniscorthy, where eighty-two girls had been assisted in emigrating to the colony the previous year and where there was an expectation that further groups would be sent out.[78] It resulted in claims that the Poor Law unions were dumping their 'permanent deadweight' on the colony, and after repeated warning the authorities sent back three paupers from the New Ross workhouse, 'owing to their ill health and infirmity rendering them unable to support themselves in this country, and dependent on casual public charity'.[79] Assisted emigration became an important aspect of Poor Law union policy from the late 1840s in order to counteract the burgeoning workhouse population. While the unions were initially reluctant to utilise the provisions which allowed them to send their paupers to the colonies because of ratepayer opposition, it was not long before it was realised that it was the panacea for that section of the workhouse population who would otherwise remain a permanent long-term burden on the system. Outside influences initiated the process, and in particular the demand for female labour in Australia and Canada, and to a lesser extent South Africa, resulting in a more positive attitude to assisting the young female pauper population to settle abroad. As the workhouses in the late 1840s reached their capacity financial motives took precedence, with the argument that the cost of sending a pauper to British North America was less than their annual maintenance in the workhouse. At the same time there was a clear desire among the inmates to be sent to a foreign destination, as even when those selected changed their minds there were others willing to take their place. For the pauper inmates whose future was as permanent residents in the workhouses or being admitted on a continuous basis, the emigration had many social and economic advantages. The Poor Law schemes were their only realistic opportunity to move from Ireland and leave behind a life of destitution and pauperism, and offered them the hope of a new life and a new beginning in a foreign land where they could not be stigmatised for being a workhouse inmate. At the same time the guardians saw it as an opportunity to send their undesirable and refractory paupers to the colonies, a process which was increasingly causing alarm among the Canadian authorities. While the main function of the Poor Law during the Great Famine was to provide relief for the starving and destitute poor, its role as a vehicle in the emigration process has been largely ignored or overlooked by historians. Although research into the Female Orphan Scheme to Australia has shed light on emigration to Australia, emigration to Canada has not yet been adequately examined or assessed. These were 'the invisible emigrants' of the Great Famine, and have been marginalised because of the massive exodus that took place between 1845 and 1855 when just over 2 million people left the country. Without the Poor Law intervention, these paupers could just as easily have become part of the mortality statistics of the calamity that was the Great Famine.

2

The mechanics of assisted emigration: From the Fitzwilliam estate in Wicklow to Canada

Fidelma Byrne

In December 1914, as the First World War raged on the battlefields of Europe, tremors of a different kind were pulsating throughout the city of Winnipeg in Canada. On 26 December, Nicholas Bawlf, one of the city's most prominent businessmen, died suddenly at the age of 65. As Allan Levine states, 'if one man symbolised the rise of Winnipeg as the grain centre of Western Canada, it was Nicholas Bawlf'.[1] Bawlf was born on 17 July 1849 in Smith Falls, Ontario and educated locally. He initially honed his trade as an apprentice moulder with G.M. Cossitt Bros. at the Smith Falls Agricultural Works, a company that specialised in the manufacturing of agricultural implements. The business had a second premises in the town of Almonte, approximately 25 miles north of Smith Falls, which Bawlf also occasionally worked in, and it was here that he met Catharine Madden, his future wife.[2] On 6 February 1877 the couple married and shortly thereafter, like many others of the time, decided to head west to seek their fortune.[3] It was a decision that would change the course of their lives and the trajectory of Canadian agriculture.

Upon arrival in Winnipeg, Bawlf established a flour and feed business on Main Street South. Success resulted in expansion, and within a few years he had relocated to larger premises at Princess Street. As the 1880s progressed, he advocated the establishment of a central grain exchange though few shared his vision at that point. It was only with the advent of the railway in 1886, coupled with a burgeoning wheat market, that the leading grain producers began to envision the benefit of such an enterprise.[4] Thus, in 1887, the Winnipeg Grain and Produce Exchange was founded by Bawlf and a number of the leading traders in the region. In the early years, the company traded out of a basement at City Hall before relocating to a three-storey building owned by Bawlf at 164 Princess Street. As the wheat economy grew exponentially so too did the business. Diversification into Asian export markets and Bawlf's independent business interests in the manufacture of grain elevators only added to his increasing wealth and prominence within the city. Consequently he was offered a number of directorships, including on the Winnipeg Board of Trade and Bank of Toronto.[5]

Bawlf lived his life by the motto 'be sure you are right, then go ahead' and he was seldom wrong. Personally and professionally his life emitted an aura of success. With increasing wealth and notoriety, the family outgrew their modest dwelling on Main Street and relocated to an impressive residence at number 11 Kennedy Street. Here Nicholas and Catharine raised six sons and three daughters. The family were of Roman Catholic persuasion and active participants in the local Catholic church, St Mary's. Furthermore, Bawlf's faith extended into the realm of politics where he advocated for the inclusion of more Catholic senators in what was arguably, a Protestant-dominated political sphere.[6] Undoubtedly, Bawlf's life was one well lived, exceptional in many respects and extraordinary given the fact that he was the son of Irish emigrants who left the Fitzwilliam Estate in south-west Wicklow during 1847 (Black '47) as part of a Famine assisted-emigration scheme.

Assisted emigration from Irish landed estates was commonplace during this period. Patrick Duffy contends that irrespective of whether a landlord owned 26,000 acres, as in the case of the Shirley estate in County Monaghan, or 120,000 acres, such as the Lansdowne estate in County Kerry, many landlords engaged in the practice as a method of 'disencumbering [their] crowded places'.[7] Several schemes received negative publicity such as at Strokestown in County Roscommon whose schemes resulted in the murder of the landlord, Major Denis Mahon. In this instance, Mahon was reputedly shot for two reasons: 'his refusal to continue the conacre system [which generated ill-will between himself and his tenants, while] his clearing away of what he deemed the surplus population' who refused to emigrate was denounced from the pulpit.[8] Equally, the Lansdowne scheme in County Kerry was also viewed with contempt. Here estate officials shipped a labouring class described by Anbinder as 'the most wretched people upon the face of the globe' across the Atlantic, 'dumping' them in the notorious Five Points district of New York.[9] And yet, the Fitzwilliam assisted emigration scheme, one of the largest and prolonged in the country, appears to have received negligible criticism or indeed commentary. This was despite the fact that it systematically transported almost one third of the estate's tenantry to Canada over a nine-year period from 1847–56.[10]

The Fitzwilliam estate, or Coollattin as it was known locally, was County Wicklow's largest estate, acquired in the seventeenth century by Thomas Wentworth, Earl of Strafford. Over the ensuing century, numerous childless heirs resulted in the estate eventually passing to a female line and ultimately, into the possession of the Earls Fitzwilliam.[11] The estate which Fitzwilliam inherited had been vastly improved throughout the tenure of his maternal uncle. As leases expired, Charles had inserted covenants into new tenancy agreements which required the lessee to maintain, and where possible, improve their holding. Conditions also extended to textile manufacturing, and while some engaged in small-scale production of linen, such endeavours became extinct due mainly to adverse climatic conditions.[12] However, Charles' greatest gift to his nephew was his attempt to eradicate the middlemen resident upon the estate.

The system was widely believed to have been the ruination of landed society. Terence Dooley, in his analysis of nineteenth-century management practices, suggests that initially landlords 'perceived the middleman system to be a convenient means of relieving them [the landlord] from the troublesome collection of rents from a mass of tenants'.[13] Indeed, with a core estate that included fourteen civil parishes it is plausible that Wentworth was of the same mindset. However, with lengthy leases and vast tracts of land, these *de facto* rent collectors became an untouchable class that wreaked havoc on land, economy and people well into the nineteenth century as a consequence of exorbitant rents. It appears that despite the benefits of this division of labour, Wentworth recognised the dangers of this malign structure. In less than four decades, he managed to break the system as the number of tenants with holdings in excess of 300 acres fell dramatically 'from 40 per cent to 13 per cent'.[14] Consequently the estate that FitzWilliam acquired in 1782 was arguably more streamlined and economically viable than in the preceding decades. However, one fatal flaw remained: the system was shattered but far from eradicated, and this middle tier would in fact prove disastrous in the pre-Famine period. Equally, regardless of the three-way division of labour, the conditions of the sub-tenantry remained dire as their 'standard of living fluctuated sharply in good and lean years'.[15]

By 1838, the estate totalled 79,225 acres, or approximately 20 per cent of the entire land surface in the county, and was three times greater than the county's second largest estate owned by the See of Dublin.[16] Despite the scale of the Wicklow estate, it was but one holding in an extensive property portfolio that included estates in North and South Yorkshire, Northamptonshire and Huntingdonshire as well as a few hundred acres scattered around each country.[17] The English estates, particularly those of Yorkshire, took precedence over the Irish holdings as they possessed a dual economy in the form of agriculture and coal. Thus, despite its scale, Coollattin was viewed as a recreational retreat, a location to escape to once or twice a year at best. All too often, the visits were more infrequent, with successive earls choosing to reside in Yorkshire all year round. As an absentee landlord, Fitzwilliam devolved the management of the estate to a resident land agent who controlled the land and those that lived upon it from the administrative base at Coollattin Park.[18]

The various land agents that managed the day-to-day running of the Wicklow estate for the first half of the nineteenth century were all Yorkshire born, though this is where the similarities end. Arguably, the most trusted, loyal and well-loved by his adopted nation was William Wainwright, who managed the estate for thirty-three years until his demise in 1813. In a glowing epitaph, the fourth earl conveyed the essence of Wainwright's management skills and morality in which 'the tenant felt that his comforts were well provided for – the landlord, that his interests were fully considered'.[19] Contrastingly, Wainwright's successor, William Haigh, was universally despised. In correspondence with Fitzwilliam, a head-tenant from Tinahely described him as 'a man of unfeeling and brutal conduct' and one which 'all classes of people hate'.[20] Arguably, this negative depiction stemmed from the fact that throughout his tenure Haigh affection for economics outweighed his affection for humanity. Hence, his propagated policies of ejectment, land consolidation and assisted emigration as a means of dealing with arrears and curbing sub-division on the estate were reviled by every strata of tenantry.[21] In hindsight, though his methods were draconian, perhaps he was unjustly criticised for attempting to eradicate the very system that had slowly strangled the estate the century before. Though exact numbers are lacking for this early stream of migration, records pertaining to the 1830s and 1840s provide ample evidence to its existence.[22]

Haigh was relieved of his duties in 1826 and the Chaloner family took up residence as land agents of the Fitzwilliam estate. Their arrival coincided with a new era of professionalism that was infiltrating the position. Robert Chaloner Senior was part of the Yorkshire squirearchy. He had presided over a landed estate in Guisborough, North Yorkshire and was successful in financial affairs until the pecuniary crisis of 1825 to 1826 left him bankrupt.[23] From 1826 until his death in 1842, Chaloner Senior oversaw the running of the Irish estate and he was succeeded in 1842 by his son Robert Junior. This was the man who was single-handedly credited with relieving the estate of in excess of 5,500 people. Given his financial background, Chaloner Senior was acutely aware of the need to make the land pay in order to maintain a viable business.

The single hindrance to the continued durability of the estate was, as he saw it, the practice of sub-division. Thus, in 1831, Chaloner Senior wrote to Fitzwilliam to advise him that owing to consolidation of uneconomic holdings it would be necessary to 'turn several families adrift'.[24] Adrift in this instance referred to the practice of assisted emigration. Between April and mid-May 1831, a Mr Dempsey received three part payments which totalled £556 in respect of his role in removing 'sundry persons' from the estate to Canada. Although research to date has not uncovered the final figure of those who left during this early migration stream, Jim Rees contends when the amount paid to Dempsey is examined in the context of the cost charged during the Famine years, it appears that approximately 160 individuals left at this point.[25] Some of those that left the Fitzwilliam estate found employment as labourers on the Rideau Canal. The canal was constructed between 1826 and 1832 as a means of connecting Ottawa to Kingstown and employed a predominantly Irish emigrant labour force.

In 1829, almost 700 labourers signed a petition in response to a government inquiry into allegations that the Peter Robinson assisted schemes of 1823 and 1825 were nothing more than 'a system of transportation and banishment'.[26] In addition, to the particulars of each employee, details of their relatives in Ireland were also recorded. Those from the Fitzwilliam estate included John Byrne of Ballynultagh, his wife, four sons and a daughter. Byrne stated his father Matthew held a large holding at Nakerumkal (Knockatomcoyle), near Tenehala (Tinahely), leased from Abraham Jones.[27] William Hopkins, entry number 233, was a native of Kolekenno (Coolkenno). William stated that his father Edward, an under-tenant of Captain Nickson, had a very large family and was 'desirous of coming to Canada'.[28] Back in Wicklow, in 1832, Chaloner pleaded with the earl to introduce a total ban on sub-division on the Irish estate 'except in the most urgent necessity' as he recognised the holdings were too small to remain economically viable either for the estate or the families they were expected to sustain. Fitzwilliam refused to impose such a sanction, opting instead to assess each situation on an individual basis.[29]

The fourth earl died in 1833 and was succeeded by his eldest son Charles. From his acquisition of the estate in 1833 to the first signs of blight twelve years later, it would appear from estate records that the fifth earl employed assisted emigration in a concerted attempt to curb sub-division on his estate. Maps of the Shillelagh estate drawn in 1842 by Rogers and Smith testify not only to its existence but its proliferation throughout every townland.[30] In Kilquiggan, for example, the townland comprised 224 acres 3 roods 19 perches divided into fifty-five holdings. Thomas Wall was the chief-tenant, leasing the entire townland directly from Fitzwilliam. He worked twenty fields himself (with a total acreage of 89 acres 3 roods 20 perches) and leased the remaining thirty-five fields to more than eighteen under-tenants. These fields varied in size from Dick Hopkins' 1 acre and 20 perches to Michael Gehon & Partners' five fields with a combined acreage of 34 acres 1 roods 12 perches.[31] Undocumented on these maps is the sub-tenantry who eked out an existence from these under-tenants who further subdivided their lot, thus in many respects shrouding the full extent of sub-division throughout the estate. That said, the land agent was acutely aware of its existence.

When Robert Chaloner Senior died in 1842, his son Robert Junior took over the day-to-day running of the estate. Standing before the Devon Commission, an inquiry into the state of land occupation in Ireland in 1844, Chaloner Junior gave evidence of practices upon the Fitzwilliam estate. When asked about the size of holdings he replied there were some 'as large as 600 to 800 acres but then there are small farms down almost to any size', a great many of which were under 10 acres. He conceded 'we are sorry to have farms of a small size, but there they are, and it cannot be helped they are generally smaller than they ought to be', highlighting the prevalence of sub-division on the estate and his knowledge of this.[32] As questioning continued discussions of management practices, valuations and improvement gave rise to the conditions experienced by the tenantry. It was blatantly obvious that a year before the Famine struck, the estate was drowning in debt as tenants struggled to pay rent and many relied on loan funds to make ends meet.[33] Chaloner described the conditions of the under-tenants of these as being 'in a very bad way' mainly as a consequence of middlemen charging excessive rents and the estate's inability to interfere.[34] The final two questions put to Chaloner concerned emigration, namely was there 'extensive emigration from this district?' and had the landlord 'pursued a system of giving assistance?', to which he replied, 'we have done a good deal in that way. We take every opportunity we can in doing so'. Chaloner went so far as to explain how he used it as a means of regulating the estate, a tactic 'of bringing the supply and … the demand of labour on an equality'.[35] Such revelations by Chaloner are highly significant given that the year was 1844, three years before the estate commenced its Famine assisted emigration scheme.

Analysis of the estate records housed at Sheffield Archives sheds more light on this pre-Famine emigration. Account rentals pertaining to the Irish estate indicate that the emigration of 1831 was not an isolated occurrence. By 1836, a steady trickle of emigrants were leaving the County Wicklow estate. In June, sixty-nine persons, four single individuals and seven families, received assistance totalling £77 4*s* from the estate. Individual remunerations ranged from £1 to £25. In addition, Messrs Scott & Co., shipping agents from Dublin, were paid £66 8*s* 1*d* for arranging passage. The following year, on 21 July 1837, the estate paid out £137 10*s* in assistance to aid emigrants in their new life on the other side of the world. However, even at this early stage, emigration was no less problematic than it would be during the Famine years; on 27 November 1837 Messrs Scott & Co. refunded the estate '22 pounds 11 shillings' in respect of twenty-three persons who refused to go after their passage had been paid.[36] It would appear that even the most experienced in the process of emigration could not convince some to leave, for in 1838 the same Mr Dempsey that had assisted in removing the 1831 emigrants from the estate was advanced £10 to enable Michael Bolan and his family to emigrate. However, Dempsey had to refund the money to the estate because when they reached Dublin port Boland refused to go.[37] It is unclear whether those who refused to go were allowed to return or whether the practice of 'house to be thrown down', a common feature of the Famine emigration lists, prevented this. That said, records do indicate that some went voluntarily, like Cathe [*sic*] Palvey who was listed in October 1839 as having received £4 to emigrate 'to join friends'. In total £48 16*s* 6*d* was paid towards emigration expenses that year.[38]

With the exception of a few schemes, such as that of the Gore-Booth estate in County Sligo, benevolence tends to have been lacking in a great many instances of assisted emigration during this period. That said, regardless of the motive, Fitzwilliam was more than generous to intending passengers. In May 1840, he paid William Cullen 'to support 30 emigrants in Dublin for 1 day', perhaps owing to the late arrival of a ship. He also advanced John Carey £3 10*s* 0*d* to buy clothes, before paying James Keoghoe to transport the Carey family to Dublin.[39] As the years moved on, oblivious to the catastrophe that was to beset the country, the numbers leaving the estate continued to rise. In the spring of 1842, 312 people were listed as having left the estate.[40] While these figures appear to fade beneath the deluge which left during the Famine period, the presence of this pre-Famine scheme is highly significant on a number of levels. Firstly, the existence of a pre-Famine scheme demonstrates that assisted emigration on the Fitzwilliam estate was not a Famine phenomenon and, most notably, its presence provided a strategy and framework by which the estate could unburden itself when faced with adversity at various junctures. Equally, the fact that the mechanism of assisted emigration was in place fourteen years before the onset of Famine no doubt rendered it an efficient enterprise in comparison to those that initiated schemes in the midst of the crisis. Equally, as Gerard Moran contends, the existence of pre-Famine schemes protected proprietors from the negative criticism experienced by those who became involved in such endeavours from 1847.[41] Hence, landed families, such as the Fitzwilliams, the Wandesfordes of County Kilkenny and Gore-Booths, who engaged in assisted emigration pre-1845 were less vilified.

Despite the onset of the potato blight in Ireland in August 1845, it took two months to reach County Wicklow. This created a false sense of security amongst the tenantry which was quickly dispelled in November as reports circulated indicating that the problem was far greater than first realised. Ironically, in its initial phase the crop on the Fitzwilliam estate remained largely intact with approximately 20 to 33 per cent affected. Consequently, in 1846, 95 per cent of the normal acreage was replanted. Reduced availability of foodstuffs coupled with higher prices and competition for what little had survived made life particularly harrowing for the lower strata of tenantry. Yet optimism remained until July when the extent of the catastrophe became apparent. Everywhere foliage became infected as the blight moved like a rabid disease across the land.[42] Interestingly, the previous March, Chaloner enquired of the North American Colonial Office what, if any, was 'the advantage to Lord Fitzwilliam for emigrating persons from this estate to America', indicating that the idea of emigration had again resurfaced on the estate.[43] Arguably, this perhaps was more a question of business than Famine relief.

By September 1846, conditions on the estate were dire. As the various relief committees completed questionnaires for submission to the Poor Law Commissioners in respect of funding, the extent of the want experienced by the tenantry was exposed. According to Henry Braddell, a chief-tenant in Ballingate, the labouring class of Carnew consumed potatoes supplemented with a little oatmeal. He estimated they would run out of supplies by November. There were no employment schemes or prospect of labour and those that managed to earn a wage could no longer afford to purchase food due to escalating prices. Throughout the other townlands a similar picture of impoverishment was reported.[44] As winter set in, workhouses, designed to deter, began to flood with bodies devoid of hope or alternative. The Shillelagh workhouse, built to accommodate 400 people, reached capacity on 12 December 1846. Soup kitchens in the urban centres offered some relief but only to those able to access them; for the most part, the rural poor on the estate continued to starve.

Thus in February 1847, Famine emigration began in earnest on the Fitzwilliam estate at a level not witnessed previously. Over the course of the next ten years, twenty-four ships transported the tenantry across the Atlantic, including the *Aberfoyle*, *Star* and *Dunbrody*, although this number is far from definitive. In this instance, two variances differentiate this later phase of migration from the earlier stream. Fitzwilliam chose William Graves & Son, shipping agents of New Ross, as opposed to Messrs Scott & Co. from Dublin, while New Ross replaced Dublin as the port of departure for all intending passengers.[45] Chaloner entered almost 6,000 names in the emigration books during the years 1847 to 1856. Closer examination of these challenge some widely-held beliefs and numbers, for a sizeable portion consist of a combination of duplicate entries, either families who did not leave when initially listed only to re-appear in subsequent years or, conversely, families members who simply refused to go. In addition, a number of names were scratched from the list, possibly as a consequence of death occurring prior to travelling.[46] Pat Monaghan, for example, his wife Alice and their two adult children rented a cabin and kitchen garden from John Carr in the townland of Coollattin. In 1848, Monaghan was listed for emigration as he 'pays no rent'.[47] However, the family did not leave at that time. They were subsequently listed the following year, although Pat had died in the interim and Alice, now a 65-year-old widow, her daughter Margaret and son Pat left New Ross aboard the ship *Jane* on 10 April.[48]

There was no discernible geographical pattern to the selection of emigrants. Over the course of the scheme every parish on the estate was affected by emigration, suggesting that tenants voluntarily chose to leave and presented themselves to Chaloner for inclusion in the scheme. Equally, an element of coercion can be seen in some instances with comments such as 'rejected', 'ejected' and, interestingly, 'a person it would be advisable to get rid of'. Then of course, there were tenants who simply refused to leave, which appears to suggest that an element of force was eventually used.[49] In a great many instances families that emigrated included extended family members, suggesting that emigration from this estate was final. Similar to the geographical spread, holdings relinquished varied considerably from the most destitute, owning nothing more than a cabin, to the more affluent, who leased in excess of 26 acres.[50]

Undoubtedly, the process of assisted emigration was beneficial to the estate. In the majority of cases, it was decided that land 'given up' would be absorbed by the head-tenant, eradicating, in theory, the worst excesses of the middleman system. Simultaneously, the departure of so many of the lesser strata of the community alleviated the financial burden on the estate, discharging it of various tithes and taxes.[51] However, the expense of initiating and sustaining emigration over a decade was substantial to say the least. Graves & Co. charged the estate £4 17*s* 2½*d* for each adult shipped to Canada.[52] In addition to passage, Fitzwilliam provided rice and oatmeal to sustain the emigrants during their time at sea, which averaged approximately forty-two days. The estate engaged the services of Joseph Exley to provide families travelling with a sea-chest to carry what little belongings they possessed. In addition, arrangements were put in place to facilitate the transfer of people and luggage to the port of New Ross. Arguably, the most significant cost was that of persuasion as tenants were compensated for relinquishing their holdings.[53] Rees calculates that it cost £16,342 11*s* 1*d* to conduct the scheme between 1848 and 1856.[54] Undoubtedly, the cost of 1847 far exceeded subsequent years as evidenced by the sheer exodus that year. An account pertaining to emigration from Coollattin to June 1847 records a total cost of £4,197 3*s* 10*d*, two thirds of which was paid to William Graves & Co. in two separate instalments in respect of 'passage of emigrants up to the 9th inst.' Joseph Exley received £99 1*s* 8*d* in respect of 'expence [*sic*] of materials and making of 173 sea-chests' with the balance pertaining to 'support, getting clothes, paying for cars (carts) to take their luggage' to the port.[55] To date, no other record has been located pertaining to costs incurred during 1847. However, if one was to the take this as a half-yearly estimate the total cost for the first year would be in the region of approximately £8,500, bringing the total cost of assisted emigration to approximately £25,000.

Arguably, the cost would have been substantially greater were it not for the agents' bookkeeping methods. Children were classified as those under the age of 14 and what can only be described as some dubious accounting that might warrant a tribunal today took place throughout these years! The manner in which the figures were made to tally is exemplified in the case of the Murphy family formerly of Knocklow, subsequently inmates of Shillelagh workhouse. Mary, aged 44, was listed as a widow and head of the family, which included four children. Her youngest daughter Catherine, originally recorded as 14 years old, was subsequently amended in the ledger, getting younger with time. Significantly, 13½ rendered her a child as opposed to an adult and consequently cheaper to emigrate. The reasoning behind this is evident in the note attached to the entry. It appears that Chaloner had asked the ratepayers in the district to contribute half the emigration expenses of the family. However, on 18 April 1854, the sum gathered was found to be short of the amount required. Hence, minor adjustments were made to ensure the Murphy family emigrated to the USA.[56]

It would be remiss to consider emigration from the Fitzwilliam estate solely as an attempt at estate restructuring, though arguably, in many respects, this is what it facilitated. Examples exist throughout the emigration books of people forfeiting pensions and large holdings in order to leave, including, for example, Pat Byrne of Ballinguile, near Kiltegan, who surrendered 45 acres.[57] Correspondence between Chaloner and Fitzwilliam in March 1849 appears to suggest that people were by this point more than willing to leave. Forty-three families, equating to 220 adults, were ready to leave New Ross on 29 March. This left 193 families waiting 'far more than [Fitzwilliam's] present directions would meet'. Chaloner requested an additional £2,000 which he estimated 'would land 400' and would relieve the situation somewhat as applications were arriving daily.[58]

As to the fate of those that left the south-west Wicklow estate during the Famine years, Canadian census records reveal that many families did extremely well in their new surroundings. The Hagerty family from the townland of Kilcavan sailed on the *Aberfoyle* in April 1848. They eventually settled in Frontenac County, Pittsburgh Township, Ontario, where they are listed on the 1861 census. By then the family were recorded as living in a one-and-a-half-storey log cabin. Peter and Catherine were not listed, perhaps married in the interim, but the other family members were, including Sarah, aged 7, who was born in 1854, first-generation Canadian.[59] Similarly, the Mellon family who left the estate in 1850 were listed a year later as residing in York County, Canada West, Ontario. Peter and his son John were listed as labourers while Jane, the matriarch of the family, was listed as house-keeping. No occupation was given for 20-year-old Jane but the family circumstances had changed considerably and they were living at that time in a one-and-a-half-storey frame house, a far cry from the cabin and 3 acres they had in the townland of Coolboy in County Wicklow.

That said, prosperity was not always instantaneous. The Redmond family of Cronyhorn townland in the parish of Carnew appeared to have swapped destitution in Ireland for destitution in Canada. The family rented a cabin from William Driver in Cronyhorn but took the decision to emigrate from the estate in 1849. John, his wife Ann and daughter Mary sailed out of New Ross aboard the *Bridgetown* on 18 April 1849.[60] It is likely that Ann was pregnant at the time of departure for in 1851 the Two years later, the family now included Annabelle, aged 3 (who was perhaps incorrectly recorded as being born in Ireland), and they were living in a Huron County, Ontario 'in a shanty'.[61] However, by 1861, the family's prospects had improved considerably. John, then 40 years old, had established himself as a farmer while Ann looked after their eight children who ranged in age from 14 to 1 year.[62] John died of dropsy aged 53 on 4 March 1871. At the time of his death he reputedly owned 100 acres of land, a dwelling house, two stables and numerous farming implements.[63] Similarly, the Kavanagh family from the townland of Parkmore left the Fitzwilliam estate in 1852 aboard the ship *Confiance*. John, his wife Catherine and five children arrived safely in Quebec on 16 June 1852. Their eldest daughter, Mary, aged 21, appears to have remained in Ireland.[64] By 1861, the family had settled in the town of Barrie in Simcoe County, approximately 60 miles north of Toronto. There they resided in a timber-frame two-storey house, with John and his eldest son Patrick employed as labourers.[65]

Though these case studies were not without hardship, these emigrants were in many respects the lucky ones. A large number never set foot on Canadian soil, succumbing to disease during the course of the voyage and buried at sea. For others that docked on the other side of the Atlantic, they did not survive the quarantine station at Grosse Île, particularly it seems for many of those who sailed aboard the *Progress* in 1847.[66] However, for those that managed to reach their destination, Canada offered them far greater opportunity than a poverty-stricken townland in south-west Wicklow. Arguably, no family epitomises this sentiment more than the Bawlf family of Hillbrook. In 1847, Nicholas Bawlf Senior relinquished a cabin and kitchen garden to an under-tenant and made the decision to emigrate. This one decision transformed his family's fortune and indeed, the agricultural pursuits of a country that provided refuge to so many Irish emigrants in a time of great need. Therefore, perhaps it is only fitting that when Nicholas Bawlf Junior died in December 1914, he felt compelled to leave a portion of his wealth estimated to be in the region of $660,000 to various 'public and charitable institutions' in Winnipeg.[67] These included St Boniface Hospital, Winnipeg General Hospital and Misericordia Hospital, to which he bequeathed the sum of $5,000 respectively. Similarly, St Joseph's Orphanage at 1476 Portage Avenue, which was run by the Grey Nuns, the Home of the Good Shepherd and the Roman Catholic church of St Mary's, where he had worshipped with his family, received a gift of $5,000 each, while the St Vincent de Paul Society and associated charities were willed $1,000 each.[68]

Assisted emigration from the Fitzwilliam estate in County Wicklow was not a Famine phenomenon; it had existed as early as the end of the Napoleonic wars although the figures during the early years were miniscule in comparison to the 1840s. By the mid-1830s, Fitzwilliam emigrants had settled and established communities throughout Canada. They had laboured and lost lives during the construction of the Rideau Canal. For those that remained in County Wicklow the onset of the Famine would alter land and lives irrevocably. Its longevity facilitated the propagation of assisted emigration on an unprecedented scale. In the initial years, it appears that the Fitzwilliam assisted emigration scheme was very much a question of business, as the issue of sub-division and escalating debt needed to be confronted. However, evidence suggests that, in its latter years at least, it became one of choice as O'Gráda contends 'the poor professed an eagerness to go, if subsidized', with tenants applying annually for the opportunity to leave.[69] Undeterred by the gruelling voyage, the prospect of death or the unknown, the Fitzwilliam Famine emigrants that made it safely to Canada prospered in a way they never could in Wicklow – asphyxiated by a system that ironically, as Griffith's Valuation suggests, ten years of sustained assisted emigration failed to exterminate entirely.

3

The experience of Irish women transported to Van Diemen's Land (Tasmania) during the Famine

Bláthnaid Nolan

Irish people have always left the island of Ireland. At various times they 'have trickled, rushed, flowed and been flushed out of their homeland to various destinations'.[1] To date, there has been particular interest in the large number of young, largely unmarried, Irish women who travelled alone and who accounted for more than half of the emigrants leaving Ireland from the mid-nineteenth century onwards, crossing the Atlantic to Canada and the USA. Notably, the works of Hasia Diner, Janet Nolan, Carol Groneman, and Kerby Miller have discussed the motivation behind these women's decision to leave Ireland, their choice of occupation and how they formed social and cultural support networks in the USA. However, in contrast, relatively little is known regarding the fate of women who were forced to make the arduous and dangerous journey to the southern hemisphere, to the Australian colonies, during the Great Famine period. This chapter discusses in detail the fate of Irish women transported to Van Diemen's Land (Tasmania). Using archives and records which exist for Irish female transportation, records that have been underutilised in Irish women's history, this chapter addresses a significant lacuna in the story of Irish global migration.

Mainstream historical discussions of the migration of generations of young women have not encapsulated the diverse and complex experience of every young woman who left Ireland. There are as many 'pasts' or 'stories' as there are interpretations. Moreover, convict transportation portrays a very different story; one of the forced migration of a population that has hitherto remained largely unexamined. Altogether, 162,119 men and women were transported to Australia from its establishment as a colony in 1787 until the last convict ship docked in 1868. Of this number, some 24,658 were women, of which 8,686, or more than a third, were Irish.[2] From 1842 until the end of transportation to Van Diemen's Land in 1853, over 3,000 women were transported on nineteen ships from the Grangegorman Penitentiary in Dublin to Hobart in Van Diemen's Land, now Tasmania. Convicts in Australia were the most documented individuals of the British Empire.[3] However, as very little is known about working-class individuals, particularly women, a unique exploration of the lives of these Irish women who were transported is possible. By following individual case histories through the archival records of Van Diemen's Land (Tasmania), it is feasible in some way to redress this imbalance between trans-Atlantic migration and trans-Pacific forced migration.

Details about convict women's family lives and the circumstances surrounding their crime can be found in Convict Reference Files (CRF) in the National Archives of Ireland. The CRF usually begin with a petition, or petitions, either by the convict themselves or someone on their behalf. Also included in the CRF are notes and letters from the individuals connected with the case, including judges, governors and physicians. Finally, the files indicate what sentence was imposed on the individual and the nature of the crime committed. Importantly, the information in these documents describes the case from various points of view. Petitioning the Lord Lieutenant was a strategy utilised by convicts sentenced to transportation, although Irish women did not petition as often as men. According to Rena Lohan, between 1791 and 1853, around 7,500 petitions were received from men, whereas less than 1,000 were received from women.[4] The number of men and women tried in Ireland and transported to Van Diemen's Land from 1803 to 1853 amounted to 7,301 and 3,687 respectively.[5] Perhaps due to more impoverished circumstances, convicted women were unable to procure the services of a legal clerk to write a petition on their behalf. As Peter King explains, upon receipt of a petition, the judge was requested to report on the case and 'since their reports were highly confidential the judges were usually prepared to be relatively open in explaining their attitudes to the accused'.[6] This is evident in the judges' letters within the CRFs. Corresponding to these files are the Tasmanian Conduct Registers, which include information on every ship that transported women from Britain and Ireland to Van Diemen's

Land. Indeed, each ship during the years 1844 and 1853 kept a Conduct Register. Arranged alphabetically by the woman's surname, every convict was allocated a page, thereby offering unique information on individuals. In this analysis, seven of the nineteen ships that sailed from Kingstown (Dún Laoghaire) in Dublin, to Hobart in Van Diemen's Land are referred to.

Table 1 below illustrates the names of seven sample ships, their dates of departures and arrivals, the number of women and children on board and the number of deaths suffered during the voyage. The average length of the journey was three months, although the *John William Dare*, which departed in 1851, had the unusually long voyage of 5 months. On the seven ships, carrying a total of 1,095 convict women, only thirty-four deaths were recorded. This is a remarkably low when compared with death rates on emigrant ships crossing the Atlantic. However, there was precedent for such successful voyages to Australia. Meredith and Oxley, for example, refer to the First Fleet in 1787 as 'a veritable convict Armada', pointing out that convicts transported to America in the eighteenth century had done so under private and commercial contract, whereas the government legislated, controlled and covered the cost of those transported to Australia.[7] It was a tremendously successful sea voyage given that the fleet of eleven vessels had travelled for 252 days for more than 15,000 miles without losing a ship. There was a very low death rate of just over 3 per cent, an astonishing figure given the severe demands of such a journey and the lack of medical knowledge and proper equipment, coupled with problems of navigation and the seafaring inexperience of the convicts accommodated in overcrowded, foul-smelling and compact spaces.[8]

Ship Name	*Date of Departure*	*Date of Arrival*	*No. of convict women on board*	*No. of children of convict women on board*	*No. of deaths on board*
Greenlaw	7 March 1844	2 July 1844	120	28	10
Phoebe	22 September 1845	2 January 1845	128	28	1
Waverley	19 July 1847	25 October 1847	134	33	7
John Calvin	24 January 1848	18 May 1848	171	33	5
Australasia	26 June 1849	29 September 1849	200	28	6
John William Dare	28 December 1851	22 May 1852	172	20	4
Midlothian	17 November 1852	22 February 1853	170	19	1

Table 1: List of the sample ships which carried convicts to Van Diemen's Land, 1844-53[9]

The average age of female convicts transported to the Australian colonies during the Famine was 27.[10] Of those transported from Grangegorman in County Dublin, the average age was 29 during the years 1844 and 1845, but decreased to 26 in the period from 1847 to 1849.[11] From this evidence, it can be argued that the authorities were transporting women for their productive and reproductive labour, characteristics that were crucial to the survival of the colonies.[12] The high numbers of women transported during the Famine years can be accounted for in a number of ways. Firstly, the government was clearing large numbers of peasant women from the most densely populated and impoverished country in Europe. Secondly, due to the temporary suspension of male transportation during 1847 and 1848, which was an attempt to address sex imbalances in the colony, while there was a greater demand for female convict labour. The transportation of even greater numbers of women in later years can also be explained in terms of this demand for convict labour. The majority of the women transported on these ships were young, single, Roman Catholic, illiterate and over half had been convicted of just one or two crimes before. The majority were transported for larceny (theft) and sentenced to seven years. Official records both in Ireland and Van Diemen's Land place the women in a wider context of convicts' narratives and reconstruct, in part, the lives of convict women through the petitions sent to the Lord Lieutenant in the Vice-Regal Lodge. The genre of writing utilised in convict petitions was formulaic and formal. In some cases the judgements of the cases were analysed. The following takes a case-study approach and uses as examples the personal histories of some of the women transported from Grangegorman during the Famine years.

Mary Byron from County Carlow was transported for seven years on board the ship *Waverley* in October 1847. Described as being 46 years old and could read, her case study is significant as it sheds light on the desperation that many were subjected to during the Famine. Married with three children, Byron, a Roman Catholic, was convicted of stealing clothes. A serial offender, she had been convicted four times prior to her transportation. Twice she had been sentenced to six months for stealing potatoes, twelve months for stealing a pot, and six months for stealing a pen. This might lend some credence to habitual criminality but in reality she and her family were destitute and these were the worst years of the Famine. Interestingly, Byron was 20 years older than the average age of transported convict women. There is confusion in the records as to how many children were transported with her. According to Catherine Fleming, the Chief Secretary allowed her two youngest, Matthew and Bridget, to travel with her.[13] However, Byron's Conduct Register account states that there was only one child on board with her.[14] Both of these records also state that she claimed she had four children, although her own petition only mentions three. The other children probably remained in Naas workhouse.[15]

In October 1846, as conditions worsened following the second failure of the potato crop, Mary Byron travelled from Carlow to nearby Athy in County Kildare (a distance of approximately 15 miles), accompanied by her husband Peter and children. Having had former convictions, she and her husband were again convicted of stealing clothes, 'a crime of total despair' resulting in little hope of clemency.[16] The couple petitioned on their own behalf, professing that they had 'three children, one male aged eleven years; one male aged eight years and one female aged two years', all of whom were with them in Athy Gaol.[17] In the petition Byron argued that the children were destitute of any friends in the neighbourhood, and 'under the circumstances petitioners most humbly hope that your Excellency will be pleased to take their distressing case into your humane consideration and order that the children may be allowed to proceed with them – otherwise they will be left destitute'.[18] Unfortunately, no further records could be found of their children in Ireland.[19]

Upon arrival in Van Diemen's Land Mary Byron secured work as a 'farm servant' after the report of her voyage had noted that she was 'quiet'.[20] Having a clean Conduct Register was an incentive for mothers, as their children were taken into the government-run orphanages. Having said that, Byron was soon in trouble with the authorities after she was found with 'a man in her bedroom', for which she received six months' hard labour. It was also recommended that she 'not be allowed to enter service in Hobart Town' and was 'to be hired in the interior' (meaning the rural interior) of the colony.[21] Although this was her only offence in the colony, it would have been viewed as grossly immoral – defying the strict moral code demanded by the convict system.

Within these prisons or 'female factories', as they were known, the management of convict women was carried out through order, daily routine, gauged tasks and regulated penalties.[22] Within the system there were various categories of convict. At the lower end of the scale was the third or 'Crime Class' of women who suffered disproportionately. This comprised two types of women: convict women who had broken a rule of assignment (usually minor) and were sent to the factory by their master for punishment; the other was unmarried pregnant women unable to perform their duties. Tony Rayner describes it thus:

> Perhaps the worst crime committed against women in history has been to degrade those who became pregnant whilst unmarried, or who through poverty asked a living by prostitution, whilst ignoring the most basic fact that procreation requires both a man and a woman.[23]

Men did not receive such punishment, nor were they legally obliged to provide financially for their offspring. Following the birth of the child, after whatever amount of time was deemed sufficient by the authorities, these women still had to serve a six-month sentence of hard labour for becoming pregnant. Their diet was poorer than the other classes and they had to wear coarse and plain clothes with a large yellow 'C' sewed on the back of their jacket, sleeves and shifts of their uniform.[24] What is clear from the outset is that many of the offences in Van Diemen's Land consisted of minor infractions, such as: absence without leave; neglect of duty; insubordination or other trivial infringements. The convict women in this sample were mostly punished for social and sexual misbehaviour. It could be hypothesised that female Conduct Registers reflect the high moral expectations as well as high labour demands that Victorian middle-class employers (or those who aspired to be perceived as such) had of their convicts.

Although Mary Byron received her ticket of leave in 1850, it was revoked two years later in September 1852, when she was fined 5*s* for being 'drunk and using indecent language'. This punishment coincided with her petition for the remainder of the family to join her, which was refused. However, by February 1853 she was recommended for a conditional pardon and eight months later, despite the earlier decree of not being allowed to enter service in Hobart, she gained her certificate of freedom and was living there.[25] Having arrived in the colony in October 1847, she was free after six years and one month, a recurring theme of the case histories. Her 3-year-old daughter Biddy was admitted to the Queen's Orphanage, New Town, on 29 October 1847, where she remained until June 1851 when she was discharged to her mother.[26] This was a relatively happy ending, although it can be assumed that she never saw her other children again.

Catherine Colligan, from County Tipperary, was aged 35 when convicted of the murder of her landlady, Margaret Foran, with whom she lived with her husband and child in County Kildare. Colligan, one of the few Protestants in the case study, was married and could read and write. She was not a habitual offender and neither was she in the usual category of the young, 20-something-year old, who was single. Her story is interesting for a number of reasons, not least as to whether or not she actually committed any crime. According to the *Leinster Express*:

> On the evening of 22 February 1847, Mrs Foran was assaulted in her cabin with a shovel and left bleeding on the floor by the hearth with a fractured skull ... Although she could not speak and tell of her assailant, she lingered for three days before dying.[27]

While no petition survives in Colligan's file it does contain an intriguing letter detailing the circumstances from the man who found her guilty. In concluding the case Judge Crampton stated that he 'pronounced sentence of death upon the convict & fixed Wednesday the 25th April next for the day of execution'.[28] Crompton considered the convict 'tho [*sic*] neither lunatic nor idiot appeared to be very low in the scale of humanity & to have but very indistinct notions of the difference between right & wrong'.[29] He described her as a married woman and that her husband:

> (who was entirely unconnected with the crime of his wife, and his being miles from home at the time when the crime was [perpetrated]) was the first person to institute enquiry & the first to bring the Police to the scene of his wife's guilt – Ignorant no doubt he was that it was by his own wife's hand that the bloody deed was done, but he still deserves some consideration for the promptitude with which he stepped forward to appeal the cause of justice – a promptitude not of common occurrence in this country with persons of his class.[30]

While Catherine Colligan's voice is absent in the Irish records, her version of events entered into the Conduct Register in Hobart puts a very different perspective on the murder. She stated that her husband had beaten the woman to death, but that he had witnesses to state he was somewhere else. If her version of events are to be believed, then bringing the police to a murder scene when he had an iron-clad alibi, would certainly cast a shadow of suspicion on his wife. Taking this into consideration then, his need to convey the police as quickly as possible to his home could only have been beneficial to him and would frame his wife. The judge's bias was blatant, not only when referring to Mr Colligan as an exception 'in this country with persons of his class', but also when he recommended the Lord Lieutenant 'to spare the life of one who tho [*sic*] perhaps unfit to live is certainly most unfit to die & to commute the Guilty Prisoners sentence to Transportation for life'.[31] Guilty or not, Catherine Colligan, along with 133 other Irish female convicts, and thirty-three of their children, embarked from Kingstown Harbour on 21 June 1847 aboard the *Waverley*.

The significance of Colligan's subsequent story is two-fold: firstly, she was punished only twice in the colony and secondly, as with other women convicted of murder in the case histories, she had a much lower rate of recidivism than the petty thieves.[32] On arrival in Van Dieman's Land the surgeon reported her character as 'exemplary'.[33] There she again reiterated the fact that she was innocent: 'my husband murdered her but he brought witnesses to shew [*sic*] he was not there'.[34] With little evidence of the personal experience of convicts, their first-person statements are examples of the convict voice regardless of its brevity.[35] Finding employment as a 'laundress, plain cook and dairy woman', Colligan's first offence was that she delivered an illegitimate baby boy named Joseph in 1849. Three years later she was reprimanded for 'insolence and refusing to work', which earned her six months' hard labour.[36] It was also noted in her Conduct Register that she 'not be allowed to enter any service to the Southward of Oatlands'.[37] This may have been because she had been sent there as a 'murderer' and similar to others in the case histories she was required to serve twelve years before being granted a ticket of leave. Despite already being married in Ireland, license to marry Patrick Groghan was sought in June 1854. She received her ticket of leave the same year, within seven years of her arrival, and three years later was granted her conditional pardon.[38]

Another similar case was Mary Carroll, whose petition was made by her husband Patrick at the time of her transportation. A Roman Catholic, aged 37, Carroll could read and write. Again her age and marital status do not align with the majority of convict women who were transported. Convicted in Dublin for the felony of stealing money, her husband humbly 'beseeched' the Lord Lieutenant's mercy as his wife was of 'weak intellect' which could be verified by 'medical gentlemen' and because of this weakness she was influenced by a more guilty party.[39] Despite the fact that she could read and write, Patrick Carroll alleged that because of her 'weak intellect', she was 'made the dupe of artful designing [v]illains who have been her ruin and cause of her present awful situation'.[40] He implored the Lord Lieutenant to have 'mercy on her behalf and [F]our afflicted children whom with petitioner are reduced [to] the most agonising state by her misfortune'.[41] This was a feature of many petitions and, as King argued, the 'agonising state' of a defendant's dependants were criteria that judges usually took into account.[42] Once again the 'highly respectable signatures' were hoped to 'operate in her favour and prevent her from undergoing her awful sentence'.[43] Patrick Carroll pleaded for his wife's sentence to be carried out in a prison at home.

Dependence upon the woman emerges as a valid reason for leniency, either because of aged parents or in this case 'four afflicted children'.[44] Mary Cullen reminds us that women's contribution to the household income was substantial and played a vital role in the survival of the family as an economic unit.[45] Patrick Carroll's words testify to this fact, but the judges' recommendations in the letters that accompanied petitions seemed to have the final say in Dublin Castle.[46] Similar to Catherine Colligan, the judge proceeded to castigate the prisoner whilst commending the character of her husband:

> That the prisoner was, as stated in the Memorial, convicted before this one on the 27th of May last of having stolen money from the shop of Terence Brennan – that it appeared she had done so in a very artful and cunning manner. That she had been five times before tried for and twice before convicted of felonies of a similar character. I believe her husband, the Memorialist, to be a respectable man – but I am regretfully of opinion that under the circumstances the prisoner is not a deserving object of Mercy.[47]

Mary Carroll's petition was ultimately rejected. This response made it clear that Carroll's crime was not her first offence, thereby confirming her guilt in the eyes of the judge.[48] It could be deduced that since Mary

Carroll had four children and a husband that were so dependent on her, she may have stolen in order to provide for them. If this was the case then her husband Patrick was most likely complicit in her crimes. The judge, however, recognised Patrick Carroll 'to be a respectable man', whilst failing to see any grounds for clemency towards his wife and thus she was transported on the *Phoebe*. Although no record is made of her literacy, upon arrival she was recorded as a 'dry nurse' in her Conduct Register.[49] Just over three years later she received her ticket of leave in July 1848 and by 1851 she had been given a certificate of freedom. During that time her only offence was the delivery of an illegitimate child in 1846.[50]

Another of the convicts in the sample was Margaret Leavy, 23 years old, a Roman Catholic, a single woman who could not read or write. Although from Dublin, Leavy was tried in County Louth in 1843. She was transported for ten years for the robbery and felony of a bonnet and shawl, and arrived in July 1844 on the ship *Greenlaw*.[51] Prior to her transportation Leavy had been convicted once for stealing money and had spent nine months in prison. Her Convict Reference File is unique in that it presents testimonies of witnesses during the court case in which she was found guilty. Leavy appears to have been caught up in an unfortunate affair and, if the witnesses for the defence's testimony are to be believed, the woman who made the accusation fabricated the theft, committed perjury in court and bribed her father to do the same.[52] The case of Leavy also highlights how many of these women (and indeed men) were transported in the wrong and for trivial offences. The evidence provided at the trial also offers an interesting insight into Ireland in the 1840s. Although Leavy's crime involved the theft of a bonnet, handkerchief and shawl, during the course of the trial there were several references to her having 'loitered' on the streets of Drogheda. Loitering on streets was a clear intimation of prostitution. During her cross-examination, it is interesting to note that loitering on streets and drinking whiskey were underlined by the court clerk, although references to theft were not. This perhaps testifies to the Victorian moral attitudes towards the working classes. Intemperance in women repulsed a bourgeois masculinity which liked to see chastity in women that reflected the virtues of restraint, discipline and self-control.

Despite Leavy's petition claiming perjury by the Cunninghams and the evidence of the defence witnesses, she was transported for ten years.[53] There her convictions were few – perhaps suggesting that she had been the innocent party in Drogheda. Her gaol report was good, and the surgeon's report was 'good laterally'.[54] Towards the end of the voyage her behaviour may have modified as a strategy to gain favour with the surgeon. Recorded as working as a 'nursemaid' in Van Diemen's Land, she gave birth to an illegitimate stillborn daughter in September 1846, after which she would have spent six months in the 'Crime Class' of the female factory. There her conduct page records a small number of infractions, such as 'insolence' and 'misconduct in smoking at meal times'.[55] Smoking by a woman, was very much frowned upon by mid-nineteenth-century colonial society. For her misconduct she was reprimanded by being sent to the hiring depot at Launceston. Leavy finally received her ticket of leave in March 1850, five and a half years after her arrival.

Not all of the case studies had similar outcomes and the story of Mary Sullivan provides an inverted narrative. Arriving on the *John William Dare* in May 1852, Sullivan had been convicted in County Cork to two years previous for stealing quilts.[56] She had been in gaol twice before: once for stealing clothes for which she served six months, and once for stealing from Cork Workhouse, also resulting in six months' imprisonment. Given her young age (she was 17 when she arrived in the colony, therefore she would have been 15 when convicted) it is possible that she was one of the 'forsaken', as described by Dympna McLoughlin. The 'forsaken' was the term used to describe those who were brought to the workhouse as infants, or abandoned children, and who were raised there. In the workhouse they were effectively institutionalised and were unable to carry out 'respectable' work. The minute books of these institutions testify that female inmates were perceived as 'unmovable deadweight', as described by Gerard Moran in chapter one.[57] Sullivan's mental health may have suffered during this time, which might in turn explain her social (in)abilities in Van Diemen's Land.[58] Employed as a nursemaid, she absconded in July 1852 and a reward of £2 was offered for her apprehension. When she was eventually located she was brought to court and tried 'for the wilful murder of Adeline Clara Blackburn Frazer (on the 7th [of this month]), a child of two years old and sentenced to be hanged and dissected'.[59] Mary O'Sullivan was duly executed on 5 August 1852.

While the case of O'Sullivan had a particularly sad conclusion, there were others, such as the sisters Judith and Margaret Byrne from Dundalk, County Louth, for whom transportation provided a gateway to a new life. Transported in 1845 for stealing a pair of shoes, their family had petitioned for clemency on their behalf as they had an ill and feeble father who relied on them. By 1848, in their new colonial home, both Byrne sisters were married and by 1851, they were both free, again just six years after transportation. One wonders if their family in Ireland survived the ravages of the Famine and or what the sisters' circumstances would have been had they remained in Ireland? Their fortune in transportation was mirrored by others such as Mary Ryan, who, aged 16, was transported from Waterford for seven years for larceny and Margaret Leahy, aged 17 when she was transported from Cork for ten years for a similar crime. Remarkably, both women were still alive in 1909 when they applied for their old-age pension.

The Grangegorman Transportation Register, the Convict Reference Files and the Conduct Registers are an invaluable resource to the historian of convictism. The petitions and case evidence provide testimony to the existence of the women who were transported from the Grangegorman Transportation Holding Depot, while the Conduct Registers provide an official record of the women in the colony. Apart from these records, all their achievements and failures died with them. Analysis of the seven ships containing 1,095 convict women and their individual case histories allows for a penetrative insight into Irish women's history, mid-nineteenth-century Irish history, colonial Australian history and significantly what social conditions were like for women during the Great Famine. Moreover, it offers a unique insight into the fate of Irish Famine emigrants.

4

Reporting the Irish Famine in America: Images of 'Suffering Ireland' in the American press, 1845–1848

James M. Farrell

On 17 April 1847, a citizen of Boston, using the pseudonym 'A North Ender', submitted a letter to the *Boston Bee* newspaper, expressing his concern about the increase of Irish immigrants in the city:

> Of the 3,000 paupers at present supported by this city, over 2,000 are foreigners! and without taking into view this almost daily increasing burden by our 'spring ships,' there are more important and solemn considerations which are due our country in endeavouring to protect it from the baneful and deteriorating influence, which this mass of bigoted, ignorant, and vicious offscouring of Ireland and England, &c., must have upon our national character, our institutions, morals, &c. … there is a stern duty we owe our own country in the protection of its political and religious liberty, its morals, its general institutions, and the 'bone and sinew' of our land, the mechanic and laboring men, from the deadly influence of foreign imported pauperism.[1]

The uncharitable attitude of this letter writer was rather widely held by Americans in the wake of the early Famine migration to North American cities. And, while the social, ethnic, and religious differences between the 'native' Americans and the arriving Irish certainly explain a measure of the anti-immigrant sentiment, these explanations are,

I believe, inadequate to account for the virulence of anti-Irish rhetoric, and the depth of emotion with which the prejudice against the Irish was felt during the Famine migration. This chapter offers a close examination of the image of the Irish constructed from narratives of the Famine in American newspapers – daily and weekly, Whig and Democratic, secular and Christian – and aims to reveal not only why Americans so aggressively opposed Irish immigration, but also why the language of that anti-Irish discourse was passionate to the point of hysteria. Beginning in mid-1845, there was regular coverage of the Irish Famine in American newspapers. From these many press accounts of the Famine I have identified six master narratives that largely defined American newspaper coverage of the catastrophe. Together these narratives reveal how nineteenth-century Americans came to understand the Famine and its victims, and combined to create a portrait of the Irish that predisposed Americans to be passionately hostile towards Irish Famine immigrants.[2]

The potato blight first appeared in Ireland in August of 1845, but the alarming news was not reported in American newspapers straight away. The *New Hampshire Sentinel* of 24 September contained a notice about the total failure of the potato crop in Belgium, from a disease 'which begins at the leaves and gradually turns into corruption the whole plant,'[3] but most newspapers were still reporting 'the news from Ireland is not important'.[4] By early October, however, the first stories about a looming Famine in Ireland appeared. 'The disease among the potato crop seems to be universal,' reported the *Ohio Statesman*, and 'in Ireland it forms the chief food of the people'. While some districts had 'escaped the ravages of the disease', the 'injury is too wide spread not to cause alarm'.[5] During this earliest period of news from Ireland, there was, as yet, no Famine on which to report. The prevailing theme was one of apprehension. Throughout Europe, reported one paper, 'the potato crop is injured by disease generally, but in Ireland so as to threaten famine'.[6] Another warned that, 'Famine, gaunt, horrible, destroying famine seems impending. Fears have seized the public mind. In Ireland matters look appalling – in England gloomy'.[7]

There were varying accounts about the extent and severity of the potato crop failure. Reports offered a range of scientific explanations for the blight and some papers suggested adjustments in agricultural methods to prevent complete collapse of the crop. Other stories recommended changes in British economic and administrative policy as a way to avoid catastrophe. Some newspapers even emphasised that Ireland's grief was America's opportunity. While an actual famine remained an abstraction of the future, a considerable number of stories focused on the impact of the potato failure on the commodity exchange, emphasising how the markets in Europe would be demanding American grain. The *Baltimore Sun*, for example, reported that:

> The present state of things will give a powerful impetus to the feeling in favour of free trade, and rumours, even now are prevalent – mere conjectures, probably, but straws show how the wind blows – that Peel, ere long, will throw open the ports, and thus anticipate the famine which would appear to be impending over Ireland, and which cannot be unfelt in England.[8]

Likewise, the *Boston Daily Atlas* summarised the news from London by saying 'the leading topics that have agitated the public mind are, the famine in Ireland – the opening of the ports, for the admission of foreign grain' and 'the probable repeal of the Corn Laws'. The paper made sure its readers understood that 'the opening of the ports for the admission of foreign grain is of the greatest importance to commercial circles in the United States'.[9]

Still, the main attitude was one of foreboding as correspondents contemplated the human cost of the approaching Famine. It was this fear of an imminent catastrophe that was the chief element of the earliest American news accounts of the Great Irish Famine. By early November, most papers were reporting that 'a failure of the Irish potato crop' was 'now too painfully certain,' and 'a famine among the Irish people is apprehended'.[10] According to the *Southern Patriot*, 'there is now no part of the country that is not visited by the blight' and 'even allowing much for exaggerated alarm' it was clear 'the loss is tremendous'. Yet, 'the worst feature in the calamity is the uncertainty that still exists'.[11] Implicit in these narratives of apprehension is an awareness of the specific conditions of Ireland that made the crop failure something worse than simply an agricultural setback. Knowing that in Ireland the vast majority of the peasant population relied on the potato as the primary food source led correspondents and editors to the obvious conclusion that, without extraordinary measures, a potato blight almost certainly meant widespread starvation and death.[12]

Stories that emphasised anxieties about a pending disaster also tapped into a common fear among Americans, most of whom still lived in a farming economy and whose collective identity was rooted in a shared agrarian past infused with traditional pastoral values. The trepidation and disquiet that arises upon contemplation of a complete crop failure thus deeply implicates the Irish people as a population in danger. Fear is the principal emotional response to the perception of imminent danger. By sympathetic identification Americans could imagine the growing panic of Irish peasants who saw their livelihoods and sustenance rotting away before their eyes. The danger is all the more pronounced when no basis for confidence – no alternative source of food, and no remedy from science or the government – was at hand to diminish the foreboding. The Irish people, then, were constructed as a helpless population in grave danger. 'The fear of trans-Atlantic famine, or apprehension of scarcity, do not by any means appear to be feigned, as some have been led to suppose,' reported the *Baltimore Sun* in early December.[13] Using the words of a Dublin correspondent, the *Ohio Statesman* warned Americans that, 'SIX MILLIONS OF HUMAN BEINGS in Ireland and England, are within *eight weeks* of STARVATION!'[14] Indeed, wrote another correspondent to a different newspaper, there was an 'appalling prospect of a *horrible famine in Ireland*'.[15]

Once it became clear that famine had indeed struck Ireland, newspapers in America sought to offer a deeper analysis of events. The period of apprehension had passed, but now the newspapers sought some way to go beyond simply reporting that 'Famine and fever continue to prevail to an alarming extent, in Ireland'.[16] One of the ways that the newspapers struggled to explain the Famine was to characterise the crisis as an 'appalling visitation'[17] of God's justice, or as a providential chastisement of 'God smitten Ireland'.[18] In this narrative frame, the Famine is accounted for in theological terms. 'The mysterious Providence of Almighty God,' reported the *Wisconsin Democrat*, 'has deprived that great people of the principal article of its daily food'.[19] The *Connecticut Constitution* concluded, 'it has pleased God in his inscrutable providence to afflict Ireland',[20] yet, as the *Friends' Review* explained, quoting scripture, 'O the depth of the riches both of the wisdom and knowledge of God! How unsearchable are his judgments, and his ways past finding out!'[21] The editors of the *Christian Secretary* agreed, noting:

> The suffering which has been brought upon the poor of that down trodden country by the failure in the crop of a single article of food was designed, undoubtedly, by the Providence that directed it, for some wise and benevolent purpose: but it is not for us to determine what that purpose is.[22]

While it is not surprising to find this motif appearing in Christian publications across the USA, it also emerges in the secular press. Within the narrative, the Irish have no personal agency, but are acted upon by divine providence. The implication is, of course, that the Irish are being punished for their sins. Nor are readers encouraged to further investigate other causes, or inquire into the political and economic conditions of Ireland. Instead, readers are left to simply reflect on God's mysterious ways. If there was any consideration of a cause it was tightly constrained by the theological frame of the narrative. For example, the *New York Evangelist* concluded that the Famine was God's way of advancing the temperance cause. 'The Providence of God has powerfully co-operated [in that cause], by the visitation of a fearful scourge in teaching the lesson of temperance. In Ireland it is a grateful fact that temperance has greatly mitigated the evils of the famine'.[23]

Whether God's purpose could be known or not, the suffering of the Irish was held up as a moral lesson for Americans, who were invited to contemplate that they too, in God's good time, might be made the object of a similar chastisement. Indeed, this was the lesson conveyed by the editors of the *Christian Inquirer*:

> Yes, in this age of long peace and unexampled industry and overflowing abundance, a cry of famine has gone through the world; and communities, nations, pine for lack of bread. It is a most significant and startling intimation to the world of its weakness and dependence upon a Power above itself … in lowliness must we bow before the great Ruler of the world, and feel that we are poor and helpless pensioners upon his bounty: that it is not in man that walketh, to direct his steps, nor in man that laboreth to provide his wants; that power is no protection, and wealth no defence; that the ship-fever coming from the far-off shore of famine-smitten Ireland, may strike down the noblest and the strongest among us.[24]

Another characteristic gesture of the visitation narrative is the personification of Famine as a destroying angel or as the spectral instrument of God's justice. Such personification can be seen in the *Boston Transcript* story of 3 October 1846: 'Famine, with its numerous and dreadful train of diseases, knocks at the doors of the great majority of [Ireland's] brave and hardy population. Already the cry has become universal "give us food, that we perish not"'.[25] In a similar way, another paper explained: 'nor does famine march alone; the pestilence, in its most loathsome form, follows close in the train'.[26] American newspapers frequently employed such personifications to emphasise the extent and certainty of Irish suffering. 'Famine and death, grim messengers of despair, stalk boldly forth with lion front, in their most hideous form, crushing all beneath the massive wheels of their mighty juggernautal car'.[27] In another report, readers were encouraged to imagine 'gaunt famine, with raging fever at her heels, are marching through the length and breadth of the island'.[28] As Sean Ryder has observed, such images borrow heavily from Gothic literary conventions, 'the notion of the walking dead, the spectre army, the terror produced by violating the natural order'.[29] However, for nineteenth-century Americans, it was the biblical associations that resonated among a people whose worldview was an expression of their distinctly Protestant identity.[30]

The visitation narratives tended not only to discourage interrogation of the political and economic relationship between Ireland and Great Britain, they also limited consideration of available remedies. The witness to providential visitation responds with characteristic resignation and awe. Divine punishment does not invite economic change or political revolution. If any response is invited, it is that of charity, as readers are reminded that the same God who smites Ireland has also blessed America abundantly. 'Starvation and death is entering the homely dwellings of the poor of the "Green Isle",' wrote the *Baltimore Sun*, 'and it is only by the immediate and efficient aid of those whom a kind Providence has blessed with plenty that the monster famine can be expelled from their firesides'.[31]

This brings us to the stories about the charitable American response to the Famine, and the reports of American attempts at Irish Famine relief. Indeed, a significant portion of the American press coverage of the Irish Famine was not directly about Ireland or the Irish at all, but rather about American charitable efforts to ease Irish suffering. Americans were exceedingly generous to the Irish during the period of the Famine, and the newspapers were conscientious in reporting on the progress of relief efforts. Many of the stories were self-congratulatory, and no doubt gave Americans satisfaction that they were assisting in the relief of so much misery. The narratives largely confirmed the image Americans had of themselves as a providentially blessed and Christian nation, quite in contrast to the image of an Ireland abandoned by God and plagued by famine and disease.

Beginning as early as November of 1845, American papers called for charitable efforts to ease the suffering in Ireland. 'The blight that has fallen upon the potatoe [*sic*] crop has taken their only food out of the mouths of millions', wrote the *Baltimore Sun*, 'leaving them no alternative but death by starvation, should relief from without not be extended to them'.[32] As Americans responded to these calls, the newspapers reported on the relief efforts. The *Southern Patriot* (a newspaper from Charleston, South Carolina) reported on a relief meeting in Boston 'to devise means of extending aid to Ireland, now threatened by a famine, in consequence of the failure of her potatoe [*sic*] crop'. The meeting included appeals and addresses by prominent citizens and 'at the close of the speeches a subscription list was opened and upwards of six hundred dollars raised on the spot. Measures were then adopted to increase the fund'.[33] By the following winter of 1846–1847 Americans had responded to the crisis with an unprecedented amount of private charity for the 'suffering Irish'. Indeed, according to George Potter, aid to the Irish during the Famine was 'the first great nationwide free-will extension of American generosity and benevolence to other people bowed down under a natural catastrophe'.[34]

Charity narratives consisted of two main themes. The first was the appeal to readers for assistance in relieving Irish suffering. The second was the reporting on charitable efforts that often included applause for those public officials who took the lead in relief meetings. A story in the *Trenton State Gazette* demonstrates the collaboration of these themes in portraying the generosity of Americans:

> This evening the meeting called by the Mayor, for the purpose of raising money for the relief of the starving Irish, is to be held. We propose that this morning, and throughout the day, our readers should endeavour to realize the condition of the wretched sufferers. Information enough has been published and re-published, to put it out of the power of any to doubt, that all the charities we can send, will do good, and contribute to feed those who are dying for want of food.[35]

Other papers echoed the appeals to charity. The *Baltimore Sun* encouraged readers, exhorting them to continue their charitable efforts:

> With the increase of destitution and the rigor of privation, active sympathy should keep pace, and effort be enlarged. The United States is an immense field of action, and more favourable than any other land for the successful exertions of benevolent enterprise. Here, domestic charity has erected countless monuments of its steady perseverance.[36]

Likewise, the *Barre Patriot* reminded readers that:

> With us lies the power to diminish, to a great extent, the suffering which pervades the length and breadth of that land. Then arise! With all your boasted honour, virtue and goodness, ye sons and daughters of New England, and extend to them *now*, for now is the day, and now is the hour, the hand of mercy and benevolence, as hundreds and thousands are dying hourly and daily.[37]

When Americans began to respond, the newspapers faithfully reported on the relief efforts. 'The first step of the Committee,' reported the *Southern Patriot*:

> Was immediately to appoint Sub Committees in each Ward, to wait upon the citizens of their respective Wards, and solicit from them such aid, as in their liberality under the circumstances, they might be disposed to give … These committees are actively, and it is pleasing to relate, successfully engaged at work.[38]

The *Farmer's Cabinet* also dutifully reported on relief efforts:

> Subscriptions are going on in all quarters of the Union. There is scarcely a city or town in the country that is not contributing something for the relief of the poor starving Irish and Scotch. Contributions are daily pouring in from city, village and hamlet. America will make a generous offering, on the altar of Christian sympathy … Small efforts are not to be despised in such a work as this; they are the little rills that go to make up the great streams of charity, that is now beginning to swell across the Atlantic to the shores of suffering Ireland.[39]

But the charity narratives, very common after February 1847, continue to portray the Irish as helpless victims. Rarely did such stories of charity work include a reference to the Irish people without the adjective of 'starving' or 'suffering' or 'unhappy' or 'famishing'. To be sure, the charity was generous, and the appeals necessary to keep American readers active in their relief efforts. It is also the case that such narratives perpetuated a view of the Irish as forsaken and dependent. While they were perhaps a worthy focus of benevolence while suffering in Ireland, they could easily become a drain on the public treasury when planted among a prosperous people. Thus the common images constructed by the charity narratives prepare Americans for the often much less charitable response made to the Famine immigrants that began shortly to arrive on their wharves and streets.

When we turn to consider the fourth of the master narratives, the narratives of blame, we find a broad collection of disparate theories and explanations. Narratives that focused on attributing blame for the Famine are united, not by the details of the cause they identified, nor by the solution they proposed, but rather by the desire of writers and readers to make sense of this horrifying event across the Atlantic. In all cases, however, the Irish themselves are diminished in dignity, as either lacking in essential virtues or as victims of some force beyond their control. Apart from the commonplace narratives of providential visitation already addressed above, three prominent themes make up the bulk of the narratives of blame: the British Government is to blame, the Irish people themselves are to blame and the Catholic religion is to blame.

From the earliest reports of the impending Famine, some American papers held the British Government responsible, if not for the potato rot itself, at least for failure to respond with adequate measures to avert catastrophe. 'Is this, then, the determination of the British government?' asked the *New Hampshire Sentinel*. 'Seven millions of people, or, at least, the great majority, the whole of the lower classes, live habitually in scarcity – in what would elsewhere be thought famine, and are threatened with absolute want and starvation, while enormous duties are permitted to remain upon all kinds of grain; and the only suggestion in their behalf is an appeal to charity!' How is it, the paper wanted to know, that 'the government can do nothing, although there is a duty on wheat of eighteen shillings per quarter, and on other grain in proportion, standing directly in the way of the poor man's bread!'[40] Analysing the matter more deeply, the *Berkshire Whig* thought the source of Ireland's problems could be traced to the system imposed by its colonial masters:

> Press the whole population of the United States into Massachusetts; let the title to the soil in that State be in some ten thousand persons, and despite the most perfect form of government on earth, Massachusetts would be a land of famine and murder; millions would be absolutely at the mercy of the few landholders ... In Ireland, ten times the food consumed by the people is raised. It is sent out of the country and converted into rent.[41]

In a similar way, the New Orleans *Times Picayune* affirmed that the origins of the Famine were to be found in the fact that 'the British Government has confiscated nearly every acre of land on that beautiful island from the original native owners, and has bestowed them on favourites, generally non-resident foreigners'.[42] The *Wisconsin Democrat* agreed:

> One million of souls, gone to a happier world, we trust, where there are no non-resident landlords to plunder; and no government to aid and assist them in plundering. But though the victims may be better off, it would seem that a just God must deal vengeance upon those who have caused this awful havock [*sic*] and desolation.[43]

To hold Britain responsible in this way reassured many American readers. They could be confident that even with a massive crop failure a similar catastrophe was unlikely to strike them for no other reason than the fact that, unlike the unfortunate Irish, Americans had thrown off British rule. The people of the USA were not plagued by a landed aristocracy, nor exploited by absentee landlords. Their farms were their own, and the produce of the land remained in the hands of the yeoman farmers who raised it. At the same time, these narratives that blamed Britain reinforced a view of the Irish as dependent, oppressed, exploited, weak, and unlikely to possess the virtues and political sensibilities most commonly exhibited by American citizens. Such considerations, then, would have made many Americans suspicious about the political competence of Famine immigrants arriving in America and defensive against the corrosive influence of the Irish on American republican institutions.

Other papers and their readers saw the matter differently. They blamed the Irish themselves, in their character and behaviour. 'It is certain that the Irish poor are sadly destitute,' wrote the *Farmer's Cabinet*.

> And it is equally certain, that if the mass of Irish emigrants to this country were placed by themselves in the most fertile region in America, if as much land were given to them as they were disposed to cultivate, if left to themselves, they would be as poor, and as much exposed to famine as they are now, unless their character and their habits became essentially changed. There is something quite incomprehensible in the Irish character. Foresight, provident calculation, the spirit of improvement, those elements of New England character, seem scarcely to enter it all.[44]

A similar chord was struck by the *Saturday Rambler*: 'the Irish people seem to have given themselves up to despair, and are making no preparation for the next season. Agriculture seems about to be abandoned. There seems to be a total neglect of tillage'.[45] To another paper, it was 'bad government and whiskey [that] have made Ireland what she is. Make her the recipient of the world's charity, yet suffer the causes of her ruin to remain, and her miserable population will continue the unrelieved, unimproved and profitless consumer of potatoes and bread'.[46]

These narratives of blame drew upon stereotypes of the Irish as feckless, violent, lazy, savage, primitive or otherwise uncivilised. In particular, the Irish were ignorant, superstitious drunks. 'Indulgence in intoxicating drinks has been the cause of a very great proportion of this suffering', wrote the *New Hampshire Sentinel*. Intemperance keeps 'the poor depressed, and reckless of the future. Even now grain which might feed tens of thousands is daily converted into whiskey'.[47] Evidence of the defects of the Irish character could be seen especially in the reports of agrarian violence that sometimes accompanied accounts of starvation and disease. 'The country is in a frightful state of disorder', reported the *Baltimore Sun*. 'Murder succeeds murder,' and Irish peasants 'attack poor-houses' and plunder the flocks of landlords. 'The mass consists, not of paupers and famine-stricken wretches, but of strong hale young fellows, having no employment. The object is to deter from rents and rates'.[48] Another paper reported that 'bakers' shops are still broken into by mobs, and bread is carried off. Sheep are stolen from fields and carts with corn and flour, are stopped and emptied of their contents. Murders, in some counties, at noon day, are frequent, and are committed upon unoffending persons'.[49] The *Ohio Statesman*, too, described Ireland as 'again the scene of agrarian outrage and murder' and of 'illegal combinations which have been formed to resist the payment of rent'.[50] Peasants have 'attacked and demolished soup-kitchens, thus depriving others of their sole means of existence'. There has been, wrote the *New Hampshire Sentinel*, 'a system of outrage and intimidation' such that 'it has been found necessary to keep the military and police in constant requisition'.[51]

By far the most common narrative of blame was that aimed at Catholicism. The Famine was the work of 'an ignorant priesthood'[52] and Americans should feel sorry for the suffering of the 'many poor Papists',[53] who have been 'ridden, and kept in ignorance by the priesthood'.[54] 'The starvation, sufferings, and crimes which prevail among four millions in Ireland', proclaimed the *Christian Observer*, 'are the legitimate fruits of Popery'.[55] To understand the cause of the Famine, explained the *Friends' Review*, 'we need only examine the difference which exists between Episcopalian England, Presbyterian Scotland and Popish Ireland'. Who can make such examination 'and not immediately perceive the origin of the woes of the last named country?' To be sure their readers understood, the *Review* announced clearly, 'It is the priests who have made the Irish what they are; or rather it is a degrading religion which has debased alike priest and people'.[56] The *Farmer's Cabinet* editorialised about the necessity of finding 'vigilant agents' who could distribute American charity in Ireland, 'to see that these benefactions are not put into the hands of popish priests'. 'An Irishman', wrote the editors, 'would take the bread out of his living children's mouths to pay for masses for the soul of a dead child. The curse of Ireland', they concluded, 'is her popish priesthood'.[57] We find within all these narratives of blame descriptions of the Irish that were especially powerful to an intensely anti-Catholic, Anglo-Protestant readership educated to value industry, self-discipline, moral and intellectual virtues, community spirit, independent religion and public order. These images of the Irish, in other words, contrasted sharply with the images many Americans had of themselves and gave grounds to fear the disorder and foreign influences that would attend a vast influx of Irish into their community.

Most of what I call morbidity narratives presented graphic descriptions of starvation, disease and death, and were by far the most common image of the Irish people occupying the newspapers of America in the winter and spring of 1847. Typical of the morbidity narrative was this one from the *Barre Patriot*:

> A day ago I entered a miserable cabin, dug out of the bog; a poor woman sat propped against the wall inside; the stench was intolerable, and on my complaining of it the mother pointed to a sort of square bed in the corner; it contained the putrid – the absolutely melted away remains of her eldest son ... These are not fancied sketches, neither are they ideal pictures, but painful realities; and who is there that will not shudder at their truths?[58]

A similar account appeared in the *New Hampshire Gazette*, a first-hand report that had originally been printed by the *Cork Examiner*:

> We this day witnessed a most horrifying and appalling spectacle at the Shandon guard-house, at the foot of Mallow lane. Under the sheds attached to that building lay some thirty-eight human-beings – old and young men, women, children and infants of the tenderest age – all huddled together, like so many pigs or dogs, on the ground, without any other covering but the rags on their persons, and these in the last stage of filth and hideousness. – There they lay – some dying – some dead – all gaunt and yellow, and hideous with famine and disease. We have seen many sights of horror within the last month, but never anything equal to this congregated mass of human debasement. The smell that came from the unfortunates was offensive in the extreme, and was sufficient of itself to propagate disease.[59]

Not only the vivid depiction of starving bodies, but also graphic images of those suffering from disease and its effects were part of the portrayal of the Irish absorbed by American newspaper readers. 'Typhus fever, of a malignant character, rages', reported the *Boston Transcript*, 'and also a disease – for which we know no term, but of equally fatal consequences – has made its appearance. It attacks the lips first, which fester, and then the stomach, somewhat similar to English cholera; so much so, that we have heard of a great number of persons having fallen victim to this latter disease'.[60]

Another characteristic of the morbidity narratives is the frequent reliance on the 'trope of indescribability'.[61] As graphic as were the descriptions of starving bodies, correspondents often confessed their incapacity to capture the horror they witnessed or to describe the extent of the suffering throughout the regions they visited. 'Description is futile to convey any notion of the suffering in Ireland,' noted the *Baltimore Sun*, 'but some idea may be had from individual facts'.[62] In another account, printed in the *Boston Evening Transcript*, readers are prepared to learn about 'scenes of frightful hunger'. As the writer, Nicholas Cummins, entered the cabins of Famine victims in Skibbereen, he found scenes:

> such as no tongue or pen can convey the slightest idea of. In the first, six famished and ghastly skeletons, to all appearance dead, were huddled in a corner on some filthy straw, their sole covering what seemed a ragged horse cloth, their wretched legs hanging about naked above the knees. I approached with horror, and found by a low moaning they were alive. They were in fever, four children, a woman, and what had once been a man.

Cummins struggles to find words that adequately communicate the horror he witnessed and his rhetorical struggle itself becomes a measure of the dreadful reality he experienced:

> It is impossible to go through the details, suffice to say, that in a few minutes I was surrounded by at least 200 of such phantoms, such frightful spectres as no words can describe. By far the greater number were delirious, either from famine or fever. Their demonic yells are still yelling in my ears, and their horrible images [are] fixed upon my brain. My heart sickens at the recital, but I must go on.[63]

Yet even as writers confess the inadequacy of their communications, they also strive to assure readers about the veracity of their testimony. They emphasise in various ways that their description is authentic, and includes no exaggeration or embellishment. As unbelievable as it may appear to incredulous readers, these accounts were, in the words of American statesman Henry Clay, 'no fancy picture; but if we are to credit the terrible accounts which reach us from that theatre of misery and wretchedness, is one of daily occurrence'.[64]

The morbidity narratives depend on the reader's morbid fascination with the slow process of death by hunger and related diseases. They enlist all the senses of the reader in an effort to induce an imaginative encounter with the suffering of the Irish. These narratives reduce the abstract idea of a national famine to the graphic and particular representation of what Elizabeth Clark has called, 'the gruesome tribulations of the body'.[65] The vividly described deterioration of the body becomes the material evidence for the absence of food. The unseen process of starvation is physicalised in the agony of Famine victims. The response to such an account is pity. Readers, by sympathetic imagination, would be encouraged to place themselves in the scene, and identify with the suffering victim. At the same time, the pathos of vivid description kept near at hand the abiding fears of readers who were forced to confront their own mortality and consider their own vulnerability to starvation and disease. In this way, then, the graphic accounts of extreme suffering were instrumental in motivating charitable efforts across America.

These morbidity narratives also 'naturalised' the Famine as a physical, medical or scientific reality, and so removed it from the context of politics and economy. Yet, even this must have been unsettling, for the narratives then demonstrated the inability of British science and medicine to cope with the catastrophe. While the graphic descriptions of dying people and even of rotting or rat-eaten corpses, may have satisfied scientific curiosity and implicitly further subordinated social, political, or economic meanings of the Famine, they may have also strengthened the idea of 'famine and pestilence' as God's judgement. Americans may have been reassured by the belief that the Irish, suffering from a medical crisis beyond the reach of the modern science, must indeed be enduring a divine punishment. The detailed physical description of the Irish, then, becomes one way for Americans to ritually mark the morally corrupt alien. The vivid accounts of physical suffering prepared Americans to physically isolate and exclude the Irish immigrants who would soon arrive in America.

During the summer of 1847, amidst some optimistic reports of improving crops, and suffering themselves from what we might call today, 'compassion fatigue', Americans mostly stopped paying attention to the Famine, which with varying degrees of severity continued for three more years. At the end of July 1847, the *Boston Transcript* assured readers that in Ireland, 'the weather continued favorable, and there is scarcely room to doubt an abundant harvest. Even the potato appears to be very generally healthy, and to promise bountifully'.[66] In August, the *New York Tribune* reported that after a season of Famine, 'the prospects of the Harvest still continue unexceptionally encouraging, and everywhere promise a most abundant yield. Harvesting has already been begun in some of the Southern Counties. The crops of Wheat, Oats, and barley are universally healthy; the Potato, notwithstanding all that has been said about the reappearance of the disease of last year, is affected but to a very insignificant extent'.[67] Following such reports, the Famine faded from view and seldom again engaged the imaginations or aroused the sympathy of American newspaper readers, who instead became occupied with the immigrants the Famine had transplanted to their shores.[68] The final master narrative, then, consisted of stories about Famine emigration first to England, then to Canada, and then to America. The narratives generally reveal a harsh picture of the American 'welcome' for the Irish and reflect, in their portrayal of the arriving Irish, the result of so many degrading pictures of suffering Irish carried earlier in the same pages.

In January 1847, the first such stories appeared and depicted the scenes in English cities as Irish refugees fled starvation. 'Immense numbers of poor half-starved creatures find their way across the channel, and beg and exist as best they can, by appeals to the feelings of the inhabitants in the great towns of England', the *New London Morning News* reported. 'The number of these poor creatures in Liverpool, Manchester, and the manufacturing districts, natives of the sister country, who have fled from the wretchedness of their homes, is adding seriously to the local taxation of the places named'.[69] It got worse. 'Fever, introduced by Irish emigrants, is said to be prevailing extensively in the English towns near the Irish coast', reported the *Emancipator.* 'Liverpool is suffering severely from the effects of this emigration; 200,000 Irish are reported to have landed in that city within the past year, filling the city with paupers, the hospitals and temporary sheds erected for the purpose, with the diseased and dying, and burdening the city with heavy taxation'.[70] The *Farmer's Cabinet* described Ireland as 'the world's great pauper-breeding establishment'.[71] When it became clear that many of the Irish Famine refugees were headed for America, the paper asked, 'Are we prepared to have these hoards of Irish paupers become citizens on touching our soil, to be employed as the tools of priests and demagogues, in carrying our elections?'[72]

Reports also came from Canada. The *New Hampshire Sentinel*, for example, noting that:

> The tide of pauper emigration pouring into our country [by] this Northern channel is incredible, and certainly alarming. The average number of Irish people daily landed at the Quarantine of the city, during the last month, is one thousand. They arrive here in miserable plight, and while a portion of them only stop here to die, the remainder are immediately shipped like wild animals to the United States.[73]

Another alarming report from north of the border appeared in the *Trenton State Gazette:*

> Every hour furnishes some new instance of sickness, or some fresh example of its termination by death, among those we know and respect. With whatever point the stream of misery comes in contact, it leaves the mark of its passage: on the steamboats, ten, fifteen, twenty, or five-and-twenty depart in the short voyage of one night between Quebec and Montreal … In that hell upon earth, between one and two thousand sick fever patients, are constantly lying, and deaths to the number of thirty, forty, fifty, and even more than fifty take place nightly.[74]

American readers knew that thousands of these Famine emigrants were headed for American shores and cities. When one immigrant ship arrived in February, the *Boston Bee* reported the scene.

> The poor creatures, nearly naked, or clothed only in rags, were huddled together in the smallest space possible; and it appeared as if none of the filth, accumulated during the passage, had been removed. The stench that issued thence almost prostrated the visitor at the entrance, and yet cooped up in this noisome place, were several sick persons, and, in one bunk with her four children, was a poor woman, apparently just dying.[75]

All understood the implicit threat. 'The influx of pauper immigrants in squalid condition, diseased and destitute, is giving rise to serious concern in New York and Boston', reported the *Trenton State Gazette*.[76] An editorial in the *New York Sun* explained the concern:

> Let it once be understood that all the paupers are emigrating to America, and we may bid adieu to the emigration of those industrious and enterprising foreigners who have hitherto flocked to our shores in multitudes. By emptying their poor-houses and jails upon us, the European monarchies accomplish four objects. They make emigration to America infamous among the better classes of their subjects; they corrupt us by sending their criminals here; they reduce our resources by increasing our taxes for the support of the poor; and lastly, they get rid of the responsibility of supporting alms-houses and prisons.[77]

But the immigrants kept coming, and throughout the spring the papers continued to cover the arrival of the Famine Irish:

> Not only are our Alms houses and Hospitals crowded with the poor and sick who are daily flocking to our shores, but our streets are also swarming with them, and in almost every part of the city we see groups of these poor wretches, sick and feeble, resting their weary and emaciated limbs at the corners of the streets and on the door steps of both private and public houses, exciting commiseration, and, at the same time, the disgust of all who see them.[78]

A week later, the same paper reported that:

> Vessels are continually arriving here with vast multitudes of miserable human beings, from famine-stricken Ireland, who were both physically and morally enfeebled before commencing a voyage which disease tracks across the ocean with an unerring certainty … Hence cases are perpetually occurring in public institutions where foreign paupers are admitted, and in narrow streets, and old decaying tenements where emigrants congregate on reaching the city.[79]

Still another report announced:

> The tide of immigration which is increasing daily to a most alarming extent, bringing with it its necessary concomitant, poverty, sickness, and crime, has excited as it ought, the attention of the whole community, and the people in all parts of the country have at last become aroused, and are turning about to devise means to check an evil which has reached such a height that the very vitality of our country has become endangered by it.[80]

Consistent with the premises established in the other Famine narratives, Irish immigrants were viewed as bringing disease and moral corruption to America, and threatening the economy and political vitality of the nation. Those narratives that reported on Irish immigration consistently depicted the Irish as swarms, or flocks, of impoverished and diseased foreign creatures invading, polluting, and plaguing American cities. These stories and characterisations, almost entirely hostile towards the Irish, grow directly out of the predispositions formed by the other narratives of the Famine. That is, the images of the Irish composed over months of coverage of the Famine by American papers finally resulted in a response to the Irish immigrant that expressed the disgust, fear and hatred towards the Irish that Americans had been conditioned to feel.

5

Widows' and dependent parents' American Civil War pension files: A new source for the Irish emigrant experience

Damian Shiels

In May 1863, Ellen Driscoll applied for a USA pension in Angelica, Allegany County, New York. Ellen, a 60-year-old Irish immigrant, formerly made her home with her husband John and their five children in Dunamark, near Bantry, County Cork. John, described in the application as a 'poor man', had died during 'the year of the Great Famine in Ireland' in 1846 to 1847. His death forced Ellen and her five children (one of whom was crippled) to seek aid as paupers. The intervening years had seen Ellen remain in 'poor and indigent circumstances', frequently reliant on public charity. However, a number of her children had managed to emigrate to the USA and her son James joined other Bantry neighbours who settled in New York towns such as Angelica and nearby Mount Morris, where he worked as a farm labourer. In the latter town, on 11 May 1861, he enlisted in what became Company H of the 27th New York Infantry, under the alias James Driskscom. It was his intention to use his army pay to secure his mother's passage from Ireland to the USA. On 27 June 1862 James was wounded at the Battle of Gaines' Mill, Virginia, and died the following day. The money he had gathered did allow his mother to travel to America and she arrived in Angelica in the spring of 1863 where she stayed with her daughter Honora. In the preparation of her pension application Ellen was able to call on a range of Irish emigrants in New York State who had known both her and her husband in Ireland – people like Patrick and Daniel McCarthy, Timothy Crowley and John O'Leary – all of whom gave statements as to her history and circumstances. Ultimately, Ellen's application was successful, and she was granted a pension of $8 per month for her son's service.[1] Experiences such as those of Ellen Driscoll and her family afford us a rare insight. Their stories provide a window not only into life in pre- and post-Famine Ireland, but also enables us to 'follow' Irish emigrants from their original homes in Ireland across the Atlantic and to their new lives in the USA.

Despite significant research into the Great Irish Famine, there has been comparatively little study of the fate and experiences of Famine emigrants in its aftermath. Many of these emigrants, such as James Driscoll, went to the USA, where they became an integral part of Irish-American communities which were impacted by what for many was a second great trauma in their lives, the American Civil War. The Famine and the prevailing economic circumstances of 1840s and 1850s Ireland were the direct cause which ultimately led to many Irishmen donning Union blue and Confederate grey in the conflict of 1861 to 1865. Historically, we have divorced these two linked events in the history of Ireland and her diaspora. As a result, Irish historians have also inadvertently neglected a source which offers the potential for significant insight into the experiences of Irish people both in Ireland and the USA in the mid-nineteenth century – the Civil War pension files.

The American Civil War is undoubtedly one of the most significant conflicts in Irish diasporic history. At least 150,000 Irish-born men fought for the North, with a further 20,000 casting in their lot with the South.[2] Indeed, we must look to the First World War for the only other conflict in the Irish military experience in which so many natives of the island fought. A large proportion of the *c.* 1.6 million people of Irish birth living in the USA at the outbreak of the American Civil War had arrived in the country as a result of emigration sparked by the Great Famine.[3] Although no figures have been arrived at for the total number of Irish who died, it certainly ran to tens of thousands. Irish involvement in the conflict remains a popular topic in the USA. Much of this research has focused on assessing the military prowess of ethnic Irish formations – notably the Irish Brigade – but increasingly there is a move towards a more inclusive analysis, in turn incorporating many aspects of social history.[4] Despite the significant work that has taken place in recent years, many opportunities remain to assess the impact of the war on Irish-Americans, particularly at a macro level. This is especially true with regard to that majority of Irishmen who have heretofore been overshadowed by the celebrity of those who fought beneath the green flag, namely those who did not serve in ethnic Irish units. As well as providing us with insights into the wider experience of Irish emigrants, the Civil War pension files also offer us an opportunity to gain a fuller picture of the social impact of the American Civil War on Irish Americans.

On 14 July 1862, Abraham Lincoln signed into law an act that provided monthly pensions for widows and men totally disabled by the American Civil War.[5] The motivations behind the act lay in a desire to recognise the sacrifice volunteers were making for the war effort and also as part of a series of measures in the summer of 1862 to increase mobilisation into the Federal military.[6] Over the course of the next three decades the pension system would be expanded and refined through a series of additional acts that would see the number of pensioners grow, so much so that by 1893 a staggering $165.3 million was spent annually on military pensioners – some 40 per cent of the entire Federal budget.[7] A significant proportion of these pensions were paid to the dependents of veterans, who usually fell into categories of widow, dependent mother, dependent father and minor children. It has been estimated that at least 108,000 widows were directly created by the American Civil War.[8] A large proportion of these women, many of them Irish, went on to claim Federal pensions based on their husbands' service. Moreover, women would make claims following their veteran husbands' deaths in the decades that followed the conflict. By 1890 a total of 145,359 widows of Union soldiers and sailors were recorded.[9]

The initial act of 1862 entitled the widows of privates to a monthly rate of $8 per month, with a $2 monthly supplement for each child under the age of 16.[10] The same monthly rate was generally also paid to dependent parents. Although the pension was originally restricted to the widows, dependent mothers, dependent sisters and minor children of veterans, the law was altered in 1866 to allow dependent fathers to benefit.[11] The basic $8 per month rate was increased to $12 for widows and dependents in 1886. This represented a total of $144 per year and equated to a third of the average American annual wage in 1890, highlighting just how economically significant the pensions were.[12] The expansion of eligibility and general improvement of the pensions available was a feature of the nineteenth-century pension acts. From 1868 widows and dependents were entitled to the payment of the pension from the date of death of a soldier, provided they had filed within five years of his death. In 1879 Congress altered this, allowing payment from the date of death no matter when the claim was filed – facilitating the payments of a lump sum to pension recipients.[13] Similarly in 1873 the law was altered to the benefit of dependent parents. Whereas prior to that date mothers and fathers had to prove they had been financially dependent on their deceased son, they now only had to show that their son had aided them financially or contributed to their support 'in any other way'.[14]

The most significant alteration to the pension system came with the Dependent and Disability Pension Act of 1890. In that year pensions were made available to disabled veterans unable to perform manual labour regardless of the cause of their disability, which could include old age. It expanded the eligibility of widows who could now claim regardless of the cause of a soldier's death (previously death had to be a result of war service) as long as they had been married prior to the 27 June 1890. Similarly the act benefitted all parents who were without means of support and whose son's death had been a result of war service. The only additional requirement was that the servicemen on whom the pension was based had served at least ninety days in the Union army or navy and had been honourably discharged.[15] The 1890 Act effectively created an old-age pension system for veterans and dependents.

Pension files relating to Federal American Civil War service come in a number of forms. The National Archives in Washington DC today houses well over 3 million pension applications of Federal veterans or their dependents made between 1861 and 1917. The vast majority of these relate to the American Civil War and includes *c.* 2,000,000 applications made by US Army veterans, *c.* 26,000 applications by US naval veterans, *c.* 1,280,000 applications made by US Army widows and other dependents, and *c.* 20,000 applications by US naval widows and other dependents. Many thousands of these files are concerned specifically with Irish-Americans. Among the richest from a social history perspective are those that relate to the widows and dependent parents of Irish soldiers and sailors who died in Union military service during the Civil War era.

Among the key pieces of information that widows were expected to supply in their applications were proof of marriage and of continued widowhood. The files usually also contain an affidavit from the widow outlining her former and current marital status. For those Irish women who had married after their arrival in the USA this proof was generally provided in the form of a marriage certificate or through the baptismal records of children born subsequently. Women who had married in Ireland often struggled to obtain this information, and in many cases submitted the affidavit of a clergyman from their home parish outlining details of their marriage and/or the birth of their children. When Maria O'Neill's husband Richard died on 22 May 1863 of wounds received with the 154th New York Infantry at the Battle of Chancellorsville, she moved quickly to procure the information she required from home:

> This is to certify that Rich. O'Neil [and] Maria Heaphy were married as appears from the Parish Register on the 31 day January 1852 in presence of Thomas Heaphy and Joanna Connery by the Rev. Mr. McGrath. Richd O'Brien P.P., June 26th 1863, Knocklong, Co. Limerick.[16]

However, it was not always possible for a widow to access this information so readily. Mary Sullivan was originally from Kenmare, County Kerry, where she had married her husband Michael on 25 February 1843. Michael later died in the notorious prisoner-of-war camp at Andersonville, Georgia on 18 August 1864, while serving as a private in the 69th New York Infantry. Mary was unable to procure an affidavit from Ireland due to her limited means and 'the great expense which she is unable to bear', as well as the 'great distance to the place of her marriage'. Instead she had to rely on the statements of two deponents, John O'Neil and Nelly Galway, who swore that they had personally been acquainted with the couple and that they had lived together as man and wife.[17]

Other widows were able to draw on statements from friends in the USA who had known them at home, and who claimed to have been present at their marriage. These affidavits indicate that many Irish emigrants maintained close bonds in the USA with people whom they had known in Ireland. Honora Murphy had been unable to get proof of her 1843 marriage in Ireland when she sought a pension based on her husband John's service. The private in the 31st New York Infantry had died of chronic dysentery in Washington DC on 24 September 1862.

Honora's friend William Flanagan stated he had known her for twenty-eight years and that he had been 'a resident of the town of Malow' before his emigration. He had a 'perfect recollection' of their marriage twenty years previously. He even added that before the marriage had taken place it had been 'much talked about' around the County Cork town. Another Mallow native, Denis Collins, also gave evidence to state that he had been a witness at the wedding ceremony.[18]

In cases where women did not have access to such witnesses, or where they sought to provide irrefutable proof of their relationship, they sometimes resorted to providing letters written to them by their deceased husband. In many cases these must have been treasured possessions, submitted with applications out of dire economic necessity. The widows never received these possessions back and they remain in their files to this day. This was the choice Sarah Jane Cochran faced when she went in search of a pension. The Limavady woman had been married to her husband Richey at the 9th Presbyterian church in Philadelphia on 25 June 1856. Richey, a member of the 63rd Pennsylvania Infantry, lost his life at the Battle of Glendale on 30 June 1862. Three days earlier he had written what ultimately proved to be his last letter to his wife. He let her know that he was in good health and hoped 'that this few lines may find you all enjoying the same'. Outlining how he and his unit had been having a 'fairly hard time of it' in the fighting up to that point, he signed off by asking Sarah to 'remember me to all the folks'. Left widowed with two small children, Sarah clearly felt she had little choice but to submit the letter to the Pension Bureau and insure a successful application. It was approved, but the pension did not insulate her from further hardship; her youngest child William died just short of his third birthday in March 1864 and Sarah returned to her family in Ireland with her daughter.[19]

Occasionally the wartime letters provided by widows spoke to their husband's final moments. Ann Scanlan had married Irish labourer Patrick Scanlan in Charleston, South Carolina, on 29 April 1851. They moved to New York in the late 1850s, where they lived with their four children at the outbreak of war. Patrick was serving with the 63rd New York Infantry of the Irish Brigade when he was wounded at the Battle of Fredericksburg on 13 December 1862. A bullet penetrated his right knee, an injury that eventually necessitated the amputation of his leg. Repeated haemorrhaging ultimately caused his death on 14 January 1863, but not before he had dictated his final message to his wife through one of the hospital staff:

> After I am dead, write to my wife and tell her that I died a natural death in bed, having received the full benefits of my church. Say that I felt resigned to the will of God and that I am sorry I could not see her and the children once more. That I would have felt better in such a case before I died. It is the will of God that it should not be so, and I must be content to do without.[20]

The file of Anne Cairns is another that reveals the extended family ties throughout the USA and Ireland during the nineteenth century. It is also an example of the poignant details contained in the applications. Anne's Scottish husband, Colin, was in America serving with the 10th New Hampshire Infantry when he was captured in Virginia during 1864; he died the following January as a prisoner of war in Salisbury, North Carolina. Anne had stayed at home in Ireland during Colin's service, with the intent of following him to the USA once he had become established. Colin had carried a Bible with him during his imprisonment; when he was found dead it was opened to reveal the following message:

> Miss Helen Mitchell, Care of Mrs. Greeley – 19 South High St. Baltimore, Maryland. Should this Book be ever found on my dead body let the party know of the above address, who will acquaint my wife & family with my fate. Colin Cairns.

Helen Mitchell was Anne's sister. When Union survivors of the prison camp passed this information to her in March 1865 she was able to write to Anne – then in Tralee, County Kerry – to inform her of his fate.[21]

The widows' files can also provide an insight into the social and economic difficulties that many Irish women and their families faced in the nineteenth century. Ellen Martin from Coleraine, County Derry, lost her husband Patrick during the war, another victim of the Confederate prison at Salisbury, North Carolina. Ellen struggled with alcoholism in the years after the conflict; she was eventually placed in New York's Bellevue Hospital for treatment. Her difficulties evidently continued, as she was later accused of abandoning her children who sought to have her pension diverted for their own support.[22] Economic destitution remained an ever-present threat for many of these women throughout their post-war lives. When Mary Butler from Dungarvan, County Waterford, was faced with the prospect of losing the pension she received for her husband's service in the 12th New York Cavalry, she wrote of her fear of ending up in the local workhouse were the payments to stop.[23] Such a vista became all too real for Mary Daly, whose husband had also died while a prisoner of war. She collected her pension in County Kildare, but was soon to find herself in Celbridge Union Workhouse. When she died on 29 December 1905 she did so as an inmate of Carlow District Lunatic Asylum.[24] Occasionally pension applications reveal the prevalence of bigamy in nineteenth-century society. John D. Murray had served in the ranks of the 99th New York until his death due to disease during the Civil War. In later years his son Michael went in search of a widow's pension for his mother, only to discover what he thought to be an impostor already claiming it. Investigation revealed that the woman – Barbara Murray – was in fact his father's legitimate wife – they had married in Dublin in 1844. John Murray had abandoned her before marrying Michael's mother, who he in turn appears to have abandoned prior to emigrating to the USA.[25]

Prior to 1873 dependent mothers and fathers were required to show that their deceased son had financially contributed to their support. This often took the form of a statement from a former employer regarding the son's earnings, affidavits of friends or neighbours attesting to dependence, or wartime letters from their son which indicate a portion of his earnings were being given over to his parents.[26] Where a husband was still alive, mothers were required to show why they were reliant on their son as opposed to their spouse for support. In cases where a woman's husband had died (such as that of Ellen Driscoll discussed above), files usually specify if this took place in Ireland prior to emigration or following the family's arrival in the USA. In cases where a dependent mother's husband was still alive, and in dependent fathers' applications, it became necessary to show that the men were disabled and unable to work, something usually achieved through the statement of a physician. As with widows' files much of the key social information is contained within the statements of deponents, be they the parent themselves, members of the extended family, or friends and acquaintances. In another similarity with the widows' files, information on the soldier's service and occasional statements from his comrades can also be found within.

The nature of the evidence required of dependent parents' means that their files often contain detailed information regarding the family's ante-bellum life. In Mary O'Dea's application she outlined how she had emigrated from County Clare to Cuba, New York with her husband and sons in the 1840s. Her first husband died in 1850, leaving her financially vulnerable with three small children to support. Mary remarried in just a few months, wedding an Irishman named Michael Foran, but he too passed away in 1854. Now living in Salamanca, she came to rely on the assistance of her son Patrick to maintain their modest 7-acre farm. Patrick supplemented this income by working at the nearby Hemlock Mills Lumber Works, before war came and he joined the 37th New York 'Irish Rifles' in whose service he lost his life.[27] In another example Mary Horan of Tralee, County Kerry, told how her husband was infirm and unable to work, forcing her son Denis to seek work in the town's Mineral Water Factory at the age of 11 in order to support the family, a job for which he received 9*s* a week. He spent the next thirteen years there, before deciding to travel to the USA in search of increased wages. He first spent six weeks in an oil and guano factory before finding work as a longshoreman. After six months in America, Denis enlisted in the 8th US Cavalry – he died of cholera in Virgin Bay, Nicaragua, in 1866 while enroute to his regiment.[28]

As was the case with widows, the efforts of parents to prove their relationship with their son often reveals the extremely close ties emigrants from certain localities within Ireland maintained in the USA. Mary Sheehan lost her son John at the Battle of Gaines' Mill, Virginia, on 27 June 1862. He had been her main support, her husband Morris having died on 11 July 1836. Mary had married Morris in Cork city's North Chapel in 1824, emigrating to the USA in 1833. Despite the passage of time, she was able to call on 70-year-old Daniel Harrigan and 65-year-old Ann Murphy for affidavits in 1862. Both swore that they had known Mary and Morris for 'over forty years', that they 'knew them in the city of Cork, Ireland and knew them here in New York' and that they had come to America on the same ship with them almost thirty years previously.[29] Similarly, the dependent mother's application of Catherine Henry reveals information about the decision behind her son Mathew's emigration from Ballyjamesduff, County Cavan, and his decision to locate himself in Newark, New Jersey. When he followed his sister across the Atlantic in 1859 he went to Newark to live with the Boyles, family friends from Ballyjamesduff who had settled there two years previously. In 1861 these ties led him to enlist in a Newark company which became part of the 72nd New York Infantry; he was killed in action at Williamsburg, Virginia, on 5 May 1862.[30] Another similar case is that of Jeremiah Durick, who left Nenagh for West Rutland, Vermont, in the 1850s to join other Tipperary locals working in the region's marble quarries. He first boarded with John Barrett, who had known him since he was a boy and had attended his mother's funeral in Ireland. Following Jeremiah's death in the ranks of the Irish Brigade at the Battle of Antietam, Maryland on 17 September 1862, his father Timothy was able to call on John Barrett's testimony to prove his relationship with his son.[31]

Even where emigrants had not known each other in Ireland, there is still evidence to suggest that they often situated themselves within social groups from their home region. When Ann Divver (*sic*) went in search of a dependent mother's pension following her son Daniel's death as a lieutenant in the 11th New York Infantry at the Battle of First Bull Run in 1861, she called on her friends James Friel and Catherine O'Donnell to provide affidavits. Although both had known Ann for over ten years, neither had met before her family's arrival in New York. However, all three of these surnames have extremely strong links to north-west Ireland, particularly counties Donegal and Derry. It seems highly probable that Ann had become friends with them in this context, as people from 'her' part of Ireland.[32]

The initial requirement that dependent parents provide evidence that their son had financially supported them (a requirement relaxed in 1873) means that wartime letters are substantially more prevalent in parents' pension applications compared to those of widows. Each of these letters frequently included a reference to their son either sending a portion of his pay to his parents, or his intention to do so. In addition, parents often included multiple letters from their child to demonstrate that this support took place over a sustained period of time. These letters contain significant detail as to these men's experiences of the war and their thoughts about home, family and friends. Patrick Kelly, for example, from Ballinasloe, County Galway, had emigrated to Boston with his parents, where in 1860 he (along with many Irish emigrants in Massachusetts) was working in the leather trade. He was killed in action on 3 December 1863 while on picket duty (a task which saw small groups of soldiers placed on watch) with the 28th Massachusetts Infantry. His mother Mary included eight of his wartime letters in her pension application. Patrick touched on many topics in his writings. These included expressions of patriotism for the Union and Ireland, as he boasted how he intended to 'shoot Jeff Davis' and how for the Irish regiments 'Faugh a Ballagh is the war cry and no turn back'. More than just bravado, the letters also contain an insight into his personality; a love for music is apparent as he asked his parents to send 'a guitar and some song books if you can get the guitar cheap' and in later correspondence that 'I want Father the next letter he writes to write off the song called Mary Le More I want to learn it'.[33] Some of these letters highlight the homesickness, insecurity and loneliness that many young Irish emigrants felt in the USA. Patrick Finan was a Second Class Fireman aboard the USS *Wabash*, which formed part of the Union blockading squadron off the Confederate coast. He was scalded by the ship's boilers and died of his injuries on 5 April 1864. At home in Sligo town, his father John included three long letters written by his son in his pension application. Patrick had clearly spent a lot of time thinking of home; he asked his father to let one of the neighbours' children know that he intended to 'bring him home a suit of Man O'War clothes and make a regular Jack Tar [sailor] of him' and asked his father to send his best to 'all my old comrade boys of Sligo and not forgetting the young girls'. Patrick was also quick to express his disappointment that friends from home who had recently emigrated had failed to contact him, noting of one that he was 'like all the rest of them that is here he soon forgot me'. His isolation and distance from family also sometimes got the better of him: 'I don't know the reason of it when I was in England I never used to think half so much of home as I do now, but I am not the same since my Mother died. I feel very lonely and down hearted'.[34]

***

The potential for integrating information contained within widows and dependent parents' pension files with other forms of research presents an opportunity to explore ordinary Irish emigrants' lives in often unprecedented detail. This can reveal just how hard life could be once families took the emigrant boat. One example is the experience of Charles and Marcella O'Reilly, who left for the USA at some point during the 1840s, settling in Auburn, New York. The 1860 Census shows them living in Auburn's First Ward where Charles worked as a labourer.[35] A third son James was born in 1861. The rosters of the

9th New York Heavy Artillery record that the couple's eldest son Anthony enlisted in Auburn on 15 August 1862, becoming a private in Company F. He was joined in the unit by his then 44-year-old father Charles who signed up a year later, on 20 December 1863.[36] The next chronological reference to the family appears in Alfred Seelye Roe's 1899 history of the 9th New York Heavy Artillery. In recalling the regiment's actions at the Battle of Cedar Creek, Virginia on 19 October 1864, Roe remembered one particularly harrowing scene which occurred as the Confederates attacked:

> Here one of our boys, Anthony Riley, was shot and killed; his father was by his side; the blood and brains of his son covered the face and hands of the father. I never saw a more affecting sight than this; the poor old man kneels over the body of his dead son; his tears mingle with his son's blood. O God! what a sight; he can stop but a moment, for the rebels are pressing us; he must leave his dying boy in the hands of the devilish foe, he bends over him, kisses his cheek, and with tearful eyes rushes to the fight, determined on revenge for his son.[37]

Marcella O'Reilly went on to receive a Federal pension following the war, but it was not based on her son's sacrifice. Charles was still in the 9th New York Heavy Artillery as 1865 dawned, engaged in the operations then taking place around Petersburg, Virginia. The rigours of campaign had taken their toll on the Irish emigrant and as the end of the war neared he fell ill. He was removed to City Point where he died on 20 March 1865.[38] Marcella had now lost her husband and eldest son. As well as the emotional impact of these events she also faced the economic reality of life without her two main breadwinners. She successfully applied for a pension of $8 per month as a widow, supplemented with an additional $2 per month from July 1866 for each of her surviving children under 16 years of age.[39] However, it seems that this was not enough, as evidenced by Marcella's appearance in the pages of the Auburn *Daily Bulletin* of 7 March 1873. Under the heading 'Sherriff Sale' it is recorded that the disposal of her property, ordered in 1871 by the County Court of Cayuga, was now due to take place.[40]

The pension files of women such as Ellen Driscoll and Marcella O'Reilly provide us with what must surely be our best opportunity to examine in detail the lives of Irish emigrants around the time of the Famine, both before and after they left Ireland. Theirs are just two of many thousands of stories relating to Irish emigrants which are held at the National Archives in Washington DC, the vast majority of which await discovery. Their potential value as a historical source for nineteenth-century Ireland is clear. It is a consequence of the burden of proof placed on pension applicants that the documentation these files contain is of considerable social, historical as well as genealogical significance. This is particularly relevant given the relative dearth of material available in Ireland itself when it comes to the study of individuals impacted by events such as the Famine. However, it is appropriate to sound a note of caution when examining widows' and dependent parents' files. It must be remembered that they represent only those individuals who lost a loved one in the service – their experience is not the same as families where a soldier or sailor made it through their military service. It is also true that many of these files can contain fabrications; the pensions were a major financial asset to those who received them, and applicants were not above lying or embellishing the truth in order to secure the payments. Despite this, Civil War pension files are not only an invaluable tool for studying the impact of the American Civil War on Irish-Americans, but also have the potential to be a major resource for those researchers who are interested in the social history of both the Famine and Irish emigration. Within their pages can be revealed a vast range of information touching on every aspect of Irish emigrant lives, be it financial, societal or emotional. They also serve to re-establish an important link, often forgotten in Ireland, by illustrating that people's experiences – and in many cases their hardships – did not end when they decided to become emigrants and took ship for a new life at one of Ireland's ports.

6

From emigrant to Fenian: Patrick A. Collins and the Boston Irish

Lawrence W. Kennedy

Four decades after leaving Ireland during the Great Famine, a mature Patrick Collins returned to the land of his birth where he received public honours from the cities of Dublin and Cork, as well as suspicious looks from detectives of Dublin Castle and Scotland Yard. Both the honours and the suspicions stemmed from his new life in America, a life marked by his continued and deep love for Ireland. Collins in the 1860s was a Fenian recruiter before turning to city, state and national politics and as late as the 1880s was scolded in Ireland by British officials who suspected him of continued support for violence in the republican cause. Despite these British concerns, in the 1890s, this former Famine emigrant was received by Queen Victoria as the US Consul-General in London.

Patrick A. Collins left Ireland for Boston in 1848, at the age of 4. In his new life he experienced hardship and prejudice as he made his way in a variety of trades. By his early twenties, through good luck, hard work and steady determination, he managed to earn a law degree from Harvard Law School. He served four terms in the Massachusetts state legislature and three terms in the USA Congress. Collins aided Ireland as a founder and president of the American branch of the Irish Land League in the 1880s, and in the 1890s was rewarded for his Democratic Party service by his appointment as US Consul-General in London. His political career culminated in two terms as Mayor of

Boston. Patrick Collins's life and career illustrate some of the problems and opportunities facing nineteenth-century Irish emigrants in one major American city.

Bartholomew Collins and his wife Mary (*née* Leahy) resided in a two-storey thatched cottage in the townland of Ballinafauna, on the south bank of the Blackwater River in east Cork when their third child and first son, Patrick Andrew, was born on 12 March 1844. Two days later the infant was baptised at the parish church in Fermoy.[1] According to the words of Patrick Collins's short autobiography, Bartholomew was a 'strong' farmer and came from a family of farmers, all of 'intense national spirit'.[2] Bartholomew Collins built the family home on some 200 acres of land leased from the Earl of Mountcashel. The house was situated on a high range and commanded a view of the Galtee Mountains in the distance. Collins also related how Daniel O'Connell, reputedly his father's friend, and one day his guest at the house in Ballinafauna, 'took the small boy in his great arms and kissed him and hoped he would grow to be good and useful to his native land'.[3] This was obviously a story that remained with Patrick Collins all his life, and gave special meaning to his continuing interest in the affairs of Ireland, long after he had left for a new life in America. Although he had managed to maintain his holdings during the first years of the Great Famine, Bartholomew died in 1847. Collins described in his autobiography how, after his father's death, his mother 'sold the lease of the Mountcashel farm and gave to her brother-in-law the lease of another nearby, and set out with her three children and the children of her late husband by a former marriage for America'.

Crossing the stormy Atlantic in an emigrant ship during early 1848 was, as has been so well shown, fraught with incredible hardships. Passengers were responsible for their bedding and food and frequently ran short of the latter during the crossing. The crowded decks and cramped sleeping quarters were further woes and 'ship fever' claimed many victims.[4] It was in the midst of such conditions onboard *The Hibernia*, that the Collins family endured the bitter ordeal of the North Atlantic crossing. Mary Collins, with her children – Patrick was the youngest – survived the weeks of seasickness, crowded quarters, and meagre provisions until, in March 1848, they finally landed in Boston. Although Patrick may have been too young to recall much of the experiences that had brought him to the New World, the stories his mother later told him about his father, the struggle for Irish independence, and their life before the Famine, made him conscious of the need for adequate political representation of poor working people, and turned him into a champion of every constitutional measure that would promote the cause of Irish freedom.

At the time the Collins family came ashore, Boston was a city with a population of about 127,000 people. James K. Polk was President of the USA and much of the country was experiencing a heady sense of national pride as a result of its one-sided victory in the brief war with Mexico. Puritan Boston, however, offered no welcome to Irish immigrants - especially those of the Roman Catholic persuasion. It was, in truth, difficult for foreigners of any kind to settle permanently in a city like Boston where a solidly homogeneous Anglo-Saxon-Protestant establishment still dominated the community's political, social, and economic resources, and resented any outsiders who might threaten the safety and security of that order. Previous immigrant groups had tended either to sidestep Boston entirely, or to move away as soon as possible, not only because of the town's pronounced anti-Irish bias, but also because of its lack of work. With its capital invested in such outlying areas as Lowell and Lawrence, Boston itself had no major industrial centre or manufacturing outlet capable of employing large numbers of unskilled labourers. Most immigrant families had neither the money to move nor the willingness to leave their friends, their families, or their church. Packed into hovels and cellars along the crowded waterfront, or lodged in factory-converted tenements in the least desirable parts of the city, the immigrants from Ireland lived in deplorable conditions.

Epidemics of typhus, typhoid tuberculosis, and other diseases broke out with ever-increasing frequency among the destitute and impoverished newcomers, claiming the lives of such a large number of young people that an 1845 census report observed that the children of Irish families seemed literally 'born to die'.[5] Another contemporary report stated that one immigrant section of Boston had 3,131 residents with an average of thirty-seven people per house. The committee asserted 'here is a density of population surpassed, probably, in few places in the civilized world'.[6] Oscar Handlin, in his 1941 classic *Boston's Immigrants,* wrote that in accommodating the immigrant Irish 'enterprising landowners utilised un-remunerative yards, gardens, and courts to yield the maximum number of hovels that might pass as homes. The abundant grounds surrounding well-built early Boston residences, and the hitherto unusable sites created by the city's irregular streets, once guarantees of commodious living, now fostered the most vicious Boston slums'.[7]

In this alien and hostile environment, the Irish huddled together for warmth, worked together for survival, and did what they could to help one another gain a more permanent foothold in their adopted country. After a short stay in Boston, the Collins family took the ferry across Boston Harbour to Chelsea, where a number of Irish immigrants had already taken up residence because of the availability of work. It was here in Chelsea that Mary Collins met and married a fellow countryman, John Burke, with whom she had four more children. Despite what must have been a poor and crowded household, Patrick Collins later recalled he went to primary, 'intermediate' and finally to the grammar school.[8]

Patrick Collins and his siblings grew up at a time when the unprecedented growth and expansion of the Irish Catholic population produced a violent backlash among those native-born Americans who feared the worst from these 'Papists'. Believing that this mass migration was actually a part of a papal conspiracy to establish the power of the Catholic Church in the USA, various political organisations were established to defend the nation against the inroads of the 'Catholic menace'.[9] In 1847 the *Pilot* commented on nativism:

> The Natives are beginning to be heartily discouraged, and well may they be. Their late meetings and all the paraphernalia attending them have proved failures, and have excited the disgust and reaped the ridicule and contempt of the well-disposed and high-minded citizens of the community … Boston has always been looked upon as the hot-bed of this fanatical spirit, and once put down here, its dirge may be sung throughout the Union.[10]

This hope proved premature.

In the 1850s native-born Bostonians played a prominent role in what became popularly referred to as the 'Know Nothing' movement, a group whose members were determined to stem the tide of future immigration and, by threats and intimidation, to keep those foreigners who were already here in a clearly subservient position. The American Party, its official name, was formed as a national political organisation designed to protect the USA from foreigners. In Massachusetts, the party succeeded in electing the governor, all state officers and virtually all members of the state legislature.[11] Once in office, these legislators pushed forward a program that called for the elimination of 'Rome, Rum, and Robbery'.[12] It was during this period of Know-Nothing bigotry that the young Patrick Collins witnessed at first hand the degree to which the fear of Catholics aroused the nativists, and the extent to which their hatred would go. Among the itinerant preachers who blossomed during the anti-Catholic revival of the period was the eccentric John S. Orr, who was convinced that God had given him a mission to bring about the destruction of the Roman Catholic Church. Dubbed the 'Angel Gabriel' because of his flowing white garments and the loud blasts that came from his brass trumpet, Orr made his initial appearance in the Boston area during the spring of 1854. To those who would listen to him, he proclaimed himself to be the 'trumpeter of the approaching King', and launched into wild harangues that incited his followers to various forms of violence.[13] As the *Pilot* reported:

> J. S. Orr, the lunatic, who under the cognomen of the 'Angel Gabriel,' has been lingering in our midst for the past few weeks, has at last raised a disturbance in the neighbouring town of Chelsea, in which some blood was spilt, but fortunately no lives were lost, in the forenoon of Sunday. Orr preached at Medford; from thence, he was taken to Chelsea in a carriage drawn by six horses, where at 12 o'clock he commenced preaching in the square. For about an hour and a half he discoursed to a considerable crowd on the evils of popery, creating some little, but no serious disturbance. After concluding, Orr proceeded to East Boston and attempted to speak in Maverick Square. This he was not however, permitted to do, and with a crowd of followers he again went to Chelsea. The mob, headed by the now infuriated preacher, went immediately to the 'Irish Settlement', so called, and finding a crowd of the sons of the 'Green Isle' there, attacked and drove them into the houses. The police was sent for [and] the crowd was soon dispersed, though not until a young man from Charlestown, a member of an engine company, but whose name we did not learn, received some dangerous wounds on the head from bricks thrown by some of the Irish.[14]

The mob next gathered at the Catholic church on Mount Bellingham, which they threatened to tear to pieces. It was stated that 500 Irishmen were in the church, fully armed, and determined to protect it at all hazards.[15] The *Pilot*, quoting the *Commonwealth*, reported:

> A fence around the church was partially torn down, and the cross upon the Church was wrested from its place and hurled to the ground, by a lad, the son of a *Protestant Irishman*, residing in East Boston, who reached it by climbing up the rain-spout and lightning rod. The cross had no sooner reached the ground than it was seized and cut into a thousand of pieces, each being eager to obtain a piece, either as a trophy, or 'sacred relic'.[16]

Although Orr did make a return to Chelsea at a later date, by that time the number of his followers had decreased and no further disturbances broke out. More than ever, however, the frightening incidents of that year made young Collins more keenly aware of the depth of Boston's animosity against Irish Catholics, and the reality of his own status as a member of a despised minority – indeed, in a very painful way. Collins was among those who were injured in these anti-Catholic disturbances. In his autobiography he referred to these events and to himself in the third person: 'He had his forearm broken and a few bruises, but all were healed; his heart was Irish, and the world was before him'.[17]

This broken arm apparently was less painful to young Collins than the taunts at school where he was one of the few 'Paddy boys'. Collins wrote in the autobiography that 'he never wanted to fight, but he had to'. Furthermore, he wrote, 'the majority of his classmates were tyrants' and 'he had to fight to get to school, at recess, to get home, to go anywhere'. He continued: 'nothing especially distinguished the boy at school. He learned fairly what was taught; nothing more'. Collins left school before reaching the age of 12 and later concluded that 'he knew how to spell as well as anybody, to read and write and cipher. He knew nothing of the rules of grammar whatever'.[18] If he could get books he could learn and set about doing that for the rest of his life. In his autobiography he wrote: 'I simply got books and read them in the old days in Chelsea, about the fires in the mining camps and woods of Ohio, and later on through the Boston public library, [and on] to his own home collection'. The 'mining camps and woods in Ohio' is a reference to a brief sojourn on the American frontier but before this venture young Patrick had a variety of work experiences to supplement family income and to learn a trade. After leaving school 'he engaged in the ancient industry of New England' where he became 'a boy-of-all-work in the fish and oyster shop of Nehemiah Rich in Chelsea'. He remained there some months, opening oysters, dressing cod and haddock, keeping and delivering books.[19]

Around this time he was confirmed as a Catholic by Boston Bishop John Fitzpatrick and became a Sunday school teacher in his Chelsea parish. Among the worshippers was a black man named Robert Morris, a leading lawyer in Boston, noted for defending his Irish clients. Morris hired young Patrick as an office boy where he remained for many years and later wrote of the time that 'he thought a lawyer, black or white, was a favoured being, and a judge like the "great white czar". In those days he did not think it possible that ever he could be the one or the other'.[20] As it turned out, ten years after leaving Morris and heading to Ohio with his family, Collins took up the study of law, first in the Boston law office of James Keith and then at Harvard Law School.

In the late 1850s the financial condition of the Collins family went from bad to worse, as Massachusetts and the nation were experiencing a serious financial depression. Chances for unskilled employment became practically non-existent. Reports of opportunities for work in the mines, on the farms, and in railroad construction projects throughout the Midwest offered an inviting prospect for hard-pressed members of the Collins family, several of whose relatives had moved west soon after they came to the USA. With relatives in the west, miners and farmers, a move was alluring. In March 1857, the family moved to Ohio, where for over two years Collins worked on farms, in a coal mine, in a grindstone and whetstone mill, with a machine shop attached. His last work in Ohio was in running the engine for the mill. Struck with fever he returned to Boston in September 1859.[21] Physically exhausted, and disheartened with the appeals of the West, Collins found lodging for himself in a cold-water flat in South Boston. This neighbourhood, where Patrick Collins now made his home, had developed as the result of the numerous small factories, iron works, foundries, glass works and machine shops that had been established during the early 1800s. It was an area easily accessible to the thousands of Irish immigrants living in cellars and congested tenements along the Boston waterfront and desperate for work of any kind. Moving across the channel and settling into newly constructed boarding houses, brick tenements, or small clapboard houses, these immigrant labourers quickly turned the area into an Irish-Catholic enclave.

The distinctive ethnic character of this section of the peninsula was even further defined during the Civil War years, when additional workers were brought in to increase the industrial production of the South Boston factories in order to meet the wartime demands of the Union army and navy. Boston Iron Works supplied iron bars and ship chains, cannons and shells; City Point Works turned out marine engines, boilers and new ironclad warships called 'monitors', and the Globe Works produced excavators, steam shovels and locomotives that eventually saw service in every state in the Union. The district was a clearly distinguishable working-class, ethnic neighbourhood.[22] With his slight physique, Collins was turned down for employment as a machinist in the local factories, a disappointment for him because, as he wrote in his autobiography, he had hopes of becoming a mechanical engineer. He did get a job, however, as a furniture upholsterer with the F.M. Holmes furniture establishment on Hanover Street, Boston, where in three years he rose to the position of foreman.[23]

Although he had now been in the USA for several years and was settling down to a promising future, Patrick Collins, like most other immigrants of the period, kept in close touch with what was going on back in Ireland. Of course news from Ireland was reported in the columns of the *Boston Pilot* and with his own childhood memories of the Famine years that had led to the death of his father and forced his family into exile, Collins became involved in the Fenian movement. Fenianism, a movement that emerged from 'the wreckage of the 1848 rising', drew upon 'the as yet untapped financial and sentimental resources of the Irish American community'.[24] The participants in this movement referred to themselves as part of the organisation or brotherhood. As R.V. Comerford observes 'the terms Irish Revolutionary Brotherhood and Irish Republican Brotherhood ("I.R.B." in any case), and "Fenians" were adopted or imposed. For convenience we can refer to the organization from its inception as the I.R.B. and to its members as Fenians, though strictly speaking these terms are anachronistic for the early years'.[25]

James Stephens founded the IRB in Dublin on St Patrick's Day 1858 as 'a sister organization' of the Fenian Brotherhood, set up by John O'Mahony and others in New York City. However, as Comerford argues 'O'Mahony and Stephens were the leaders of their respective organisations but there was never a satisfactory understanding about how they stood vis-à-vis one another'.[26] Despite the organisational and personal conflict, there was unity about goals. As Kevin Kenny puts it, 'the aim of the Fenians and IRB was to rid Ireland of English rule by providing

American money and manpower to encourage insurrection'.[27] By sending out speakers, launching publicity campaigns, sponsoring picnics, outings, and dances, the Fenians sought to recruit new members, form new chapters and solicit contributions from Americans for the cause of Irish freedom.[28] This was a cause that Patrick Collins was to soon dedicate himself in a full-time paid position. As a 14-year-old in 1858, however, he was not quite ready. Nor, as it turns out, was the USA, which was shortly to be rendered by internal conflict that took the lives of hundreds of thousands of Americans.

The very existence of the USA was challenged by sectional conflict over slavery; consequently Fenian action in Ireland was delayed. For the Fenians, the American Civil War was both a problem and an opportunity. The positives clearly outweighed the delay because it was immediately apparent that the war meant that thousands of emigrant Irishmen were available as recruits for both armies, North and South. This meant that, from their ranks 'seasoned military officers and men could be drawn for a future rebellion in Ireland'.[29] Furthermore, 'hopes were high of escalated tension between the American government and Great Britain, resulting in a war that the Fenians could profit from by launching a simultaneous rebellion in Ireland or by allying themselves with the federal army'. The Fenian hopes were to be dashed.[30]

Prior to that disappointment, the infamous New York City draft riots in 1863 required Union troops be dispatched to put down the violence directed against African-Americans. Many or most of the rioters were Irish.[31] The *Boston Pilot* observed in an editorial that 'riots of a serious character have occurred in New York, Newburgh, [and] Buffalo. This is to be deplored'. Sadly, however, the *Pilot* went on to blame 'nigger-worshippers who were responsible for the antagonism by telling the black man that he is equal to the white'. Seizing the opportunity in the situation the editor expressed the 'wish that the black man was employed for all the drudgery [found] in our cities and manufacturing towns, thereby driving the Irish labourer where his services will be rewarded'. In the West the Irish labourer 'can be secure from the taunts of the Know-Nothing, and where he can bring up his children in the faith of his father's without molestation' before concluding that 'we deprecate and enter our protest against this rioting between white and coloured labourers. All who participate in the crimes committed are accountable to God for the bloodshed, and it will surely fall upon them'.[32] There was also rioting in Boston at this time but 'the situation … was different and it was shaped by the peculiar animosity that existed between the Yankees and the Irish'.[33] According to Jack Tager:

> Boston had few black residents, less than 1.3% of the population … The Boston rioters, solely Irish, did not attack blacks, however, they vented their wrath upon the symbols of Yankee oppression visible in their own neighbourhood. In fact, the spontaneous outburst of the Boston Irish had a very specific goal – to get arms to protect themselves from the draft marshals.

Their targets were armouries, gun and hardware stores. Estimates of the number of rioters killed range from eight to fourteen. Observers also commented on the noticeable involvement of women among those attacking these places.

Despite these conflicts in 1863, Fenians moved forward in the USA, though the enduring personal conflict between the founders hindered the effort. From the beginning, O'Mahony 'was in an ambivalent position … as he drew his authority from two sources. He had been elected president of the American organization in New York City at the end of 1858 when it had a total membership of forty, and he had also received his appointment from Stephens'.[34] In the autumn of 1863 a financial crisis and subsequent recriminations finally spurred O'Mahony to assert his equality with Stephens. Subsequently, a national convention of the Fenian Brotherhood met in Chicago in November 1863 and elected O'Mahony as the head. Some eighty-two delegates were present at this first national convention, and the principal task of the three-day meeting was 'the drafting of a constitution embodying the principles set forth by O'Mahony'.[35]

The Brotherhood grew and fourteen months after the first convention, a second such gathering, which included Collins, met in Cincinnati in January 1865 with some 348 delegates.[36] The 21-year-old Collins, who had only joined the South Boston circle in the fall of 1864, was selected as a delegate to this second congress.[37] William J. Hynes had been named recruiting agent for the New England region earlier in 1864, but organisers felt that a second full-time agent was needed.[38] Collins appears to have impressed his fellow members by his respectable appearance, his knowledge of Irish history and his public speaking ability. At any rate, Collins started out on his recruiting work in February 1865, heading to areas in western

Massachusetts where clusters of Irish immigrants had moved to take advantage of jobs building canals, laying railroad track, labouring in the various lumberyards and in woollen mills and paper factories that were scattered throughout the countryside. Collins' success was due in no small measure to his insistence on careful planning and thoughtful organisation. Whenever he arrived in a town, he would immediately contact the most prominent Irishman in the district, identify himself, explain his mission and then organise a local committee to arrange a public meeting and publicise the project. He would also try to have groups of Fenians from neighbouring districts march through the town in uniform just before the meeting to dramatise the event and promote the establishment of another chapter.[39]

Evidence of Collins's work and success is to be found in a column titled 'Fenian Circles' that was published regularly in the *Boston Pilot*. This column reported organising efforts throughout the New England states and other parts of the North, all this during the Civil War. For example, a 25 February 1865 letter to the editor from Amesbury, Massachusetts, stated that the Fenians of the town were favoured the previous evening 'with a right sound address delivered by P. A. Collins, Esq., of Boston, Assistant Fenian Organizer for New England'. The letter writer described Collins as a 'youthful patriot and orator' who:

> began in a clear, audible tone of voice, and continued thus for more than an hour and a half, in a most sound and forcible manner, evincing a thorough knowledge of his subject. There was nothing exaggerating nor bombastic connected with his speech; but, on the contrary, something clear and practical, which seemed to give the utmost satisfaction to the entire assembly. It is entertained as the general opinion that those who selected Mr. Collins to supply a great defect in that department erred not in their appointment.[40]

Similarly, but with less flourish, a letter from West Randolph, Massachusetts, stated:

> The most respectable and largely attended meeting of Irishmen ever held in this town was addressed by P. A. Collins, Esq., Central organizer, F. B., in Stutson Hall, Feb. 25, 1865, who most eloquently defined the principles of the Brotherhood, and the necessity of its organization for the regeneration of our long-lost nationality. The spirit and enthusiasm

> displayed by the meeting during the long delivery, clearly proved to the speaker that the Shamrock was not yet decayed in the hearts of the Irishmen of Randolph, and also proved to him, by their enthusiastic interruptions, that they will not stand behind their countrymen, where chivalry and patriotism are to be displayed.[41]

Some of Collins's speeches were made in Boston, his home base. The *Boston Pilot* reported that a meeting of the friends of Irish nationality was held in March 1865 in historic Faneuil Hall, under the auspices of the Fenian Brotherhood. 'The hall was crowded to excess, and the audience was very enthusiastic'.[42] American and Irish flags were displayed on either side of the rostrum and John O'Mahony, Head Centre of the Brotherhood for the USA, was introduced. The *Pilot* observed that O'Mahony had 'not risen to the head of the order in this country by his excellence as an orator, but by toilsome, painful and silent work'. Whatever his oratorical skills, O'Mahony proclaimed 'the day of peaceful agitation and petition is gone. The sword alone can win the liberty of that green isle'. Collins also addressed the meeting, and his remarks were 'heartily applauded'.[43] At this stage of his career it is clear that Collins was a 'physical force man', convinced that only direct military action could succeed where parliamentary manoeuvring had failed.

The Civil War ended in the spring of 1865 and Patrick Collins redoubled his recruiting and fundraising efforts. By early April the New York headquarters could report that their young agent had founded fourteen new Fenian chapters in Massachusetts.[44] Through the summer and into the autumn of 1865, Collins organised more chapters and raised more money. For example, in June 1865 the *Pilot* reported:

> The Irishmen of this town have lately aroused themselves to a thorough sense of the duty which they owe their native land, and being determined that they should be no longer behind the rest of their countrymen in their efforts to free that dear old land from the yoke of tyranny and oppression, and again give to the Irish people their happy homes and altars free ... Another grand public meeting was held in Ripley's Hall on Friday evening, 13th ult.—P.A. Collins, Esq, of Boston, Central Organizer, F. B., delivered an able and eloquent address, in which he explained thoroughly the principles and objects of the Fenian Brotherhood, and the duty of Irishmen in America.[45]

With the conclusion of the Civil War, the Fenians had greater expectations of action against Britain and also greater divisions over the best strategy. However, the movement in America had continued problems with the Catholic hierarchy. As he travelled throughout New England, Collins became acutely aware of the hostility of many Catholic clergymen to the political goals and militant activities of the Irish Brotherhood. In Boston, for example, Bishop John Fitzpatrick was outspoken in warning members of his flock against dangerous movements that might infiltrate the Catholic Church in America, especially in the guise of secret societies or fraternal organisations that could well be subversive agencies promoting radical politics or outright violence. Fitzpatrick indicated his pleasure when the Sixth Provincial Council of Baltimore officially condemned all 'secret societies', and through the columns of the *Boston Pilot*, he himself constantly urged immigrants to avoid association with any type of club or society that encouraged clannishness or bigotry. It was a similar story elsewhere and during the summer of 1865 the Archbishop of St Louis, Peter Richard Kenrick, went so far as to deny Fenians the sacraments in his particular diocese.[46]

On at least one occasion, this public opposition of Catholic Church leaders to the Fenian movement provoked an explosive response from the usually calm and methodical Collins, who lashed out at what he obviously considered an unconstitutional attempt to bring religion into American politics. 'There are too many in this country prone to confound the religious with the political opinions of a clergyman, and willing to concede to him the privilege of using his clerical influence for the enforcement of his political views', he wrote in response to what he considered a particularly unfair diatribe in the *Pittsburgh Catholic*.[47] 'I am not one of that kind', he responded in no uncertain terms:

> I am inclined to accept the lamented Mulligan dictum – as a soldier I obey my general, as a Catholic I obey my bishop. But I will not obey religious commands from the general, or political orders from the bishop ... A clergyman has no more right to mark out for an Irishman his course in Irish politics than he has to dictate to an American whether he shall vote the Republican or Democratic ticket.

In his study of Fenianism William D'Arcy noted 'that the collapse of the brotherhood was brought about, not by the opposition of the

American hierarchy, but by the inability of the Fenians to bury petty jealousies and differences of opinion in their striving for a common goal. A fatal weakness of the movement was the inability of its members to recognise and admit an honest disagreement. A difference of opinion was branded as treason and the culprit accused of selling out to 'British gold'.[48] The more serious problem of the movement, then, was factionalism. As Eileen Reilly argues:

> In America, the movement split into two factions. One group, led by William R. Roberts, advocated an ambitious if quixotic invasion of Canada in order to provoke a conflict between America and Britain. The other faction, headed by O'Mahony, was still determined to launch a rebellion in Ireland. The arrival of Stephens in New York did not heal the rift but precipitated further hostility after his appropriation of O'Mahony's position. The Roberts faction attempted their invasion three times – in 1866, 1870, and 1871 – before they finally decided it was a futile strategy.[49]

The Fenian weakness for factionalism was obvious when its third convention, attended by 600 delegates, was held in Philadelphia in October 1865. As D'Arcy writes:

> The convention was a stormy one and the friction between O'Mahony and the members of the central council was evident. The revision of the Constitution left O'Mahony with shorn powers and a hostile senate with which to contend. The 'men of action' had gained ascendancy over O'Mahony.[50]

Within months some of these men of action would invade Canada, an approach of which Patrick Collins did not approve. He was a follower of O'Mahony and believed in the idea of raising money and men in America for revolution in Ireland. Despite the incipient factional split, at the convention, Collins was elected secretary.[51] He was also named a bond agent at an annual salary of $1,200 and was given an office in New York City.[52] As part of his job, early in 1866 he joined others who went on the road to emphasise the importance of buying Fenian bonds and supplying the funds that would enable a rising in Ireland.

It was at this time that events in Ireland spurred a crisis in North America. Towards the end of February 1866, news arrived in the USA that the British Government had suspended the Habeas Corpus Act in response to reports that American Fenians were beginning to arrive in Ireland. In the weeks that followed the news from Ireland, there was a flurry of excitement among members of the Fenian groups throughout the USA who concluded that the opening stages in a new struggle for Irish independence had already begun. What was needed at this point, declared Collins in one of his fundraising appeals was 'something more than cheers and plaudits. Money, not soldiers', was the immediate need.[53] Collins continued his speech by insisting that the idea of a raid into Canada was contrary to the designs of the leaders in Ireland and assuring his listeners that if they would supply the means, then some 300,000 men in Ireland were ready to do the fighting.

Collins argued night after night, that the 'hopes of Ireland are brighter than before', and so was the need to purchase more Fenian bonds. For example, on 4 March 1866, a large number of Irish-Americans assembled at Jones' Woods in New York City and listened to Collins advocate the use of force to achieve Irish independence, though he still insisted that the actual fighting should be done in Ireland by Irish soldiers.[54] Collins called upon his listeners to translate their sympathy into practical aid in order to 'make the Irish republic a fixed fact, free and independent'. The very next month, according to Kevin Kenny, a Fenian 'attempt to seize the Canadian Island of Campobello in the Bay of Fundy was thwarted at Eastport, Maine. The British and American navies cooperated in intercepting a shipment of arms, and US troops under Major General George Meade forced the Fenians gathered at Eastport to disperse. On 1 June, Colonel John O'Neill crossed the border and defeated a Canadian militia company before retreating to Buffalo'.[55] These Fenian efforts in North America in 1866 were doomed and the Fenian Rising in Ireland the following year was also unsuccessful. So too were subsequent invasions of Canada in 1870 and 1871, but it didn't take the practical-minded Patrick Collins that long to abandon the movement. After sixteen months of labouring for the cause, Collins settled into a new life in which he became a prominent Democratic Party politician in Boston, Massachusetts and later throughout the USA. Having served in the Massachusetts House of Representatives (1868-69) and the Massachusetts Senate (1870-71), Collins was appointed Judge Advocate General of Massachusetts in 1875 and was a delegate to

Democratic Party national conventions in 1876, 1880, 1888 and 1892. He served in the US Congress from 1883 until 1889 and was consul general in London from May 1893 until May 1897. In addition, he was Mayor of Boston from January 1902 until his death in September 1905.

Thomas N. Brown saw Collin's Fenianism as opportunism: 'When Fenianism swept into the East in 1864, shrewd young politicians like Patrick Collins joined up, and from then on Fenians were too frequently aspirants for public office'.[56] More recently Kerby Miller wrote that 'it was certainly true that many nationalist spokesmen were self-serving 'professional ethnics' like Thomas Francis Meagher and Richard O'Gorman [and] many Fenian leaders, such as Roberts and Patrick Collins of Boston, also used nationalism to promote careers in mainstream politics'.[57] Whatever the merits of these comments, throughout this American career, Collins retained his interest in Ireland. Collins was among the leaders who greeted Charles Stewart Parnell in Boston when he went to America to raise funds in 1880. Collins was subsequently elected president of the American branch of the Irish Land League and during the time of his presidency, he helped to raise $350,000.[58] A few years later, Collins proudly related, 'Mr. Parnell and the Home Rule members entertained him at a notable public dinner in London'. This was the occasion, he noted, 'at which the Irish leader made the famous pronouncement upon which the general election was fought that year'.[59] F.S.L. Lyons writes of this August 1885 event that Parnell 'presided at a dinner given at the Café Royal for General P.A. Collins, one of the more moderate luminaries of the Irish National Land League of America'.[60]

Two years later, in the summer of 1887 while touring Ireland, both Dublin and Cork officially recognised Collins's efforts on behalf of his native land by granting him the 'freedom of the city'. Collins wrote that in each city the vote was unanimous: 'the Orangemen and extreme Tories refrained from voting against the resolutions'. It was during this journey that detectives from Dublin Castle and Scotland Yard also took interest in Collins and followed him through his journey to Belfast and the north. They were reportedly looking for dynamite in the luggage of this man who was at that time a member of the US Congress.[61] The British Government were apparently unconvinced that Patrick Collins's Fenian associations were over and these suspicions raise some interesting questions.

Subsequent to his London posting, in 1901 Collins was elected Mayor of Boston, a position in which he served ably. He was re-elected in 1903 and died suddenly in office in 1905. His life was celebrated and memorialised by the local community and many others who attended his funeral. Bostonians lined the streets in respectful silence as the funeral cortege made its way from the cathedral to Holyhood Cemetery in nearby Brookline where Collins was laid to rest in a grave near that of his mother and only a short distance from the tomb of his close friend, the poet and editor, John Boyle O'Reilly. The two men represent much of the Irish experience in America where they both made their mark. Even in a sometimes hostile land, Collins was always assured of his place in Irish-American history because 'his heart was Irish, and the world was before him'.[62]

7

The women of Ballykilcline, County Roscommon: Claiming new ground

Mary Lee Dunn

Slieve Bawn, your ghosts are reticent;
They haunt shy corners of the past.
If we want them to speak to us
Truthfully, they have to be asked.[1]

If historian Robert Scally wrote little about the women of Ballykilcline in County Roscommon in his 1996 book *The End of Hidden Ireland*, it was likely due to their near invisibility in Famine-era records, his primary sources.[2] Scally could not draw on archaeology either since such excavations in the townland were only just beginning, carried out by Charles E. Orser and others.[3] However, the women of Ballykilcline are present in the Crown's list of evictees as it administered its emigration scheme for the hundreds of residents of the troubled neighbourhood in 1847 and 1848. Here we find the tenants' names, ages, and their contexts in nuclear families. The survival of this list meant that it was possible to trace these immigrants in the USA. Indeed, only two years after their arrival in New York, in 1850, the federal census began recording data on all individuals rather than just naming the heads of families and the age groupings and gender of wives, children, and others as had been the custom in the past. Moreover, journalism and other public record-keeping were evolving so that the sources that named individuals – such as court and police records, newspaper accounts, school and church data – multiplied to the extent that we can begin to characterise the immigrants and trace their lives with greater detail and confidence. Fortunately, in the case of Ballykilcline, which was part of the civil parish of Kilglass, we can also access troves of family records due to the organisation in 1998 of the Ballykilcline Society, which is devoted to the descendants' family history, genealogy and local history.[4] Thus, increasingly, a picture of these emigrants becomes clearer. This chapter examines the women of Ballykilcline, their work, family and social lives over several generations. It also draws on more recent research than was available to Scally and the knowledge gathered by their descendants to help characterise them. And so we ask questions of the new sources and new data; as poet Kieran Furey suggested above, to know more, 'they have to be asked'.[5]

Ballykilcline is located near the River Shannon where counties Leitrim, Longford, and Roscommon come together near Rooskey, a few miles north-east of Strokestown. In 1690, during the 'War of the Two Kings', in which William of Orange defeated James II, Ballykilcline was seized by Crown forces. A century later in 1793, the land was leased to the Mahon family of Strokestown (barons Hartland after 1800), whose estates amounted to just over 11,000 acres. The Mahons' lease on Ballykilcline ended in 1834 when they declined to renew it and the townland again reverted to the Crown. This development initiated a rent strike which continued until 1848 when the Crown evicted the inhabitants, paying for their passage to New York City in an effort to rid the area of the trouble they had incited.[6]

Trouble in Ballykilcline began in 1834 when Crown agents retook administration of the townland. A handful of tenants began a rent strike and over the next few years other residents joined the strikers, out of either conviction or pressure from their peers. Eventually nearly the whole populace engaged in the protest. Legal actions and evictions of the strike's leaders ensued but the tenants reclaimed their homes which inexplicably had been left standing. Special deals were offered to the tenants, which were rebuffed or, finally, not answered at all. When the Famine commenced in 1845, protracted negotiations were underway and Ballykilcline started counting its hungry and dead. The inhabitants became dispirited and morale dissipated. Nearby townlands imitated the Ballykilcline strike by withholding rents as well and the clamour of local landlords, including the targeted Mahons, over the strike, increased.

In May 1847, authorities began the first of a series of evictions that extended to the spring of 1848 and as many as 368 people were transported to New York City at the Crown's expense. For some, the strike had lasted more than a dozen years. The removal of the Ballykilcline tenants was replicated at Strokestown where Major Denis Mahon sent 1,490 of his tenants to Quebec on so-called 'coffin ships'. A few months later Mahon was assassinated and residents of Ballykilcline were suspects in the case, although none of them ever went to trial for the murder.[7]

Interestingly, some of the Ballykilcline tenants had family members who emigrated on their own accord in the previous two decades, including dozens of people from the townland and surrounding Kilglass parish who had gone to Rutland, Vermont.[8] Thus, many of the Crown's evictees settled there after landing in New York. Within a decade they had dispersed but in Rutland the female evictees (some 48 per cent of Ballykilcline's population) appear more visible. This chapter then focuses on the first two generations of these immigrant families from Ballykilcline and in particular the fate of its female inhabitants. Using primarily government records, Robert Scally wrote the first extensive account of the strike and emigration of the Ballykilcline tenants, but provided no focus on the women of the townland.

In his view, females had 'always been among the missing' in Ballykilcline.[9] And so they are in his story. In 1841, he noted that the townland was home to 236 females but five years later that number had decreased to 199. By and large Scally drew his picture of women from numbers. For example, women, he found, were four times more likely to be in domestic service than were Roscommon men and four times as many women in the county were paupers.[10] Just over 3,000 women in the county were employed as 'servants & labourers' (meaning farm workers), whereas 46,000 Roscommon men did such work. Seven times as many boys as girls under 15 were farm workers elsewhere. Scally also pointed to an abnormally high mortality among women in the townland, but also to a higher rate of single emigration of women in the early years of the Famine and to women returning to households of their birth as eviction was imminent.[11] Although by 1851, there was an increase in women in County Roscommon (and Strokestown in particular), in the parish of Kilglass the opposite was true. There, unmarried women, largely aged between 15 and 40 were missing, due, he suspected, to the threat of evictions, although it is likely that emigration contributed to the decline.

At the onset of the Famine no unmarried women lived alone in Ballykilcline and there was only one household which was solely women, where a widow and her spinster sister resided. In 1846 there were fourteen widows, which increased to twenty-five two years later, as Famine and emigration worsened. Women, it has been argued, lacked 'formal economic or political identity' while a male head of household was alive.[12] Society seemed to accord certain deference to males. Three times as many males as females could write English (because they stayed in school longer), although more women than men could read. Indeed, among a number of local schools, several small private ones were operated by women. Of the fourteen widows in 1846, six were heads of households with land leased in their names and unmarried offspring living among them. Widows were also part of joint holdings. As Scally concedes, these facts must have given them a say in what happened, though it might not be evident in the written record:

> In the absence of a record of their own minds, it is impossible to know just what part the women of Ballykilcline played in the events that ended with the community's destruction. But that alone cannot be taken to mean that they were either silent or without influence in those events, perhaps even decisive influence.[13]

Charles E. Orser and David Ryder, archaeologists who carried out excavations at Ballykilcline in the 1990s, took issue with the characterisation of the Ballykilcline people drawn by Scally and the 'culture of poverty' model he imposed on them, which, they said, scholars in other disciplines had rejected.[14] They noted:

> Our research suggests instead that the Ballykilcline tenants understood their circumstances and were wise enough to manipulate and use the system to their advantage. Only the eventual potato blight and its attendant horrors precluded further resistance. The evidence indicates that the tenants were part of a complex land system that represented an ingenious adaptation to both the social and the material environments.[15]

The archaeologists contended that Scally erred in distancing the tenants so thoroughly from a 'growing consumerist marketplace … Ballykilcline … was an extremely dynamic place with a vibrant culture and a complex social structure', they said.[16] Fellow archaeologist

Katherine Hull examined the role of females in the townland through artefacts found in their excavations. The items included sewing implements, a partial ceramic 'nesting egg', fragments of vessels used in milking, table utensils, and parts of an iron pot and imported ceramics. 'The sewing scissors and thimble indicate maintenance tasks and cabin crafts, the milk pans and pitchers reflect butter production, the iron pot reflects traditional cooking methods, and the imported ceramics reflect the transformation of tradition', Hull explained. 'In this way, archaeology can be used to develop sketches of the women's responsibilities and influence'.[17] Women's domestic functions in Ballykilcline as childbearer and caretaker, meal-maker, and in making and caring for clothing were also evident. Women produced textiles to sell outside the home, including lace, knitting, linen work and so forth, to augment the family's income. They cared for livestock (cows, pigs, chickens, and sheep), and the home garden plot. A wife might, for instance, sell butter and eggs at the local market. Hull concluded that such work might have earned nearly half of the income of an Irish household.[18]

Historical archaeology, she said, provides means and opportunities to examine pre-Famine women's roles as 'makers and modifiers of tradition'; that is, as 'active participants in the cultural transformation that occurred during the mid-19th century' since 'as household managers, women were the primary vectors through which English culture, as represented by material goods, could enter the realm of traditional Irish culture'.[19] Studying this material record gives precedence to 'the items chosen, made, used, and discarded'. Women's roles extended far beyond the concerns of kitchen, barnyard, and garden as 'actors in the manipulation of and resistance to elements of the landlord system and English capitalism itself'. The women purchased English ceramics and adopted individual plates at meal times and 'were involved in larger cultural issues'.[20] The mechanisation of agriculture and labour in textiles during the Famine period forced women to factories and domestic service at home and elsewhere.[21] Such images underscored those of Isaac Weld, who, in his 1832 survey of Roscommon, delighted in watching the scene at a market day in nearby Strokestown, which he called the 'most picturesque in Ireland'. He noted:

> The colours of the dresses and the scarlet cloak or mantle still worn by the older women. Younger women wore vivid scarlet shawls and 'the fondness for finery amongst the female peasantry and the eagerness with which they survey it in shops and windows almost surpasses belief.[22]

Emigration from Ballykilcline had begun in earnest in the pre-Famine decades; John and Sabina (Brennan) Hanley and family who settled in Rutland, Vermont about 1830 were among the first Irish documented there. Daniel and Nancy (*née* Winters) McGuire also went to Rutland during the 1830s. Indeed, research to date has found more than twenty-five men, some with families, who named their home places as Kilglass or Ballykilcline when they filed for naturalisation in Rutland before 1847. Roger Mullera, for example, left Ballykilcline about 1834 and went to New York before moving on to Kentucky. This early wave of emigrants proved enormously helpful to the Famine evictees, providing support, lodgings, employment and social relations once they landed in the USA. When the evictees arrived, Rutland was on the verge of a commercial boom, thanks mainly to the new railroads which provided ready employment for Irish immigrants. In addition, the railway opened up Rutland to marble production, although at some cost as these new transport networks also hastened a decline in sheep farming in Vermont by helping Western farmers get their sheep to market. While the men found work building and operating the rail lines and in the numerous marble quarries, young Irish women worked in hotels, boarding houses and the homes of Rutland's elite, whose fortunes grew from the mid-1850s due in no small way to the burgeoning marble economy. According to Blaine Edward McKinley 'in the 1850s, in the urban East, Irish-born women constituted the largest single group among servants'.[23]

Many of these immigrant women lived in the homes of Rutland's 'Yankee' natives – that is, descendants of the early British settlers in New England – where the women served as domestic help. In 1850, for example, Kilglass native Ann Colligan, aged 22, lived in the home of John A. Hicks, an Episcopal clergyman, while Margaret Winters, aged 23, and Margaret Foley, aged 17, were counted in the house of marble businessman, William F. Barnes. Honora Winter's daughter and namesake appears (under the diminutive Ann) in the home of attorney Charles Williams and ten years later Catherine Foley worked in the home of another marble entrepreneur, William Gilmore. By 1860 William Ripley, another marble businessman, employed Margaret Hanley in his house.[24] Domestic service was comparatively well paid and the work offered other advantages as well, ones that did not come in mill or needlework. Moreover, those who could speak English – as the Kilglass people often did – had an advantage in the service marketplace.[25] Thus, Kilglass people had an inside look at the lives, homes, and habits of some of Rutland's social leaders, and one wonders how their positions influenced their new life and what they absorbed from their new environments. How important was this experience as they became Americans?

When they married, the Ballykilcline immigrants tended to choose spouses within their own group – that is, someone from their Irish townland, parish, or home county. Numerous examples illustrate the point. William Brennan married Bridget Geelan, his brother Daniel married Maria Kelly, while Michael Igo married Catherine Geelan. All were from Ballykilcline. However, domestic service sometimes led to marriage with Americans as well, as was the case with two Colligan sisters, Mary and Ann, who married into their employers' families, the Butlers and Caprons.[26] Naturally, not all marriages were approved of; that of Annie Kelly and Edgar A. Batchelder of Dorset, in Bennington County, being a case in point. Kelly, the daughter of an Irish marble cutter, James Kelly, born in the 1820s in Strokestown, met Batchelder when she worked in his family's home.[27] Their families' reactions to their marriage, which crossed social and religious lines, were strained, as their daughter recalled in a note to a cousin:

> My Father was a Congregationalist. My mother's parents were very strict Catholics. They did not know of the marriage at the time. When her parents did find out they were furious. Her mother, especially, never got over the fact that her daughter married out of the faith. They finally did forgive her, but it took a long time. My mother's sisters never did relent. For the same reason the relationship between my grandparents Batchelder and my parents was no less strained. In fact, my Grandmother never, as far as I can remember, came down to my parent's [*sic*] farm. Mother went up there, but never received much welcome. In time because of Father's good nature, there was a detente between the families, although the women never were themselves.[28]

The transition to life in the USA would have been far easier for many Irish women, given their domestic and farm work in Ballykilcline, had they been able to buy land in Rutland and move into more familiar roles. The night that Nancy McGuire (*née* Winters) died, for example, she was taking butter to Rutland (selling butter was something she often might have done in Kilglass, as Hull's research, described above, explained). However, many jobs open to women in Rutland seemed to depart from the familiar farm-based tasks to which they were accustomed. Few of the immigrant families could afford a farm for years, if ever, in Rutland. And the town had few of the mill jobs that attracted young immigrants in southern and central New England. Some women, especially widows, likely did sewing or worked as laundresses. In their earliest years in Rutland, some families took in boarders, but one of the mysteries is how Irish women in Rutland contributed to household income during their child-bearing years. Or did supporting family and household shift entirely to the men and their older children? Men's wages in railroad and quarry work were not sufficient, as shown by several quarry strikes in Rutland after 1859 and continuing outlays of public funds to care for those affected. Lists of those recipients included Kilglass or Ballykilcline people among them, especially widows, children and the elderly, and more particularly in the early years after their arrival.[29] Indeed, Rutland's quarry strikes cost some evictees their homes (for the second time in their lifetime) when owners turned strikers out of company housing.[30]

Analysing the Irish in Vermont, Vincent Feeney argues that marriage meant a woman left her job 'thus it was mainly young, single girls, along with spinsters and widows, who made up the female Irish work force'.[31] Many of the immigrant children left school at an early age to start working, something which, because of a lack of education, penalised them later when it came to finding better jobs. The literacy of the evictees was germane in appraising their sense of agency, which I attempted to do in my book *Ballykilcline Rising*. The changes in the US census in 1850, when the government began to ask about literacy and later censuses asked separately about ability to read and write, facilitated an assessment. No information in known Irish records told how many of the rent strikers could read and/or write. Of these immigrants, data for fifty-eight individuals (thirty-seven subjects were men, twenty-one were women) has been examined. Evictees comprised 56 per cent of the group; the rest were linked to Ballykilcline by other records. In compiling this dataset I sought to identify people who had at least two responses to census enumerators; in fact though, the number of replies for each individual is one to three over four censuses. In answering census-takers, forty-three people, or 74 per cent of them, asserted one to three times between 1850 and 1880 that they were literate and never reported that they could not read or write. The oldest person in the study group, Honora Winters, born in 1787, twice reported that she could both read and write.

While weaknesses are apparent in the data, nevertheless, it seems that the people of Ballykilcline were more literate than many Irish immigrants, particularly those from the western Irish counties. This fact corresponds to Ciarán Reilly's findings for the nearby Mahon estate at Strokestown where there was a high level of literacy.[32] Ballykilcline's literacy levels may have been influenced by the presence of a priest, at least one teacher and an aide to an attorney who lived in the townland, while there were a number of schools nearby. A significant portion of the Kilglass populace spoke English by the early 1800s, while many were bilingual. This naturally helped them secure employment elsewhere and by the 1840s, women from Ballykilcline were in domestic service in England. Indeed, Bridget Wynne, when her family were assisted in emigration by Crown's agents, had such a job.[33] And hundreds of Kilglass men – approximately 425 in 1838 – were seasonal labourers, or spalpeens, in Scotland and England who brought more commercial ideas with them when they returned home from these temporary jobs each season.[34] Undoubtedly, this form of economic support for Roscommon families and farms, which meant the harvesters were away from home for long periods each year, also meant that the women had to develop a measure of self-reliance, economics, and independence to manage farm and family alone for a time year after year.

The importance of education in Ballykilcline was also reflected in the lives of the immigrants in Vermont. In the early 1850s a school attached to St Bridget's church was established in West Rutland, catering for more than 126 pupils. By 1860, there were more than 200 students in attendance. The majority of this parish were Irish and many of them were former tenants of Ballykilcline or Kilglass.[35] There was a growing appreciation for the need to educate their children and some were sent to boarding school, including two Colligan sisters, who were sent to a convent school in Montreal, Canada, where they learned French and music. Likewise, three daughters of William and Bridget Brennan (Ann Elizabeth, Mary Ann and Margaret) became teachers, while their brothers became a doctor, a lawyer, and an engineer respectively.[36] Catherine Riley, the daughter of Kilglass immigrant John Riley in Connecticut, joined a religious order and studied in France. Later, as Sister Jeanne Teresa, she taught briefly in Lee, Massachusetts, and then helped found St Francis Hospital in Hartford, Connecticut, heading its nursing school for thirty-five years. In turn younger family members followed her into nursing at the school. Her older sister Mary

Ann tutored the children of a local 'Yankee' family and then taught in a one-room schoolhouse. And Kilglass women and their children excelled in other areas. These included Alice O'Brien, who with her husband, ran Halcyon House at Watch Hill on the southern Rhode Island coast, a summer resort of celebrities in the later 1800s. Her name alone appears on a number of property deeds in the area, which suggests she was a business woman of some independence. Ann Tully's daughter, Mary Malone (*née* McLaughlin), worked as both postmistress in Manchester, Vermont, and as a 'stringer' (freelance journalist) for three newspapers.[37] A daughter of young Ballykilcline evictee Luke Caveney, whose family lived in Lawrence, Massachusetts, became one of the first female graduates of the medical school at the University of Colorado in 1896. She later became the head of the Colorado Sanatorium and Hospital Association.[38] And finally Eliza Butler, the daughter of an 1848 evictee, became a postmistress in Utah.

By 1900 many Irish immigrant women and their children, like the aforementioned Brennan and Riley sisters, were school teachers. That tendency arose early, according to Feeney who noted that:

> the one genteel occupation where Irish women in Vermont had a noticeable presence – particularly among first-generation Irish Americans – was teaching … By the late 1800s, dozens of public schools in villages and towns throughout Vermont had teaching staffs that were primarily Irish. As early as 1869, West Rutland's Public School No. 7 – the 'Catholic' school – had five female teachers, all Irish … But even elsewhere in Vermont, wherever there was an Irish community of significant size, the public schools had large numbers of Irish teachers.

However, the job was poorly paid, standards for teachers were low, and districts set their own curriculum. Facilitating the Irish influx in the schools, young teachers could board in their students' families' homes. However, that influx also drew resistance. There were several incidents where Protestants objected to the hiring of Catholics in the schools, including the appointment of a Catholic as the principal at Rutland High School in the late 1870s.[39] Despite these inherent problems and tensions the occupation continued to draw Irish immigrant women, underlining their determination to leave the household in search of work.

In the early 1980s, Hasia R. Diner produced a notable study of Irish domestic workers in the USA in the years 1840–1900. In it, she said:

> Irish women viewed themselves as self-sufficient beings, with economic roles to play in their families and communities. The ways they migrated clearly established their ability to make decisions for themselves. In a larger sense, their work histories and involvement with trade unions put them beyond the pale of that cult [of American womanhood] as did their assertive family life and frequently boisterous public behaviour. They reckoned that they could support and succour brothers, sisters, parents better from America than on the 'ould sod' … [but] they did not remain deaf to the resounding debate on the roles, rights and responsibilities of women that engulfed American society from the 1840s onward.[40]

Diner noted too that as domestic workers and schoolteachers they filled 'occupations [that] constituted a restricted and, in a sense protected labour market for Irish women, and it did not change as rapidly as did the larger market for unskilled industrial labour'.[41]

Away from work and the home place, Kilglass immigrant women invested time and energy in church, charity, nationalist efforts and social events. The parish of St Bridget's, for example, had an Irish band, a night school, a lending library, a debating club, a cemetery, and the pastor was involved in the Quarryman's Aid Society. Also operating in Rutland in the 1860s were various Fenian circles, while the Ancient Order of Hibernians was active in Rutland by the mid-1870s. Unsurprisingly, a number of women became active in church affairs. Daughters of evictee Richard Padian in Maryland and John Riley in Connecticut regularly maintained and worked at their local churches.[42] Irish women invested time and effort in other community efforts including the numerous organisations that sustained community life and brought people together for shared interests. Doubtless the women were involved in multiple capacities in these group efforts; newspaper notices in Rutland showed they raised money for Irish causes well past 1900.

Working and being involved in local community did not deter the women of Ballykilcline from raising large families. For many, ten children was not uncommon; indeed the largest in this case study was that of Michael and Margaret Hackett who had eighteen children. Familiarity with evictees and their records also suggests that Kilglass people may have had a higher-than-average chance of twin births; there were three sets of twins, for instance, among the offspring of the seven immigrant Riley siblings, while many other examples exist.

Of course these large families were the result of early marriage rates, with women marrying as young as 15. Interestingly, there is evidence of only one divorce in the cohort of Ballykilcline evictees, despite the fact that it was not uncommon among the general population in Rutland in the later 1800s. Bridget Mullera divorced from her husband Terence Maguire, and her young son lived thereafter with her brother in LaSalle County, Illinois.[43] Despite the large families, Irish couples often made room for elderly parents or children of misfortune. Honora Winters lived with a son in later years; the older McCormicks in Albany, New York, took in their younger siblings after their father's death; while John Riley and wife in Hampton, Connecticut, became guardians of his deceased brother's youngest children.[44] In addition, Mary Butler and her husband opened their Rutland-area home to her widowed mother and unmarried sister; the widowed Anne McGinty had three nieces living in her Minnesota home in 1880;[45] while after her husband died, Mary McLaughlin Malone returned to her parents' Vermont house to care for them.[46]

Among the Ballykilcline and Kilglass immigrant women a number stand out for their longevity: Honora Winters and Bridget Brislin, for example, both lived to advanced old age, outliving children they had followed to the USA.[47] It was surprising given the fact that the average age at death in America was 37 years in the post-Civil War period. Between 1857 and 1873, the most common causes of death in Rutland were consumption, pneumonia, and fevers. More than half of the deaths from tuberculosis were people under 40 years of age and it occurred more often in women than men, whose jobs in the quarries or on the railways were the source of many fatal and trivial accidents. For example, William Colligan's wife was widowed with six children after an injury he sustained in a marble quarry became infected in the early 1850s.[48]

For the Kilglass immigrants and their children the attachment to Ireland remained. Those who stayed in Ireland were never forgotten and remittances were sent in an effort to bring relatives or friends over in what is called chain migration.[49] At the time of Ireland's Famine emigration, the Americas, including the native-born, experienced great mobility due to the opening of western territories and uncertain economic conditions so that immigrants sometimes lived in two or more localities before finally settling permanently. No source of specific information on that subject became apparent in Rutland to me except that some followed earlier immigrants from Rutland to LaSalle County, Illinois, and after a few years to Minnesota. But scholars have demonstrated that Irish women were particularly diligent in helping their families to emigrate. According to Diner, domestics and mill girls 'made a staggering contribution to the Irish economy in the form of these remittances'.[50] In one instance, the captain of an American ship said that remittances arrived 'by almost every packet that reached Liverpool'. He continued:

> I had occasion, when in Ireland, when visiting a large union workhouse, containing between two thousand and three thousand inmates, to enquire if many such sums found their way to the paupers in that establishment, and I was informed that from six to eight persons weekly on an average were enabled to leave the workhouse by this means, and to pay their passage to America.[51]

The testimony of the land agent, Joseph Kincaid, in 1847 may provide evidence of this occurring at Ballykilcline. Appearing before the Select Committee of the British House of Lords on Colonization from Ireland, Kincaid told them that 'the best proof that I can give is the numerous instances of small Sums of Money being sent over by Persons who emigrated in former Years both to the USA and to Canada, to assist other Members of their Families to go out this Year'. Kincaid had visited Ballykilcline only three weeks before giving his testimony and he knew Kilglass well.[52]

A strong sense of identity and community motivated the generation of the immigrants and their children, many of whom devoted themselves to their communities. Others devoted themselves to the Church, as did Catherine Riley of Connecticut, later Sr. Jeanne Teresa who gave long service caring for the ill and educating nurses at St Francis Hospital in Hartford. Other examples are provided in three hand-drawn family trees, which I became aware of after the publication of *Ballykilcline Rising*. These family trees were sent to the Ballykilcline Society by a descendant of the townland whose ancestors went to Rutland and Dorset, Vermont. The intersecting family trees each begin with a Kilglass couple born in the 1700s and describe multiple generations of their descendants in both Ireland and Vermont. In all, the trees name approximately 350 individuals and provide some detail about their lives. For example, that of James and Ellen (McGuire)

Reilly lists a half-dozen descendants who were identified as priests or nuns and family knowledge has added several more to that count.[53] As Diner asserted, the immigrants retained their unique cultural values and 'the distinctive cultural traits of Irish-American women remain strong today'.[54]

Religious life was not the only expression of their values and concern. In the next and later generations, that legacy also manifested in pursuit of governance through political and administrative offices. To this point, the story of six remarkable women is worthy of mention. They were the aforementioned Sister Jeanne Teresa (Catherine) Riley, Mary Featherstone Prendergast, Sarah Palin, Josette Sheeran, Mary McAleese and Mary Pat O'Hagan. Prendergast's grandmother (Ann Riley) and her first husband, Peter Featherstone, were both immigrants from Kilglass. Mary, who was born in 1879, became the second wife of Rhode Island mill owner and banker William Prendergast of Burrillville, Rhode Island, just after the turn of the twentieth century. A few years after William died in the 1920s, Mary became the first woman ever to run for an alderman's seat in Providence, although she was ultimately unsuccessful.[55] Nevertheless, it was a breakthrough forward-looking action, a challenge on her part, an expression of her sense of civic responsibility and her desire to serve.

This interest in politics was also evident in another descendant of Kilglass Famine emigrants. In 2008 Americans witnessed the rise of Sarah Palin, then governor of Alaska, when Senator John McCain of Arizona named her as his 'running mate' for the vice presidency in that year's national election. Through much of the campaign, Palin's Irish background from her mother's Sheeran line remained something of a mystery. After Palin's selection, an internet genealogy list buzzed that her great-great-grandfather Michael Sheeran was born in West Rutland.[56] With that fact confirmed, I looked for her family surname on a database I had constructed of naturalisation records of immigrants from Roscommon who settled for a time in and around Rutland. Listed there was an earlier Michael Sheeran, born in 'Nokall' (that is, Knockhall) in Kilglass in 1823. Knockhall was particularly affected by the Famine. In 1841 it had a population of 1,200 people but ten years later that number had decreased to 470 people through death and emigration. This Michael was Palin's immigrant ancestor. The evidence also revealed that Michael's wife's maiden name was Cline, a name present also in nineteenth-century Ballykilcline.[57] Sarah

Palin's ancestors had followed the same route that John McGinty did, leaving Rutland for LaSalle County, Illinois, and eventually moving on to Minnesota. Before he died in Minnesota several years ago, Joseph Sheeran, who carried out extensive family history, endorsed this finding about the Kilglass roots.[58]

However, the Sheeran story does not end there. When Palin's roots in Kilglass were disclosed, some Sheerans born in Kilglass and now living in the eastern USA contacted me. From them, I learned that another woman in that extended Kilglass family (there was only one Sheeran in Kilglass in the Synge census of 1749), Josette Sheeran, was then the head of the United Nations' World Food Program. Since then she has served as Vice Chair of the World Economic Forum, and in May 2013 was named president of the Asia Society, an educational organization to promote linkages in culture, policy, and business between Asia and the world. Indeed, further recognition of her achievements is evident in the fact that *Forbes* magazine named Josette Sheeran as the world's thirtieth most powerful woman in 2011.[59]

The heiresses of Kilglass's local history bear the imprint of its history in a consciousness that has informed their individual achievements and commitments and the collaborative efforts in which they have invested themselves. Witness the Irish National Famine Museum, which is located on an estate where the immediate past President of Ireland found that her ancestor, Mary Lenihan, received a gift of meal during the early months of the Famine in June 1846. Mary McAleese's ancestor was not spared the horrors of the Famine however, and lost two children – as did so many more Strokestown and Kilglass descendants in New England, New York, and elsewhere in the USA. Increasingly, more of their stories are made known.[60] Some of these stories, however, are tinged with sadness. In November 2013 the town of Sheffield, Vermont, dedicated a playground to the late Mary 'Pat' O'Hagan, whose Hanley and Brennan ancestors had emigrated from Ballykilcline to Rutland about 1830. Pat and Ed O'Hagan, early members of the Ballykilcline Society, had retired to Sheffield from Massachusetts. After her husband died, Pat stayed on there and became greatly engaged in the area's many organisations, craft circles, and historical societies, volunteering at a school and a food bank, activities that are the lifeblood of small communities everywhere. In September 2010 Pat disappeared and a search went on until her body was found about three weeks later. She had been shot during a burglary in her home and her body left in a wooded area. Police and prosecutors are working diligently on the case which attracted national headlines and some in County Roscommon. A speaker at the Sheffield playground dedication extolled O'Hagan as 'an excellent example of good citizenship', while her son, Shawn O'Hagan, told assembled Vermonters that 'we learned late in life what it means to give back to a community. Our mother taught us that and it's a lesson you all could learn and bring forward for a long time'. As her Ballykilcline forebears had done before her, Mary Pat O'Hagan passed on a spirit and commitment to community that these Irish made their own.[61]

8

Constructing an immigrant profile: Using statistics to identify Famine immigrants in Toledo, Ohio, 1850–1900

Regina Donlon

In 1852 Stephen J. Pickett, the son of Irish Famine immigrants, was born in Toledo, Ohio. His father, Stephen, had travelled to the USA in 1848 and was followed two years later by his wife, Margaret and their eight children. After initially settling in New York, within two years of their arrival the family had migrated to the Midwest and chosen Toledo as their new home. Shortly after arriving in the city, their ninth child, the aforementioned Stephen, was born. Educated in St Patrick's Parochial School, where his family were all members of St Patrick's parish, at the age of 19 Pickett began learning the brick-laying trade and after a few years established his own construction business. Gradually, his reputation increased and during the second half of the nineteenth century he was contracted to build many of Toledo's landmark buildings, including the Roth Knitting Works Building and the city's 'Blade' Building.[1] Undoubtedly, Pickett's story was characteristic of many Irish immigrants whose experience has formed part of our diasporic legacy. Writing in 1983, Thomas Archdeacon argued that 'the historian who describes how people have come from all over the world to North America … must answer several basic questions'. The questions, he notes, 'seem simple but beneath their appearance lies a reality that involves complicated questions of definition and judgement'.[2] This chapter aims to examine this reality by using census schedules to establish and construct a profile of the Irish immigrant community in Toledo during the second half of the nineteenth century. Using these schedules as the primary quantitative source, this chapter also seeks to demonstrate immigrant life by using examples of qualitative material to further illustrate the Irish experience in Toledo.

In assessing the composition of post-Famine Irish immigrant communities in the American Midwest, an interpretation of census records provides valuable answers to the 'several basic questions' Archdeacon alludes to. The value and limitations of using census transcripts have long been debated by historians and genealogists. Census records provide researchers with a unique snapshot of immigrant life. However, this in turn can itself prove problematic at times and any analysis of census schedules must be conducted objectively. Despite this, when used in tandem with qualitative data, census schedules enable researchers to construct a concise ethnography of post-Famine Irish immigrants in Toledo.

The principal theoretical framework of this study is derived from the sociological research methodology known as grounded theory. This method essentially allows the collected data to form the theory itself rather than manipulating the data to suit an already existing premise, arguably a strategy suited to a proportional ethnographic study such as this. As Charmaz argues, 'the logic of grounded theory prompts going back to data and forward to analysis'.[3] Given the extensive quantity of census material pertaining to the Irish immigrant community in Toledo during the period from 1850-1900, this study identified a region in the city to undergo micro-analysis. This area focuses on the ethnically Irish neighbourhood around Swan Creek in Toledo. Consequently, the findings of this study are both proportional and representative, but nonetheless retain a level of accuracy as they focus exclusively on a well-established region of Irish influence.

The information extracted from these census schedules concerned only immigrants whose stated place of birth was Ireland and their descendants. Prior to 1880, descendants were identified by their place of birth and their direct relationship to the head of household. However, after 1880 it was possible to identify generational members of the community based on their place of birth and that of their parents. Thus, from 1880 onwards, not only second generation, but third and, in some isolated instances, fourth generation immigrants were identifiable. The information was transcribed according to the way in which it was recorded on the census schedule. However, for the benefit of quantitative analysis supplementary classifications were added. For example, in determining and classifying generational elements of the Irish immigrant group, a generational category was also added which was denoted by the terms 'I1' and 'I2'. This was extended to third and fourth generations where applicable.

In classifying the occupations of the recorded immigrants, the census bureau guidelines for 1900 were incorporated. However, they too were modified separately to provide a more accurate account of Irish occupational trends. Finally, in assessing immigrant marriage trends, additional classification categories were also required. Accordingly, four types of immigrant marriages were identified. These included marriages that took place both within and outside the immigrant community itself. They were also reflective of the influence of generational marriage trends within the group as a whole. Upon completion of the census transcription for the area under analysis, a concise profile of the Irish immigrant community in Toledo was apparent. However, despite the obvious benefits of working with census schedules and using them to establish a profile of an immigrant group over an extended period of time, there are a number of limitations to working with census material. Specifically, a researcher is reliant on the level of accuracy deemed appropriate by the census enumerators. In some instances, the diligence of enumerators is questionable as important information relating to occupation, property ownership or ethnicity is not recorded. On other occasions, the census transcripts present palaeographic challenges or alternatively, the quality of some of the census manuscripts can be poor. However, in other examples the diligence of the enumerator is apparent.

***

The city of Toledo is situated in Lucas County in North Western Ohio. Although established on the banks of the Maumee River, the northern part of the city also lies on the shores of Lake Erie. Toledo was founded in 1833 and initially formed part of the Michigan Territory. However, in 1837 the city was re-founded and became part of the state of Ohio. The formation of canals was one of the primary reasons motivating the development of the city in the 1830s. Crucially, the Miami and Erie Canal helped the city's entrepreneurs to form important trading links with cities in southern Ohio like Cincinnati. Furthermore, the linking of canal routes like the Wabash and Erie Canal ensured accessibility to cities like Fort Wayne, Lafayette and Evansville, Indiana. These canals ultimately provided access to the Ohio River, which in turn ensured the rapid growth of Toledo's economy. As early as 1832 there was a significant settlement of Irish immigrants in the city as many had come to find work as canal diggers. After the boom of the canal era, many Irish immigrants found a reason to stay in the city as employment opportunities increased on an almost daily basis. By 1837, the development plans for the Erie and Kalamazoo Railroad were at an advanced stage, providing further employment for many Irish immigrants. The development of the railroad combined with a swiftly expanding economy resulted in the emergence of Toledo as a popular immigrant destination by the mid-century. Accordingly, the US Federal Census transcripts for 1850 recorded that 620 of the city's 3,829 inhabitants were born in Ireland.[4] This constituted 16 per cent of the city's population and made the Irish the most dominant immigrant group in the city; a title they could claim until the 1880s when they were surpassed by their German counterparts. The arrival of Irish immigrants in the city also corresponded with the civic development of Toledo. Within five years of the city's incorporation, three distinct school districts had been created and the first public school was opened in Toledo in 1837. This was followed by the first telegraph in 1846 and the construction of the city's first sewers in 1848. However, it was not until 1855 that Toledo's first hospital, St Vincent's, was established. As more and more immigrants gradually came to the city, an Irish settlement emerged on the west bank of Swan Creek. Here, Irish immigrants established make-shift housing on the high ground and so the neighbourhood quickly became known as 'the Irish Hill'.

Historians such as Kathleen Neils-Conzen, David Ward and Howard Chudacoff have discussed at length the various formulations, structures and models of immigrant communities.[5] Ward has long argued the validity of the 'ethnic ghetto' model, while Conzen contends that the 'ethnic community' model was a more likely explanation of how immigrant communities were structured. Both theories are applicable to the Irish community in Toledo, but they were far more susceptible to forming an ethnic ghetto. Primarily this was because of their economic status upon arriving in the city, yet gradually as the nineteenth century drew to a close, there is sufficient evidence to suggest that the Irish community was leaning more towards the ethnic community model advocated by Neils-Conzen. Importantly, this reflects the economic maturity of the group as a whole.

In the middle decades of the nineteenth century, the ghetto model was evident in the high concentration of Irish immigrants occupying the lowest social classes and poorest areas of the city, usually those neighbourhoods close to the central business district, where unskilled employment was easily attainable. Irish communities throughout the USA, whether in New York, Boston or St Louis, followed this model. Emmons' examination of the Irish in Butte, Montana, for example, describes the Irish ethnic clusters of Corktown and Centreville, both of which replicated conditions outlined by Anbinder in his investigation of New York City's Five Points district.[6] Similarly, in Massachusetts, Meagher and Blanchette identify the presence of ethnically Irish clusters in Worcester and Lawrence respectively.[7] The 'ethnic community' model outlined by Neils-Conzen argues that not only residential clustering, but also local amenities such as churches, shops, schools and saloons were as important in defining the characteristics of an ethnic neighbourhood as residential concentration and this again is evident in the traditionally Irish neighbourhood of Toledo by 1900.

An interpretation of census transcripts is arguably one of the most effective ways of personifying the 'Irish Hill'. By analysing census returns for the period from 1850–1900, the dynamism and vitality of the Irish community in Toledo becomes apparent. Integral to this representation was the simultaneous transformation of the US Federal Census Schedule. In 1850, the schedule recorded only basic information about each person. Specifically, name, age, sex, colour, occupation, value of real estate owned, place of birth, whether married within the last year, whether the person attended school in the last year, whether the person can read or write and whether the person was deaf, dumb, blind, insane, idiotic, pauper or convict. By 1900 this basic information was still sought, but additional data concerning relationship to head of household, marital status, number of years married, number of children born to the mother and number of children living, place of birth of both parents, year of immigration, number of years resident in the USA and year of naturalisation was also required. Furthermore, details relating to property ownership were sought by enumerators by 1900. During the period 1850–1900, the Irish population in Toledo experienced an increase of 332 per cent.[8] This increase is explained by two factors. Firstly, there was an expanding Irish immigrant population in Toledo in the two decades after 1850 as Famine immigrants arrived in the city at accelerated rates. By 1870, the number of Irish-born immigrants resident in Toledo peaked at 3,032 people.[9] Secondly, these immigrants produced offspring which further augmented the structure of the ethnically Irish community in the city.

In building an immigrant profile of the Irish community, the age and gender composition of the cohort are quite obviously important. However, using census schedules it is also possible to examine the occupational profile of the community, examine child labour trends, marriage patterns, investigate average household size and establish an interpretation of the amount and value of property owned by a particular immigrant group. However, for the purpose of this chapter, only the age and gender profile of the Irish community, as well as their occupational and marriage patterns, will be highlighted.

Year	*No. of Irish-born resident in Toledo*	*Increase/ decrease*
1850	620	-
1860	2,467	297%
1870	3,032	23%
1880	2,941	3%
1890	2,878	2%
1900	2,684	7%

Table 2: Increase of Irish population in Toledo Ohio, 1850–1900[10]

Throughout the period from 1850 to 1900, male immigrants were frequently more abundant in Toledo than their female counterparts. Yet, in 1880, more Irish-born females were present in the city than Irish-born males. This is perhaps explained by the availability of employment in the city by 1880. Aside from domestic service, many women were also employed in manufacturing industries, and often worked in paper and box factories or in cotton mills. Perhaps, this large number of immigrant women is also explained by the effects of chain migration and the increasing popularity of Toledo as an immigrant destination.

As is to be expected, during the period 1850–1900 the average age of the Irish immigrant community in Toledo increased. In 1850, the average age of the famine immigrant generation was 31 years. By 1870, this had increased to 36 years and by 1900 the average age of an Irish-born immigrant in Toledo was 50 years.[11] This suggests that a certain portion of the immigrant population in Toledo decided to settle in the city and also confirms the decreasing rate of emigration from Ireland by 1900. Similarly, the generational aspect of the community – that is, children born to immigrants – remained under ten years until 1870. By 1900, however, the average age of second- and third-generation Irish in Toledo had increased to 24 years, suggesting again that many ethnically Irish offspring decided to remain in the city. Significantly, by 1900 the average age of members in the Irish community in Toledo was 28 years, confirming that the Irish population in Toledo was still relatively young. However, compared to cities further south like Fort Wayne, Indiana, and St Louis, Missouri, the Irish population in Toledo was older than many of its counterparts by 1900.

Toledo Irish	1850	1870	1900
Average age of 1st generation Irish (immigrant)	29 years	36.2 years	50.4 years
Average age of Irish generational composition	7.9 years	8.5 years	23.6 years
Average age of Irish immigrant community overall	22.3 years	22.6 years	28.3 years

Table 3: Representative sample of the average age composition of the Irish community in Toledo, Ohio, 1850–1900[12]

One of the most interesting ways census transcripts can be employed is in the analysis of marriage trends. In this instance, the Irish in Toledo exhibited definitive signs of assimilation by 1900. In the census returns for 1850, 73 per cent of Irish-born immigrants married spouses who were also of Irish origin. Of the 27 per cent who married outside of the ethnic group, the majority married American-born partners from Ohio, Indiana and Michigan.[13] Of those who married spouses of foreign origin, French-born spouses were the most common. This emphasises the importance of religion and the desire of Irish immigrants to maintain and preserve their Catholic faith. By 1900, however, only 14 per cent of Irish-born immigrants were married to Irish-born spouses. Yet, despite this, marriage within the ethnic group had been preserved to a certain extent, as 28 per cent of marriages consisted of one partner born in Ireland and the other partner having at least one Irish parent.[14] However, despite this, there was a distinct increase in the number of marriages outside of the Irish ethnic group. By 1900 the majority of inter-ethnic marriages consisting of an ethnically Irish partner and an American spouse of at least three generations had increased. Again, spouses born in Ohio, Indiana and Michigan were the most popular. Where other immigrant groups were concerned, marriages to English, French and Italian partners were the most common, demonstrating, as before, the importance of religion and perhaps also previous migration trends.

Toledo City	*Number of marriages*			
	1850		1900	
	No.	%	No.	%
Emigrant generation marriage	145	73	38	14
Intra-ethnic group marriage	-	-	76	28
Inter-ethnic group marriage	38	27	279	58

Table 4: Representative sample of the marriage trends within the Irish community in Toledo, Ohio, 1850-1900[15]

Census records are also an integral source in defining the economic structure of immigrant communities. In 1850, Irish immigrants were engaged in no fewer than 197 varying occupations. By 1900 this had increased to 358 assorted occupational descriptions. Undoubtedly, the majority of Irish women were recorded as 'keeping house'. Where women were single or widowed, occupations such as seamstress, paper-box maker, servant and laundress were recorded. Conversely, their male counterparts were employed in both the manufacturing trade and transportation sectors. Occupations such as railroad man, switchman, motorman, bricklayer, deckhand and peanut sorter were recorded. However, by and large, the majority of Irish immigrant men pursued unskilled labour and worked as hod-carriers, helpers or general labourers.[16] There were also examples of Irish immigrants in the professions and some worked as doctors or lawyers as well as those who embraced entrepreneurship. One such business tycoon was William Finlay, born in Drumsna, County Leitrim, in 1819. He emigrated to America at the age of 17 in 1836. Upon arrival, Finlay settled in Lockport, New York, before arriving in Ohio in 1843. After settling in Toledo, Finlay found work as a hotel porter and later became an agent for a passenger steamboat company that operated on the Wabash and Erie Canal.[17] In 1866, having gained invaluable experience in trade and commerce, he established the Finlay Brewing Company. As a reward to his employees for their loyalty in helping him establish the business he later gave them $100,000 worth of the company's stock.[18] Throughout his life Finlay also gained a reputation as a generous philanthropist and donated money to both Catholic and Protestant charities. Before his death, for example, he allotted $20,000 to buy land and establish Toledo's first Home for Friendless Women, while in his will be bequeathed $50,000 to his former employees.[19]

His entrepreneurial counterpart Edward Malone also rose to prominence in Toledo. Born in King's County (now Offaly) in 1825, Malone immigrated to Philadelphia in 1849 before migrating west to Maumee, Ohio, and then to Toledo. There he married Elizabeth Madden from Queen's County (now Laois) in 1853 and they subsequently had eight children.[20] After arriving in Toledo, Malone learned the carpentry trade in the workshop of William Hoffman, but, like Pickett and Finlay, also set up his own business, forming a partnership with fellow Irishman, John O'Neill in 1857. Together this partnership was responsible for the construction of Oliver House in 1859, St Patrick's church in 1862 and Boody House in 1871.[21] Malone also sat on Toledo's police board in 1867 and the board of education two years later. He continued to be active in local politics and was elected to the Ohio State Legislature on a Democratic ticket in 1883. Notably, it is by investigating immigrants like Finlay and Malone that the benefits of using a combination of both quantitative and qualitative research methods are most rewarding. Both could be identified in the census and because of their recorded occupations and property ownership status, further qualitative research revealed their outstanding contributions, not only to their own immigrant groups, but to the city of Toledo as a whole.

Aside from identifying these entrepreneurs, an analysis of census records also highlights the economic role of children. Although both public and religious schools in Toledo were pivotal in creating progressive immigrant communities by the turn of the century, many children were forced to work if the opportunity arose. Despite this, in Toledo by 1900, 620 children of Irish descent were regularly attending school. A further sixty-three children aged 12 or younger were also in employment.[22] These occupations ranged from simple tasks like bag folding or stove polishing in the manufacturing sector to messenger boys and pedlars in the trade and transportation sector.

While census transcripts are an essential source in attempting to construct a profile of consolidated immigrant communities, they unfortunately provide little qualitative data which would further illustrate and explain the immigrant experience. And yet, in the evenings when the mills had closed, the motormen had gone home and the domestic servants had been given a rare evening off, the social life of a nineteenth-century Irish immigrant in Toledo had many possibilities. As with most Irish immigrant communities, social and cultural activities tended to revolve around the Catholic Church. Although there were at least three Catholic churches in Toledo attended by the Irish community, it was St Patrick's Parish that served the Catholics from the 'Hill'.

Occupation	*Number*
At school	620
News boy	12
Peddler	8
Elevator boy	3
Scrub girl	11
Paper box folder	9
Laundry girl	11
Dock boy	9

Table 5: Representative sample of child labour trends within the Irish community in Toledo, Ohio, 1900[23]

St Patrick's was established in 1862 by Fr Edward Hannin, a native of Ballymote, County Sligo. Born in 1826, he was educated in a hedge school until his father founded a national school on the family farm. Hannin later moved to Dublin and became a civil engineer but the outbreak of the Famine forced him to emigrate.[24] Hannin's second migration took him to New York, where he began his theological training. Subsequently, he moved to St Mary's Seminary in Cleveland, where he completed his spiritual preparation and on 1 June 1856, the French-born Bishop Armadeus Rappe, ordained him. The Irish in Toledo had long petitioned for an Irish priest who would be able to cater to their spiritual needs. However, Rappe had taken a dislike to the Irish when he worked in Toledo as a priest and was reluctant to dispatch an Irish pastor to Toledo. Eventually, he succumbed and appointed

Hannin to St Patrick's, where he was charged with establishing a parish for Irish immigrants. Arriving in Toledo in 1862, Hannin remained there as pastor for the next forty years until his death in 1902.

Within a few weeks of his arrival in Toledo, Fr Hannin's influence on his parishioners became apparent. In 1950, an article appeared in the *Toledo Blade* newspaper which recalled an incident that occurred at the city's waterfront in 1862. After a night of heavy drinking, two Irishmen became involved in a fight and when a policeman arrived to intervene, both parties pounced on him. At the same time, a passer-by had been walking along the waterfront and heard the commotion. 'Suddenly', the paper recalls, 'the biggest of the drunken rioters staggered back from a well-placed uppercut to the chin … the Irish men stood frozen, when they saw who was dealing the blows … a young man in his thirties, dressed in a long cassock and wore the flat black hat of a priest'.[25] The young man in his thirties was Fr Hannin and after this incident he quickly began securing donations for the construction of the church. Indeed, as a testament to his character and inter-ethnic co-operation, St Mary's German Catholic parish in Toledo donated $975 and the French St Joseph's parish bequeathed $2,000 to assist with the construction costs.[26] By 1863, Hannin had collected $27,000 and, with the help of parishioners who donated materials and labour, St Patrick's church was constructed in the city's fourth ward. Taking no more than nine months to erect, Bishop Rappe held the first service in the new church on 1 February 1863 and the parish became home to Irish immigrants, primarily from counties Roscommon and Galway.[27] In addition, the construction of a school soon followed. This became known as St Patrick's Academy, and was free of charge to those attending. Staffed by the Ursuline Sisters, as well as some lay teachers, they provided courses in reading, writing and arithmetic for the Irish children of Toledo. Boys were also instructed in commercialism to benefit their employment prospects and girls were instructed in homemaking.[28] Local businessmen and prospective employers were invited to public exams so that they could scout for future employees.[29]

As the parish grew and expanded, it could no longer cater to the needs of all the parishioners. As a result, overflow parishes like the Immaculate Conception church were established to serve Irish immigrants from Kerry and Mayo. Immaculate Conception was located in the city's fifth ward, colloquially termed the 'Bloody fifth' due to the presence of raucous and unruly Irish immigrants. Fr Hannin's work continued and during the 1860s he became heavily involved in the establishment of a Catholic cemetery. In 1873, he initiated plans to erect St Patrick's Institute, a recreational centre which provided an alcohol-free environment in which parishioners could socialise. This was a much-needed centre as the Irish in Toledo had a reputation for alcohol abuse. Identifying this weakness in his flock, Hannin set about resolving the situation. Indeed even before the institute was established he had already attempted to reform the Irish social habits. In 1863, for example, he had founded the St Patrick's Temperance and Benevolent Society with a Juvenile Society being formed five years later. In addition, he established a library society and an athletic and literary society which had a monthly subscription of $25, a hefty sum in 1870.[30]

However, the Institute was intended to serve as a 'recreation centre that could compete with saloons and pool halls'.[31] Bishop Gilmour was strongly in favour of the establishment of the institute and granted $7,000 for its construction.[32] It would include 'a library with 1,000 books, a bowling alley, billiards tables, gymnasium, a hall for receptions and theatre productions and meeting rooms for organisations'.[33] Significantly, the centre did not allow the consumption of alcohol. Taking just over a year to construct, the facility was dedicated on 17 March 1874. The institute possessed the latest modern equipment and caused much excitement, not just among Fr Hannin's parishioners, but all across Toledo as well. The official opening was well attended and included the mayor and the Ohio State Governor, William Allen, and other prominent local civic leaders. The contribution of Fr Hannin to the Irish community in Toledo was both commendable and almost unfathomable. His enthusiasm and passion for enhancing the Irish immigrant experience in Toledo was widely admired by those who benefited most.

However, it was not only Irish-born men who made a positive contribution to their new homeland. The influence of Irish-born women was equally as important in the immigrant experience. One example was Catherine Duffy, who arrived in New York from Liverpool on board the SS *Winchester* in September 1853. With her travelled her mother Mary, older brother William and younger sisters Alice and Margaret.[34] During the voyage there had been an outbreak of cholera on board the *Winchester* and this particular sailing had been the most deadly of all passenger ships that entered New York harbour during September and October 1853. On 26 October the *New York Herald* reported that, 'in one vessel, the Charles Sprague, the unusually large number of forty-five persons died on the passage from Bremen; and in another, the Winchester, from Liverpool, the number of fatal cases amounted to no less than seventy-nine'.[35] Despite this, the Duffys arrived safely in New York and Catherine's father, Hugh, who had made the journey earlier in the summer, was waiting for the family. From there they made their way to Napoleon in Henry County, Ohio, approximately 40 miles south-west of Toledo. Napoleon was a small rural settlement which had developed as a result of the construction of the Miami and Erie Canal during the 1830s and 1840s, most probably the reason why the Duffys ended up in the township. By 1860, Hugh was recorded as working as a day labourer, as was his son William, while Catherine was earning a living as a domestic servant. The family did not own any property and the value of Hugh's personal estate amounted to $25.[36]

Catherine however, was not destined to stay in Napoleon. Four years later, in 1864, she entered the Ursuline Convent on Cherry Street in Toledo. The convent had been founded ten years previously at the request of Bishop Rappe. Inviting five Ursuline Sisters from Cleveland to open a convent and parochial school in Toledo, Rappe believed that the parochial and public school systems in the city were inadequately developed. At the age of 19, Catherine Duffy entered the Ursuline convent and stayed there until her death in 1918. After her investiture, Sr Catherine became a teacher at the parochial school, which became known as St Ursula's Academy. Typical of many Catholic institutions in developing cities during the mid- to late nineteenth century, Catherine was surrounded by fellow Irish-born women, as well as women of German extraction. The development of the Ursuline order in Toledo was particularly successful and by 1870 the Ursuline Sisters had a staff of twenty-five teachers, six of which were of Irish birth and which catered to the educational needs of Toledo's young Catholics. Moreover, the convent also included eight boarders ranging in ages from 15 to 8 years of age and the various parochial schools boasted hundreds of day pupils.[37] St Ursula's Academy itself taught students a range of subjects including English, German, French, mathematics, history and art and was divided into two departments, elementary and collegiate. The order continued to grow and by 1880 the convent had an academic staff of thirty-six and an ancillary staff of twelve.[38] As well as that, the academy's reputation increased and the school continued to attract students. As a result, by 1910 the Ursuline convent in Toledo boasted a teaching staff of eighty-two nuns.[39]

Fittingly, between 1910 and 1918, Sr Catherine was appointed as the Mother Superior of the convent where she had spent over fifty years of her life. During this time she had seen fellow Irish nuns like Sr Bridget Waters, whom she trained with and taught alongside for over thirty years, leave the convent and pursue other missions. Catherine remained in Toledo and died on 5 August 1918, one week after falling off a stool in the convent.

In many ways, Sr Catherine's story was typical of Irish immigrant women in smaller towns and cities throughout the American Midwest. In 1860, census enumerators documented a very bleak record of the Duffy family living in rented accommodation in a backward township in rural Ohio. The family's personal wealth of $25 represented only an average annual income and quite obviously the Duffys were subsisting rather than flourishing. Yet, despite this, Catherine was able to create a life for herself and make a positive contribution to her community. In becoming both a nun and a teacher, Catherine's life in America contrasted significantly with that which she would have had if she remained in Ireland.

The development of Irish immigrant communities in the American Midwest requires the study not only of a people and a way of life, but also of a dynamic that involves their past, their present and their future. Their past brought them to America, their present to the Midwest and their future lies in the generational development and legacies of their communities. Whether candy-makers or congressmen, the immigrant experience enveloped many different guises and it is only when these are examined and compared that a true image of the immigrant experience can be portrayed. An interpretation of census transcripts is essential in portraying immigrant life. Moreover, when utilised as a series, the development of the group becomes apparent. An analysis of census records exemplifies the diverse nature of the immigrant experience, while simultaneously highlighting those who struggled to find a place in immigrant America as well as those who seized even the smallest of opportunities. Census records illustrate patterns of assimilation and identify areas of ethnic exclusivity while concurrently unleashing immigrant portraits on each page. However, it would be remiss to interpret these communities purely as statistical specimens.

What is truly significant here is the story of the immigrants themselves. In establishing a secure environment, old-world values coupled with new-world practices ultimately resulted in a culturally conscious, yet assimilated community aware of its traditions, of their communities and of their responsibility within the wider context of their cities.

9

'The chained wolves':[1] Young Ireland in Exile

Christine Kinealy

The year 1848 is generally remembered as 'the year of revolutions', reflecting the political unrest that challenged the status quo in many countries. By European standards, the rising in Ireland that year was insignificant. It lasted approximately three hours, took place in a remote part of the country, there were no casualties and, seemingly, no outcomes. Moreover, the British press and Irish opponents of the Irish Confederation, who led the rising, were quick to characterise both it and its leaders as pathetic. However, to see the events of 1848 in Ireland simply as a failure is to misjudge the aims of those who led the rising and to underestimate the men – and women – who participated.[2] This chapter explores the fate of seven men who, in diverse ways, played a part in the events of 1848 and who, as punishment, were exiled to Van Diemen's Land. It argues that their influence extended well beyond the events of 1848 and had an impact far beyond the shores of Ireland.

When the news of the French Revolution reverberated throughout the world at the end of February 1848, radicals rejoiced. Of particular note was the fact that the abdication of the monarch, King Louis-Philippe, had been achieved with little loss of life or damage to property – both were to come during the notorious 'June Days'. Radicals and nationalists flocked to Paris to pay tribute to the new Provisional government. One of the delegations was from Ireland, a group known as the Irish Confederation. They had originally been supporters of Daniel O'Connell but, disillusioned with his prevarications, had left the Repeal Association in 1846. Initially referred to as Young Ireland, in January 1847 they had formed a separate organisation, the Irish Confederation. Within a year the Confederation had also split, initiated by John Mitchel, who had been further radicalised by the British Government's mismanagement of the Famine.

The British Government's response to the growth of political agitation in Ireland was swift and draconian. In April 1848, a Treason-Felony Act was passed, making it illegal to 'compass, imagine, invent, devise, or intend' to overthrow the Queen.[3] The act was used to arrest the outspoken John Mitchel, who was found guilty of treason-felony and transported to Bermuda.[4] His former colleagues, William Smith O'Brien and Thomas Francis Meagher, had also been arrested but were not convicted. More repressive legislation followed, including the outlawing of the Irish Confederation Clubs and culminating in the suspension of Habeas Corpus in late July. In addition, the editors of the radical press were arrested and warrants were issued for the arrest of Smith O'Brien and other leaders of the Irish Confederation. Out-manoeuvred and on the run, as a gesture more noble and symbolic than practical, a small rising took place in Ballingarry in County Tipperary on 29 July. It was easily defeated by the local constabulary.

The trial of the leaders of the Confederates was carried out by a Special Commission, held in Clonmel. The prisoners travelled there by a private train, in a first-class carriage. As they boarded the train, O'Brien was described as 'walking with a firm step, and Mr Meagher appeared quite cheerful and laughed occasionally'. The railway station was guarded by city police and those on the platform had their pistols cocked.[5] In total, about forty prisoners were tried for high treason, ranging from the aristocratic O'Brien to men described as being 'of the lowest class, dressed in rags and most dejected in their appearance'.[6] Many were charged with having been present in Ballingarry, which was regarded as levying war against the monarch. O'Brien was the first of the leaders to be convicted of high treason. A few days later, Meagher, Terence Bellew MacManus and Patrick O'Donoghue were similarly convicted. The conviction of O'Brien and Meagher was expected, but MacManus and O'Donoghue had not been prominent members of the Confederation, and had travelled to Ballingarry (MacManus from his home in Liverpool) in order to support O'Brien, an action which was interpreted in the court as an act of war. As with

O'Brien, the three men were informed that they would be, 'drawn on a hurdle to the place of execution, and that each of you be there hanged by the neck until you be dead, and that afterwards the head of each of you shall be severed from his body, and the body of each divided into four quarters, and be disposed of as her Majesty shall see fit'.[7] When given an opportunity to state why they should not receive this sentence, the prisoners used this opportunity to thank their counsel, particularly Isaac Butt. MacManus, who had worked as a shipping agent in Liverpool since he was a young man, also pointed out that his actions had not been 'actuated by animosity towards Englishmen ... it is not for having loved England less, but for having loved Ireland more that I stand before you'. Meagher, who was renowned for his passionate eloquence, concluded his speech by saying:

> I do not despair of my poor old country. I do not despair of her peace, her liberty, her glory. For that country, I can do no more than bid her hope. To lift up this isle, to make her a benefactor to humanity, instead of being what she is – the meanest beggar in the world – to restore her ancient constitution and her native powers – that has been my ambition, and this ambition has been my crime.[8]

Two editors of the nationalist press, John Martin and Kevin Izod O'Doherty, were sentenced to transportation. Their radical careers had been relatively short – both stepping forward following the earlier transportation of John Mitchel and the suppression of his paper.[9] O'Doherty, who was associated with the *Irish Tribune,* was convicted on his third trial and sentenced to ten years transportation. John Martin, long-time friend of Mitchel, who had edited the *Irish Felon*, received the same sentence. Interestingly, the more experienced Charles Gavan Duffy, proprietor of the *Nation* newspaper, was released following his fifth trial.

While O'Brien and Meagher were undoubted leaders of the Irish Confederation, MacManus and O'Donoghue were not. Moreover, both O'Brien and Meagher were from established Irish families (Protestants from Limerick and Catholics from Waterford respectively) who were politically well-connected. On a more personal level, both men were liked and respected, even by those who disagreed with their politics. Following the sentencing of O'Brien, numerous appeals were made to the Lord Lieutenant for clemency, including a memorial from

Dublin Orangemen, who, amongst other reasons, suggested: 'That the execution of Smith O'Brien under the ancient severe code will give a shock to the whole empire, create a thrill of horror in the hearts of the people, and be repugnant to the feeling of a large portion of the Protestant population.'[10]

Inevitably perhaps, within weeks of the convictions, it was announced that the death sentences would be commuted to transportation for life.[11] Logistically and legally, however, such an action proved to be a slow process, dragging on into the following year.

The decision not to execute the leaders immediately following their conviction was taken for pragmatic reasons; the government not wanting to create national martyrs.[12] For months the men languished in Richmond Prison. In July 1849, on the eve of Queen Victoria's first visit to Ireland, the death sentence was officially commuted to transportation. The convicted men resisted, even presenting a memorial stating that they preferred to die an honourable death to transportation. The first signature was that of Meagher, who added, 'the next best thing to fighting for a good cause is the suffering for it'.[13] Regardless, O'Brien, Meagher, MacManus and O'Donoghue were transported to Van Diemen's Land for life. They sailed together on board the *Swift,* a naval vessel, in relative comfort.[14] This fact was not lost on the British public, with one newspaper deprecating that, 'a roomy cabin, a capital library, a fair dinner, with a couple of glasses of wine, and cigars upon deck, form the dietary and the entertainment of the political exiles'.[15]

Sir William Denison, the Governor of Van Diemen's Land, wanted to treat the Irish exiles as common convicts and deny them all privileges, but he was over-ruled.[16] Consequently, they were each offered a ticket of leave, acceptance of which amounted to a promise not to escape. In return, they were allowed to live in relative liberty, but within their own separate districts. Meagher, MacManus, O'Donoghue, Martin and O'Doherty accepted the tickets of leave. O'Brien refused and so was sent to Maria Island, a location usually reserved for the worst-behaved convicts.[17] There, he was only allowed to leave his home accompanied by an armed constable, and his correspondence was opened. Meagher regarded their treatment as unnecessarily vindictive, writing to a local newspaper asking why, 'having separated us by so many thousand miles of all that was dear, consoling, and inspiring to our hearts, they should have still further increased the severity of this sentence by distributing us over a strange land'.[18]

On 12 August 1850, O'Brien attempted to escape from Maria Island on a schooner commissioned to collect him.[19] According to the *Irish Exile*, O'Brien failed because he had been surrounded by government informers who had betrayed him. The paper believed that his action was not a violation of honour as he had not accepted a ticket of leave.[20] More surprising, the *Launceston Examiner* sympathised with him:

> In common with the colonists generally we were gratified to hear that this gentleman had escaped from the colony. The attempt was no violation of honour for he declined to accept the usual terms, which accompanied the tender of a ticket-of-leave. We learn with regret he has been recaptured, but in the name of the community we protest against the exhibition of a spirit of revenge which petty souls, dressed in a little brief authority, are apt to display.[21]

As punishment for his unsuccessful escape attempt, O'Brien was transferred to Port Arthur, which contained a penitentiary for the most hardened of the convicts. There, he was kept in isolation. Again, there were protests in the press and from his fellow exiles. O'Brien remained in Port Arthur for only three months. At the end of 1850, he applied for a ticket-of-leave. It was an admission that he would not attempt to escape again. It was granted and he was allowed to move to New Norfolk. When he passed through Hobart, he received a standing ovation from the local population.[22] On arrival, he was secretly visited by MacManus, O'Doherty and O'Donoghue. When the Governor heard of this reunion, he sentenced the men to three months' hard labour. O'Brien took advantage of his new-found freedom to write a letter to Duffy, intended for general publication, complaining of the latest example of the harsh treatment of his friends.[23] MacManus, however, was released on a technicality and took advantage of his freedom to escape from Van Diemen's Land. The other men knew of his plans, O'Brien admitting that 'my mind will not be at ease until I hear he is safe in California'.[24] MacManus successfully reached San Francisco, where he remained until his death in 1861.[25]

O'Brien passed his time alone by keeping a journal and writing poetry.[26] Exile and isolation had not diminished his political acumen. In 1851, Van Diemen's Land was allowed a measure of self-government with the election of a new legislature. O'Brien had privately contributed to the writing of the new constitution.[27] His writings were published in 1856 as *Principles of Government or Meditations in Exile*. An unexpected addition to the exiles was John Mitchel. Immediately following his sentencing to fourteen years transportation in May 1848, he had been placed on a prison hulk and taken to Bermuda. On 12 February 1849, following weeks of illness caused by asthma, Mitchel was informed that he was being transferred to the Cape of Good Hope, with a number of other convicts, where they would be allowed to roam free but under police surveillance.[28] On 22 April 1849, Mitchel left Bermuda on board the transport ship *Neptune*. His medical attendant had thought him too ill to survive the long journey. This sentiment was echoed in the House of Commons, the Home Secretary stating that it was unlikely that Mitchel would make it to the Cape.[29] Mitchel did survive, but the arrival of his ship coincided with protests on the Cape, the settlers not wanting to accept any more convicts.[30] When they learned of Mitchel's presence, however, the Anti-Convict Association proposed to the Governor that Mitchel should be allowed to stay there as a free settler. The request was refused. Instead, the local people sent Mitchel fine wine to show their sympathy with him. He responded by toasting the protestors, saying 'Bravo, men of the Cape'.[31] While anchored at the Cape, Mitchel learned that the *Swift*, carrying his former colleagues, O'Brien, Meagher, MacManus and O'Donoghue, had arrived in the port a week earlier to take fresh provisions on board.[32]

The *Neptune* spent almost six months in the Cape. In February 1850, instructions arrived from London that the vessel was to proceed to Van Diemen's Land.[33] As compensation for the hardships of the voyage, all convicts on board received 'conditional pardons'; all, that is, except Mitchel.[34] After a further forty-two days at sea, the *Neptune* arrived in Derwent, near Hobart, Tasmania, in April.[35] Mitchel had been ill for most of the journey.[36] On landing, he was offered a ticket of leave, giving him more freedom than he had been allowed in Bermuda. The British Government had debated whether such a privilege should be afforded, but the Home Secretary had reassured Lord Clarendon that, 'you are mistaken as to his wish to renew his endeavours to revolution. From what we have heard of him while at Bermuda he seems to be deeply sensible of the extreme folly of his former violence and is thoroughly disgusted with his old associates'.[37] Not for the first time, the British authorities had underestimated Mitchel and seemed unaware that since being deported from Ireland he had been keeping a 'jail journal' in which he showed no sign of remorse. As a result of his ill health Mitchel was allowed to live with his long-time friend John Martin. What he did not know was that his wife, the fearless Jenny Mitchel, accompanied by their children, had decided to join him in the Cape. When she arrived and heard that her husband had been sent to Van Diemen's Land, she continued in his wake.[38] Jenny's decision to join her husband was praised in the nationalist press in Ireland.[39] When his family arrived in Van Diemen's Land on 18 June 1851, Mitchel simply noted in his journal: 'these things cannot be described'.[40] As the house he had shared with Martin was small, Mitchel later moved to the nearby Nant Cottage, a farm of 200 acres.

The transported men found it difficult to recreate the lives they had left behind, partly because they were all constantly short of money.[41] Meagher was frequently unable to pay his bills, surviving on credit and good will, while O'Brien was subsidised by income from his estate at Cahirmoyle in County Limerick. In 1851, he took a job as a personal tutor. O'Donoghue, who was the least affluent and well-connected of the group, was initially given money by the other prisoners.[42] He attempted to resolve his financial problems by establishing a newspaper, *The Irish Exile and Freedom's Advocate*, shortly after his arrival on the island.[43] The other exiles disapproved, fearing that he would become embroiled in the petty squabbles of the colonists.[44] O'Doherty, who had been a medical student prior to his arrest, was allowed to work, initially as an apothecary and then in a hospital.

Regardless of his youth, Meagher's exuberance and patriotism appeared undiminished by exile. He decided that while in Van Diemen's Land, he would render his surname as 'O'Meagher'. Living initially at Campbell Town and then at Ross, one of the first things he did was to have a boat built in Hobart, which was then hauled by six bullocks the 75-mile journey to Lake Sorell. He named the vessel *Speranza*, possibly in memory of his former colleague and friend at the *Nation*, the poet Jane Elgee. Significantly, he sailed it under the American flag.[45] However, because he had accepted a ticket of leave, Meagher enjoyed relative freedom of movement, although this did not extend to meeting his former colleagues. Nonetheless, he was assiduous about staying in touch with them and also with his friends and family in Ireland, even sending presents home despite being constantly short of money.[46] The territories where Martin, Meagher and O'Doherty lived all adjoined Lake Sorell and Meagher arranged for the three men to meet secretly each week on the edge of the lake, although this was forbidden by the terms of their parole. He ordered the others to bring mutton chops, ale, brandy, cigars and a backgammon board to their illicit picnics.[47] Terence Bellew MacManus, who lived at Launceston, was too far away to be involved in these gatherings. Although Meagher stayed in touch with O'Brien and MacManus by letter, he seemed to have little contact with O'Donoghue.

Despite Meagher's apparent cheerfulness, he was frequently frustrated by the petty restrictions imposed on him and his friends. He believed, however, that 'the chained wolves must have patience, and put up for a short while at all events with the grimaces and worrying of the most contemptible of the Quilps, whether they be in or out of office'.[48] Nonetheless, Meagher was restless. According to one unsympathetic London paper, Meagher was 'in excellent health, but not spirits', and he regarded Van Diemen's Land as an 'English-organised hell on earth'.[49] The arrival of John Mitchel, shortly followed by Jenny, helped to raise Meagher's spirits. Jenny brought with her copies of the nationalist newspapers from the period leading up to 1848 and Meagher used them to write a book of the events that had led to the uprising. In addition to setting the record straight, he hoped that it would provide him with an income, admitting that, 'I have set to work with the rascally intention of making it vastly marketable'.[50] The need to make money was an important consideration as, in the middle of 1851, he was forced to sell his pony to raise cash and apologised to O'Doherty for not paying him money that he owed him.[51]

Meagher was also lonely for female companionship. In Ireland, he had had a close relationship with a 'Miss O'Ryan', with whom he was secretly engaged. However, she was forced to end the association when her parents intercepted a letter from Meagher. According to Meagher, their reason being that they could 'never sanction an engagement which would be sure to end in disappointment in never being realised, since there was little or no prospect of my return to Ireland'. They asked that all of their daughter's letters be returned, and he complied.[52] Only a few weeks later, in February 1851, Meagher married Katherine (or Cate, as Meagher referred to her) Bennett, the daughter of a convict. Meagher realised that 'in the opinion of the frivolous, the fashionable, the sordid, the worshippers of the dollar, and of the flimsy phantom known as Birth', he had married beneath him. The ceremony was simple: in Meagher's words there was to be 'no gloves, no cards, everything quite quiet', although John and Jenny Mitchel, Martin and O'Brien attended.[53] He regarded the marriage as his salvation, confiding in O'Doherty that he hoped it would help him to:

> … forget the ruins that were behind me, and the waste in which I was idly living on, from day to day – feeling too every incentive to useful and elevated pursuits hourly subsiding and life becoming to me a sickening stagnation, in which the best sympathies and tendencies of my nature were drooping into death, having no object to attract them, no vital purpose to sustain and quicken them … it is no wonder that my heart should have turned to one, in whose love it felt assured that peace and health and gladness would be returned to it – on which its earlier action might be re-inspired, and its old ambitions to do something upon this earth, for the good to bless and the free to glorify, might be disengaged from the indifferent emptiness.[54]

The exiled men were desperate for news from home, and any newspaper that they received from there was circulated amongst them, even if it was months out of date.[55] However, they were despondent by the apathy and lack of political progress that followed the 'springtime of the peoples'. In August 1851, Meagher, who had just received copies of the *Weekly Freeman*, averred that 'the Irish news is utterly unattractive. The Tenant League even seems to have disappeared. There has been an election for Dungarvan … the parish priest standing "neutral", that is, deserting the popular party. Damn him and his neutrality… England is full of the Great Exhibition – an immense piece of London Puffery'.[56] They were cheered, however, to hear that John O'Connell, a long-time protagonist, was retiring from politics.[57]

By the end of the year, Kate was pregnant. Nonetheless, Meagher was finding life in Van Diemen's Land increasingly unbearable, confiding in O'Doherty, 'what a detestable country it is! What depths of selfishness, insincerity, treachery, falsehood … How my heart beats and pants for a quick deliverance from the abominable captivity, yearning for some other land, built up with sounder stuff and radiant with a purer destiny'. At the end of his letter, he made an oblique reference to the fact that he was considering escaping, asking, 'Could the "bolt" be managed?'[58] A few months later, Meagher escaped from Van Diemen's Land, arriving in New York in May 1852. His escape, like that of Mitchel's some months later, became embroiled in questions of honour and integrity – the escapees being expected to resign their parole formally in advance of escaping. Meagher had done so, but this issue was to trouble him long after he was safely ensconced in New York.[59]

Kevin O'Doherty found exile especially difficult. He had been a medical student when he was arrested. The penal authorities refused to permit him to take his final exams, but he was allowed to work in a dispensary in Hobart.[60] Later, despite his lack of formal qualifications, he was allowed to practice as a surgeon in a hospital in the town.[61] O'Brien used part of his income as a tutor to finance O'Doherty's medical studies.[62] While in prison in Dublin, O'Doherty had formed a relationship with 'Eva', the pen-name of the nationalist poet, Mary Anne Kelly. She had promised to wait for him, but he was pessimistic about their meeting again. During one of their illicit meetings, Mitchel noted that O'Doherty was 'gloomy and desponding', guessing that he was depressed because in Ireland there was 'a dark-eyed lady, a fair and gentle lady, with hair like blackest midnight'.[63] Eva, however, did keep in touch with O'Doherty, and also with Meagher and Martin.[64] Even though Meagher was the same age as O'Doherty – both had been born in 1823 – he played a protective role. On one occasion, when O'Doherty failed to meet with Meagher and Martin, who had waited five hours for him, Meagher gently chided him in a note asking, 'What's the matter with you? – Sick? Crippled or disconsolate? … You're going to Old Nick straight'.[65] Following his own marriage, Meagher offered to build O'Doherty a cottage on the grounds of his home.[66]

The harsh punishments meted out to the exiles for transgressions of their parole no doubt added to their despondency. At the end of 1850, O'Doherty, together with MacManus and O'Donoghue, visited O'Brien in New Norfolk. They were admonished by the local magistrate for having done so, but the Governor overturned this judgement and ordered that the three men be sent to the remote Tasman Peninsula.[67] The public outcry that followed, however, resulted in the dismissal of Governor Denison.[68] In 1851, O'Doherty was discovered visiting the newly arrived Mitchel without permission. He was punished with four weeks' penal servitude with hard labour. Meagher was outraged and wrote to Charles Gavan Duffy, urging his former colleague to publicise how O'Doherty was being treated.[69] The reporting of such incidents in both Irish and British newspapers kept the men in the public eye and ensured sympathy for the exiles.

Neither Patrick O'Donoghue nor Terence Bellew MacManus were as well known as the other prisoners. MacManus, born in Fermanagh, was living in England by 1848. Following his arrest, newspapers often referred to him as 'the Liverpool Chartist'.[70] MacManus was the first of the prisoners to escape from Van Diemen's Land. He did not forget how his friends had been treated while in exile. Following his settling in San Francisco, MacManus arranged a 'kangaroo court' to indict the captain who had allegedly betrayed O'Brien during his escape attempt, but the captain was freed due to lack of conclusive evidence.[71]

O'Donoghue had been born in Clonegal in County Carlow, probably in 1815, making him the same age as Mitchel.[72] Socially, he had little in common with the other Young Irelanders, having been a legal clerk in Dublin before his arrest. At his trial, he was described as looking 'about 45 years of age, of spare make, wears a dark brown wig, and has a long, pale, unprepossessing visage'.[73] When it was announced that he was to be transported, the radical press appealed for donations to be made for the family that he was leaving behind.[74] However, O'Donoghue was more politically radical than his colleagues.[75] Almost immediately upon landing he established a newspaper, the *Irish Exile*, although the other prisoners disapproved of this undertaking. When Mitchel arrived in Hobart, O'Donoghue asked him to join him in the venture, but Mitchel doubted O'Donoghue's competence to run such a paper and refused to be involved.[76] John Martin, however, contributed a series of articles in which he justified the 1848 rebellion. Moreover, the paper was successful, with distribution outlets in Sydney, Melbourne and New Zealand. It also attracted attention in Ireland, with the *Nation* reporting that the paper was getting hundreds of subscribers.[77] O'Donoghue's continuing interest in nationalist politics was evident in the first edition, which announced, 'we are, in fact, very green – as green as the shamrock that grows in our own native Isle of the Ocean'. His radicalism was also apparent; he promised that the paper would defend oppressed people everywhere, 'whether they be free or in chains'.[78] Unusually, he was a consistent defender of the rights of Tasmanian Aborigines. Initially, O'Donoghue had included articles deprecating the treatment of O'Brien, but the Governor banned him from including these reports.[79] Personally, O'Donoghue seemed to experience the same loneliness as the other exiles. Despite occasionally lecturing on the evils of alcohol, he was arrested a number of times for drunken brawls, one resulting in his being sentenced to hard labour.[80] O'Donoghue attempted to escape twice, and was successful on the second occasion in December 1852 when Irishmen in Australia paid for his eventual passage to San Francisco. While in Melbourne, he wrote a vindication of his escape, sending it to a member of the legislative council.[81] However, he was in hiding for so long before sailing that newspapers started to report his probable death.[82] As was the case with the other escapees, once he was safely in America, full details of O'Donoghue's escape were given to nationalist newspapers in Ireland. A full account was also printed in the *New York Tribune.*[83] However, on arrival in America, O'Donoghue was not feted as Meagher or Mitchel had been, although the former did greet him in person and reportedly embraced him.[84]

O'Donoghue's freedom was short-lived and he died in January 1855. He was then living in Brooklyn in New York, in relative oblivion and poverty. Poignantly, he died on the same day that his wife and daughter arrived from Ireland, but before they had a chance to meet.[85] None of the other escaped state prisoners attended his funeral, although former Young Ireland colleagues who lived in New York, including Michael Doheny, John O'Mahony and Michael Cavanagh, did, with the latter paying for five funeral carriages. According to Doheny, O'Donoghue's unpopularity in the USA had arisen from the fact that he 'had told stories about the other Irish patriots, and I did not care to meet a man who would repeat such stories, whether true or false; however, any feelings of an unpleasant nature ceased with his death'.[86] O'Donoghue was the first of the Young Ireland state prisoners to die. Similar to his role in the 1848 rebellion, his death went largely unnoticed.

Terence Bellew MacManus was the second escaped state prisoner to die in the USA.[87] In contrast to O'Donoghue, his death and subsequent funeral became an occasion of spectacle and political manoeuvring on two continents. MacManus passed away on 15 January 1861 in San Francisco, where he had been living in relative obscurity since his escape. His death was particularly mourned by Meagher.[88] Some months later, Meagher gave a lecture in the Irving Hall in New York City outlining MacManus's life.[89] Until his involvement in the Ballingarry rising, MacManus had played a minor role in the Confederate movement. However, the brief notoriety that he achieved in 1848 was exceeded by the attention he received following his death. A number of Fenians living in California, with the support of their Irish comrades, decided to remove MacManus's body to Ireland for burial in Dublin. The idea emanated from John O'Mahony, a former Confederate and co-founder of the Irish Republican Brotherhood. The journey was a long one, to be broken by a stop in New York, the heartland of much Irish nationalist activity. By the time the body arrived in September 1861, the Civil War had commenced. The Fenians asked John Hughes, the Irish-born Archbishop of New York, if the coffin could be placed in a vault in his newly opened cathedral. Hughes initially said this would not be possible on the grounds that 'the quietude of the Cathedral might be disturbed' by the crowds who would want to pay respects to MacManus.

However, following a visit from a delegation of local Irish nationalists, which included Colonel Meagher (who had enlisted for the Union army), Hughes complied.[90] Thus, in September 1861, MacManus's casket was laid in the centre of St Patrick's Cathedral. He was escorted there by a military guard of honour. Following a requiem Mass, Hughes made an address 'on the nature of lawful resistance to the state within the context of Catholic doctrine', his central purpose being 'to harmonise MacManus's actions with Catholic teachings according to the precepts of St Thomas Aquinas'. His main argument focused upon MacManus's 'love of his country'.[91] To his predominantly Fenian audience, Hughes' comments demonstrated how physical force and Catholicism could be compatible. The archbishop's involvement was surprising because, apart from briefly supporting a nationalist rising in 1848, he was publicly critical of Young Irelanders now resident in the USA, including Meagher and Mitchel, whom he accused of having 'red' republican sympathies.[92] Moreover, the Pope and leading members of the Catholic Church in Ireland were opposed to nationalism in general and to Fenianism in particular.

On 18 October MacManus's remains were taken to the New York docks for transport to Ireland. The accompanying procession through the streets of the city attracted thousands of observers, including Irish delegations from California, Philadelphia and Boston. Meagher and O'Mahony were also present.[93] The response of the Catholic hierarchy in Ireland contrasted sharply with that of Archbishop Hughes in America. Cardinal Paul Cullen refused to allow MacManus's body to be laid in the Pro-Cathedral in Dublin. Instead, it was displayed in the Mechanics' Institute, which proved too small a venue for the numbers who visited.[94] The burial of MacManus in Glasnevin Cemetery, on 10 November 1861, was attended by thousands of people. James Stephens, a veteran of the Ballingarry rising and a founder of the Fenian movement, wrote the oration. Overall, the funeral of Terence

MacManus, which took place over two continents and over a period of ten months, was a massive propaganda victory for the Fenians and the Irish Republican Brotherhood. As had been intended, it suggested the continuity between the men of 1848 and the next generation of nationalists. It also provided an early indication that nationalist Ireland was no longer confined to the island of Ireland. Moreover, it demonstrated that while the Catholic Church could pronounce against Fenianism and its evils, it could not control it – on either side of the Atlantic.

From first arriving in America, Thomas Francis Meagher had been the subject of intense public scrutiny. Initially, he was warmly welcomed, his reputation as a charismatic and uncompromising nationalist having preceded him. However, like his colleagues, he needed to earn a living. Initially, he financed himself by lecturing and writing on the events of 1848 and their aftermath.[95] The ever-restless Meagher quickly became fed up with speaking on this topic and suggested that he be allowed to talk on different topics.[96] Subsequently he studied law and was admitted to the New York Bar in September 1855.[97] Within a few months of arrival, Meagher fell foul of the Catholic Church and in particular John Hughes. As already alluded to, Hughes labelled Meagher and Mitchel and other Irish radicals as 'red republicans' because they supported Italian nationalism and were admirers of Garibaldi – a stance totally opposed by Pius IX in Rome. Privately, however, the two Irishmen seemed to enjoy a warm relationship.[98] Meagher's wife, Cate, and their son never joined him in the USA.[99] Henry Emmet Fitzgerald Meagher had died in June 1852, at around the age of 4 months, and was buried in St John's Roman Catholic Church Cemetery in Van Diemen's Land.[100] Cate visited Waterford in 1853, en route to New York. She was warmly welcomed, leading Meagher to write to the mayor thanking him for the way in which 'the companion of my exile' had been received.[101] She and her father-in-law did travel to the USA to meet with Meagher, but it seemed that outside of the confines of Van Diemen's Land, the differences between he and Cate were too great.[102] She returned to Ireland, the climate being cited as her reason for not making her home permanently in America.[103] By this time, she was pregnant and died giving birth to her second son, Thomas Bennett Meagher. Within two years, Meagher remarried, to a wealthy American woman, Elizabeth Townsend, having proposed to her on their second meeting (a proposal that was accepted despite the opposition of Elizabeth's father).[104]

Meagher appeared as restless in the USA as he had been in Van

Diemen's Land.[105] He did, however, remain unwavering in his love for Ireland and his desire for Irish independence, but did not support the Fenian movement, which had been founded in 1858. The founders of this organisation, James Stephens and John O'Mahony, had been members of Young Ireland who had participated in the various uprisings in 1848 and 1849. Meagher appeared to find fulfilment when he fought on behalf of the North in the American Civil War, as captain of a company of Zouaves in the exclusively Irish 69th Regiment.[106] He subsequently formed a New York Irish Brigade, who fought bravely – and suffered many losses – in many of the major battles.[107] Meagher himself was wounded at the battle of Fredericksburg. During the war Meagher demonstrated his prowess as a soldier and as a leader of men.[108] Ironically, 'Meagher of the Sword', who had not had an opportunity to fight for his own country's independence in 1848, fought valiantly on behalf of his adopted homeland.

Following his military career, Meagher was offered the secretary-ship of the Territory of Montana. Before travelling there, he wrote to his father explaining that the position would be 'a profitable one to me, and that it will enable me to pay you visits in France next summer'. As was his custom, he enclosed presents for some of his family, including 'dear little Bennie', the son he had never met. Two years later, Meagher wrote to his father from Montana, describing some of the problems he was having with 'the Indians on our Eastern Settlements [as] these gentlemen have been displaying for some months a very hostile spirit'.[109] The irony of his role in suppressing the native people did not seem to strike him. In his letter, Meagher talked of visiting Europe the following year and meeting his father and son. He even considered travelling to Ireland, despite the fact that he was still considered a felon by the British authorities.[110] Meagher never returned to Ireland. On 1 July 1867, he died in mysterious circumstances, apparently falling overboard on a ship, although his body was never found. His detractors claimed that he was either drunk or delirious at the time.[111]

Meagher had been the youngest leader of the 1848 uprising. Regardless of the vicissitudes of his career, he was widely mourned.[112] The Irish community in America was devastated by the news, with the *Irish People* in New York proclaiming, 'Meagher of the Sword is dead' and adding it was 'the saddest news that has befallen our lot since we made an appearance in the journalistic world'.[113] Mass meetings were held on the eastern seaboard, from Washington to Boston, with an estimated

8,000 present in the latter.[114] At a meeting at the Cooper Institute in New York City, Richard O'Gorman, a former Young Irelander, delivered an oration in which he referred to Meagher as 'the trumpet tongue that electrified his countrymen'.[115] John Mitchel also wrote a tribute to his erstwhile colleague in the American press. It demonstrated that, regardless of the ideological differences which had been evident both in 1848 and during the American Civil War, their relationship was cemented by enduring affection.[116] Meagher was aged only 43 when he died; he had spent almost twenty of those years living in exile.

John Mitchel seemed afflicted with the same restlessness as Meagher, moving around with his family, and starting a number of short-lived ventures, including some political publications.[117] Just as in Ireland, Mitchel proved to be a controversial and outspoken public figure in the USA. As had been the case in 1848, he repeatedly demonstrated his willingness to endure public opprobrium in pursuit of his political beliefs. Following his arrival in New York, Mitchel started his own newspaper, the *Citizen,* which was dedicated to Irish affairs. The *Citizen* was critical of the authoritarianism of the Catholic Church, which lost him Catholic support, notably that of Archbishop Hughes. His paper was equally disparaging about the Anti-Catholic 'Know-Nothing Party'.[118] The *Citizen* also included a weekly account of the events of 1848, commencing with his transportation in May of that year. It was based on the journal he had kept while in exile. The series was reprinted in a number of Irish newspapers, thus providing an early narrative of events, while keeping the memory of 1848 alive.[119] In 1854, his account was published as a book, with a new introduction, as *The Jail Journal*. A generally favourable review in the *New York Times* warned potential readers that 'Wormwood and hyssop are ever present as he makes up a *pleasant* draft for his reader, and when he is out of humour the amount of gall he excretes is remarkable'.[120] The book consolidated Mitchel's reputation as an unrepentant critic of British rule and as the unofficial leader of radical Irish nationalism.[121]

In 1856, Mitchel purchased a farm in Knoxville, Tennessee. It was not successful. Regardless of his notorious support for slavery, he did not utilise slave labour.[122] In 1857, he started the *Southern Citizen*, which also failed. While making it clear he was an Irish nationalist, Mitchel did not espouse either republicanism or sentimentalism in the abstract. For these reasons, he was critical of some of the pretentious and more bombastic elements within the Fenian movement, believing their policy of secret conspiracy to be seriously flawed.[123] However, while in Tennessee, Mitchel was visited by James Stephens, founder of the Fenian Brotherhood, who was seeking his support. Mitchel agreed, writing to Horace Greeley, the newspaper proprietor, asking if the money that had been raised in 1848 by the New York Directory – a group sympathetic to Young Ireland – could be given to the new republican organisation.[124] Shortly afterwards, Mitchel went to Paris, probably on Fenian business, but he returned to the USA when the Civil War commenced. His defence of the Confederacy lost him some friends and support, and it also resulted in the death of two of his sons. John Jr was killed at Fort Sumter in 1863 and William was killed at Gettysburg in 1864. Mitchel had offered his services to the Confederacy, saying that he was willing to run the blockade, but he was turned down.[125] After the war, Mitchel returned to Paris as an administrator for the Fenians, where he was visited by John Martin and Father John Kenyon. His disapproval of the fundraising methods of the Fenians resulted in his return to New York. At this stage, he was adamant that unless Britain was at war with France or the USA, no Fenian uprising could succeed.[126]

In 1874, Mitchel visited Ireland, after an absence of twenty-six years. Regardless of his chequered career, his controversial support for slavery, and his long absence from Ireland, Mitchel had not been forgotten in his native land. Moreover, in the spirit of Young Ireland, his Ulster and Protestant origins did not matter to his fellow nationalists. Wherever he went, Mitchel was treated as a hero. Despite being in ill health, before leaving he issued an address to the electorate in Tipperary, where a by-election to the British parliament was to be held.[127] In February 1875, Mitchel was elected unopposed as MP for County Tipperary, the location of the 1848 uprising. The result was invalidated by the British Government on the grounds that he was a felon. A further election was held and he was re-elected with an even larger majority. Mitchel died in March 1875, fittingly, while still in Ireland, but sadly, without the ever-loyal Jenny at his side. His death saved the British Government from the indignity of having to hold a third by-election.

Within Ireland, even those who had disagreed with Mitchel mourned his death. He was buried in Newry and, on the day of his funeral, all of the businesses closed and the mills stopped working. Flags were flown at half-mast. Sixteen Roman Catholic clergy preceded the hearse, while it was followed by ministers from the Presbyterian

Church. It was a fitting tribute to Mitchel's advocacy of non-sectarianism. Mitchel was buried with his father and his beloved mother.[128] His close friend John Martin attended the funeral, but caught bronchitis while there. It proved to be fatal. Consequently, within only nine days of each other, the two men who had been lifelong friends, political allies in Ireland, and exiles together in Van Diemen's Land, died and were buried in Ireland. Their deaths marked the end of a chapter of Irish nationalism that had been characterised by non-sectarian ideals and an unwavering adherence to principles, no matter how unpopular. A telling indication of the genuine ecumenicalism of both Mitchel and his fellow Young Irelander, William Smith O'Brien, was that they each had daughters who converted to Catholicism.[129]

In death, as in life, Mitchel proved to be a controversial figure. His detractors referred to the confusing circumstances when he had surrendered parole on Van Diemen's Land over twenty years earlier.[130] In the USA, his commitment to Irish nationalism was overshadowed by his later espousal of the institution of slavery. The *New York Times* judged his life to have been a failure, averring that 'he was undoubtedly a man of undaunted courage, but he lacked judgement and discretion … His career in this country proved a complete failure'.[131] However, it was Mitchel, rather than Meagher, O'Brien or even Duffy, who influenced the next generation of Irish republicans, with both constitutionalists and 'advanced nationalists' borrowing from his writings. Arthur Griffiths regarded Mitchel as 'the greatest figure in Irish history', while Patrick Pearse ranked him as one of 'the four apostles' of Irish nationalism.[132]

Three of the men sent to Van Diemen's Land in 1849 did not escape – William Smith O'Brien, John Martin and Kevin O'Doherty. In 1854, they received conditional pardons from the British Government, which permitted them to return to Europe, but not Ireland. This restriction was removed two years later. Following their release, each of the men continued to be involved in politics, with their influence extending far beyond Ireland. O'Brien had been a MP in Westminster for twenty years prior to the 1848 rising. Although he never formally became involved in politics again, he wrote prolifically on political topics, taking a particular interest in the struggles for Hungarian and Polish independence.[133] He visited North America in 1859, spending some time with Meagher.[134] When lecturing in Canada, he met with another colleague from 1848, Thomas D'Arcy McGee.[135] O'Brien was not afraid to court controversy and although he disliked the Know-Nothing Party, he suggested that the behaviour of some Irish immigrants had contributed to a general anti-Irish feeling in the country.[136] He opposed slavery, but deprecated the outbreak of civil war in 1861 and publicly criticised Meagher for volunteering to fight in it. Nonetheless, O'Brien offered his services as a mediator in the conflict.[137] Even in old age, he defended the actions that he had taken in 1848, as a 'Middle-Aged Irelander'. When he heard that Sir Robert Peel, the Younger, had, in the House of Commons, referred to O'Brien and his colleagues as 'the cabbage patch heroes of 1848', he challenged him to a duel.[138] When Peel failed to respond, O'Brien described him as a coward and a bully.[139] Following the death of his beloved wife, Lucy, in 1861, O'Brien's own health declined. This may have been expedited by financial wrangles with his son, who had totally rejected his father's politics. O'Brien died in June 1864, in Wales, and his remains were returned to Ireland, receiving a hero's welcome. He was buried in Rathronan churchyard in County Limerick.[140] In America also, O'Brien was remembered as 'an honest and patriotic man', although his opposition to the Civil War was regarded as puzzling.[141] The British press had a mixed reaction to his death. The *Liverpool Mercury*, while opposed to O'Brien's actions in 1848, acknowledged:

> Sincerity, disinterestedness, self-sacrificing patriotism, consistency, unblemished political integrity and personal honour are qualities so admirable that it is painful to speak otherwise than with respect of the memory of a public man who conspicuously possessed them all.[142]

In the eyes of some of his family, however, his participation in the 1848 rising continued to be a blot on his legacy, and his son did not attend his funeral service.[143] Nonetheless, within a few months of O'Brien's death, a committee had been formed in Dublin to raise a subscription in order to erect a monument to the somewhat reluctant leader of the 1848 rebellion.[144]

John Martin had been introduced to nationalist politics by his lifelong friend and fellow-Ulsterman, John Mitchel. His involvement continued after he was allowed to return to Ireland in 1856. Although a landlord himself, he immediately became involved in the Tenant Right League. Like many of his fellow exiles, Martin opposed the Fenian movement, but on the grounds that peaceful tactics were preferable to violent ones.[145] Moreover, he considered the Fenian plan of 'a combined insurrection and invasion while England is at peace with both France and America' to be 'mad'.[146] More controversially, Martin supported the right of the South to secede prior to the American Civil War, but he did not receive the same public opprobrium as Mitchel.[147] Martin's close relationship with Mitchel was further consolidated by his marriage to his sister, Henrietta, in 1868, when aged 56. The following year, the newly-weds visited America, staying with the Mitchels.[148] During the visit, Martin and Mitchel lectured together, both praising the patriotism of their former colleagues, in particular, William Smith O'Brien.[149] Martin was an early supporter of Isaac Butt's Home Government Association, which laid the foundation for the Home Rule movement although Mitchel disagreed. In a series of public letters to Martin, which appeared in the *Nation*, Mitchel pointed out to his friend the fallacy of adopting a constitutional approach to Irish politics.[150] Martin was resolute and was elected Home Rule MP for County Meath in 1871.[151] He had been victorious in spite of the opposition of many local priests.[152] As a consequence, Martin became the first Home Rule MP in the British Parliament and he was re-elected in the general election in 1874. Martin died in relative poverty, having refused to take rent from his tenants during periods of poor harvest. His funeral in Newry was attended by delegations from all over Ireland and Britain. In death, as in life, the lives of John Martin and John Mitchel remained entwined. As northern Protestants, they were outsiders in mainstream nationalist politics, which, regardless of interventions of Young Ireland, had been slowly moving towards a Catholic view of Irish identity since the time of O'Connell. The fiery John Mitchel and the gentle John Martin represented opposing sides of the nationalist spectrum, but the crucible of 1848 had brought together men and women bound by their love of Ireland. In later life, their ideological paths again diverged, but their friendship endured.

When Kevin O'Doherty received a conditional pardon in 1854, he was aged 30. He had found life in Van Diemen's Land particularly hard due to his enforced separation from fellow nationalist and sweetheart, 'Eva'. They had met when O'Doherty was in prison awaiting sentencing. Despite having published with the *Nation*, Eva was still only a teenager in 1848. Following his pardon, O'Doherty travelled to Paris to continue with his medical studies. During this time, he made an illegal visit to Ireland to marry Eva, to whom he had become secretly affianced before being transported from Ireland. O'Doherty received an unconditional pardon in 1856, allowing him to complete his studies and graduated in 1857. He initially practised in Dublin, but, in 1862, he and Eva moved to Brisbane, Australia, where he became a leading physician. His interest in politics continued and, in 1867, he was elected to the Legislative Assembly. In 1872, he was responsible for a Health Act being passed. Five years later, he transferred to the Legislative Council, but resigned in 1885 as he intended to return to Ireland. There, O'Doherty was welcomed as a hero of 1848 and granted the Freedom of the City of Dublin.[153] He was also elected unopposed as MP for County Meath. When ill-health led him to return to Australia in 1886, members of the Irish community in Brisbane organised a welcome for him and his family.[154] Even when living in Australia, he remained interested in Irish politics and for some years was president of the Australian branch of the Irish National League.[155] Although he attempted to take up his medical practice again, he was not successful. O'Doherty died in relative poverty in July 1905. Eva and one daughter survived him and a public subscription was raised to provide for them.[156] Australian newspapers were generally full of praise for O'Doherty – as a man, a doctor and an Irish patriot. One obituary explained his involvement in 1848 in terms of the Famine that was ravaging the country, asking, 'can we wonder that there sprang up in the hearts of the young men of Ireland a resolve to rid the country of this nightmare of famine and desolation?'[157]

The death of O'Doherty, the final survivor of the 1848 exiles, brought to a close an important chapter, not only in Irish nationalism, but in Irish cultural nationalism. The seven men differed in social class, education, experience and political outlook, but their experiences in 1848 and beyond not only shaped Irish politics, but politics in Europe, North America and Australasia. The fact that many of them died in poverty was a tribute to their selflessness and idealism. While the rising in 1848 may have been short-lived and unsuccessful, the subsequent lives of the people who had supported it, both directly and indirectly, were a testament to the vision and courage of the Young Irelanders. Even in middle and old age, and from a distance of thousands of miles, they did not lose their love of Ireland or their desire for their country's independence. Moreover, their actions and writings both inspired and informed subsequent generations of nationalists, of all hues of green. Most impressively, perhaps, was the inclusivity that these seven men brought to the nationalist project, symbolised by the tricolour flag that they brought back from France in the spring of 1848. The words of

Meagher, the youngest and most flamboyant of all of the exiles, spoken on this occasion, remained pertinent long after that fateful year:

> … I trust that the old country will not refuse this symbol of a new life from one of her youngest children. I need not explain its meaning. The quick and passionate intellect of the generation now springing into arms will catch it at a glance. The white in the centre signifies a lasting truce between the "orange" and the "green" and I trust that beneath its folds, the hands of the Irish Protestant and the Irish Catholic may be clasped in generous and heroic brotherhood.[158]

10

'There is no person starving here': Australia and the Great Famine

Richard Reid

Historian Kevin Whelan wrote of the Great Famine that it is 'difficult to grasp at an individual level the implications of a tragedy which wiped out one million people within half a decade'.[1] How can we generalise about the experiences of the million or so who fled the country and that other million who died, the statistically described 'excess mortality' of those years? In the wake of the disaster, the Famine emigrants would be followed by another sizeable outpouring of more than 700,000 people up to the end of 1855. Leaving aside the statistics, how was the Famine experienced in the bodies and minds of those who endured it, witnessed it and decided to leave their homeland, probably for good? Anywhere, it was said at the time, was better than Ireland and one place they went to was Australia.

Michael Tuohy died on Saturday 25 September 1915, aged 85, in the Ballarat hospital, in Victoria. The Australian Imperial Force was still engaged at Gallipoli and Australian families now knew of death experienced at places like Anzac Cove, Lone Pine and Quinn's Post. Michael was born in County Clare in 1831 and, aged 19, he sought and obtained a government-assisted passage as a single male to Sydney where he landed from the ship *Thetis* on 20 May 1850.[2] Gaining employment with a Sydney candle maker, he worked there until the lure of gold drew him to Victoria and, after the alluvial gold ran out, he became a farmer in the Ballan district for over forty years. According to his obituary in the *Ballan Times* he was a strong supporter of the democratic process and it was while making his way, although old and feeble, to vote for the local Labour candidate at the state election of 1915 that he fell from his buggy, breaking his thigh. In hospital he contracted pneumonia and, although bravely he fought off both problems, it hastened his end. Many mourners, including the well-known local MLA (Member of the Legislative Assembly), Edmond John 'Ned' Hogan, accompanied his coffin to the Ballan cemetery. His was a fairly common Irish immigrant story of moderate colonial success but that doesn't explain why the *Ballan Times* devoted two whole columns to Michael Tuohy's obituary.[3]

Part of Tuohy's obituary concerned his place of origin in County Clare – the village of Scariff in the Catholic parish of Scariff and Moynoe, located to the east of the county. The *Thetis*, the ship which brought him to Sydney, left England on 25 January 1850 and, given the administration involved, it is probable that Michael would have applied for his passage from Scariff six months before that.[4] What were conditions like in Scariff when he made the decision to leave for Australia? The Scariff Union, that administrative district of the Irish Poor Law with its Union workhouse, was, in 1849, regarded as perhaps the most wretched in all of Ireland. James Rolleston, a Poor Law official transferred to Skibbereen Union, County Cork, a location itself synonymous in much of the literature with extreme famine destitution, wrote in 1849 – 'however great the destitution in Skibbereen, it was almost nothing compared to the lamentable conditions of all classes in the Union of Scariff'.[5] In 1847, the *Limerick Chronicle* wrote this about Scariff:

> The Workhouse at Scariff, county Clare is so overcrowded with paupers that a disease almost amounting to a plague has broken out amongst the inmates – the deaths averaging from four to 12 daily. It is horrifying to behold a donkey and cart laden with five and six bodies piled over each other, going to be interred, and not a person attending the wretched cortege except the driver. The graves are so dug that the coffins are barely covered with earth, rendering the air infected. No coroner's inquests have been held.[6]

Indeed, by mid-1849 some 38 per cent of the population of Scariff Union were being kept alive by the Poor Law guardians; 1,506 in the workhouse and 18,887 on so-called 'outdoor relief'.[7]

Such terrible descriptions of the Famine are well known, but how do they relate to our young, 1849 Australia bound-emigrant, Michael

Tuohy? His obituary recalls that he had a 'keen' memory of the years 1847 and 1848 in Scariff when, as a teenager, he had assisted in the burials of Famine dead. It induced in him a great loathing of a system which could condemn his people to such suffering in a situation where agricultural produce was still being exported from the country to pay landlords the rent. Perhaps it also pushed him as a 'gold digger' to listen carefully to fellow Irishman Peter Lalor's Bakery Hill speech, delivered at Ballarat on 30 November 1854, when Lalor mounted a stump and proclaimed – 'Liberty'.[8] Tuohy was well remembered by the *Ballan Times* as one who had followed Lalor, stood his ground as the Redcoats attacked the flag of the Southern Cross at Eureka, fought, was arrested and jailed with twelve other rebels in Melbourne:

> In due course they were tried for high treason … and to the intense joy of the populace, acquitted. As far as be ascertained, the deceased was the last survivor of those who stood their trial … Australia will never forget the heroes of Eureka who laid down their lives for justice, and in the days to come, when the names of their oppressors are forgotten, the names of Michael Tuohy, and those others who fought and bled for liberty on that December morn at Ballarat, will both be remembered and honoured.[9]

There is a point to this story of the young Famine emigrant from Scariff. For all those thousands of Irish who, like Tuohy, came to Australia between 1835 and the 1860s, the Famine would surely have been one of the defining events of their lives. The post-1845 emigrants experienced it directly; those arriving between 1835 and 1845 had families in Ireland suffering its effects. It was no surprise that this generation generously donated to subsequent appeals for financial assistance at times of distress in Ireland such as in north-west Donegal in the late 1850s – through the Donegal Relief Fund – and the partial famine in the west of Ireland in the late 1870s.[10] Surely the significant sums raised to support the Irish Nationalist Party at Westminster in its struggle to obtain 'Home Rule' for Ireland – greater proportionately than money raised in the USA – had something to do with that sense of injustice born of the failure of the government and elected representatives to deal compassionately with citizens of that kingdom starving and dying in Ireland during the Famine.[11] If Michael Tuohy never forgot the scenes of those years, we can be sure his fellow Irish-Australians didn't either.

What of the families in Ireland of those who watched from far away in Australia as Famine spread throughout the homeland after 1845? It should be noted, first, that the official census of 1846 revealed that of the 184,413 inhabitants of the colony of New South Wales (which then included the Port Philip and Moreton Bay districts) 47,547 had been born in Ireland – some 25 per cent.[12] In the late 1830s and early 1840s there was quite a considerable number of emigrants from County Cavan to Sydney; among them in 1842 were a young couple, Peter and Anne Reilly. They arrived as government-assisted emigrants under what were called the 'bounty' regulations whereby for a married man and his wife, when their occupations fell into one of eight categories in demand in the colony, the shipping agent received a bounty of £38.[13] As a stonemason, aged 27, and a domestic servant aged 23, both Peter and Anne easily qualified. The shipping list also reveals that Peter could read and write, while Anne could read only. Tragically, Anne's documentation also reveals that they brought with them a child, a girl between the ages of 1 and 15, who died on the voyage. Had the Reillys arrived with a healthy, living child in this age range the agent would have received an additional sum.[14]

Imagine their alarm when Peter and Anne, not long in Australia, could read this about their home place in the *Sydney Morning Herald* on 25 July 1846:

> In Cavan the poor are unemployed and starving. Inflammation of the stomach and diarrhoea are frequent, and attributable to the use of bad potatoes. Insufficiency of food is the cause of present disease, and fever will break out to a frightful extent, in the event of scarcity of food.[15]

Scraps of news like this in the colonial press were doubtless agonised over by settlers in Australia from all parts of Ireland. The short piece would have greatly distressed the Reillys because (and this is not stated on the shipping list of the *Margaret* – the ship which brought them to Sydney in 1842), they had a young daughter still living in County Cavan. We know this because of the survival of a remarkable document – a letter written by Peter Reilly on 5 September 1846 to his mother and brother in Ballyhaise, County Cavan.[16] Hundreds, if not thousands, of similar letters must have gone back to rural locations like Ballyhaise all over Ireland during those years.

In the letter to his mother, Mary, Peter states that he had not intended writing until he had been able to put together a larger sum of money than he was now sending. He had already asked Caroline Chisholm, the heroine of mid-nineteenth-century Australian immigration, to help him get his child, left behind in 1842, out to Sydney.[17] Peter had obviously met Mrs Chisholm by February 1846 when the child was recorded by her on a shortlist of children of 'bounty' emigrants left at home when their parents came to Australia in 1841 and 1842.[18] In a letter she wrote to the *Morning Chronicle* (Sydney) at this time, Caroline touched on what was happening in Ireland and of an Australian-Irish community greatly worried about their loved ones living in Famine conditions:

> ... hundreds, to my knowledge, have sent home 30 per cent, of their earnings in this colony; the numerous letters it has been my painful lot to read, within the last three months, tell a fearful tale of the sufferings of the people at home-parents struggling with want, and children inmates of the poor-house.[19]

In his letter Peter referred to the fact that the New South Wales Government had agreed to pay the fares of these deserted children and that the money, £7, he was sending was to relieve his mother's needs and to pay for whatever his child required for the voyage. The letter also highlighted that he was well aware of the catastrophe engulfing Ballyhaise and Ireland:

> I am sorry to hear of the distressing news that I hear from Ireland, of starvation, – sickness – I thank my God for leaving it the time I did – I wish that all my friends were out of it, for it is always in poverty – this is a fine plentiful country – there is no person starving here – I am sure that the dogs in Sydney destroys more beef and bread than all the poor in Ireland can afford to eat.[20]

What Peter looked for now was that he and Anne could have 'our dear little child Mary Anne with us'.

Peter Reilly's letter also highlighted the methods by which many Irish residents in New South Wales were able to respond to the Famine, both in relation to their own families and to the situation in general. On a number of occasions large public meetings were held to draw attention to the crisis in Ireland. At one such meeting at the Market Sheds[21] in Sydney on 31 August 1846, at which the mayor, Irish-born Henry McDermott spoke, seven major resolutions were passed, including one which would have the effect of helping people to remit funds to their families in Ireland.[22] An Irish cleric, Revd John McEncroe seconded this resolution after it was proposed by the Englishman, Francis Merewether, the New South Wales Immigration Agent.[23] McEncroe also made the following interesting statement:

> … no Irishman would while he had money would allow his friends around him to starve! One fact was worth a thousand arguments, the poor emigrant girls who had come to this colony within the last two years, had sent home more than 2000 Pounds to their relatives and he was sure that 3000 would be sent this way, which was much better than laying it out in milliners shops.[24]

McEncroe was not talking here about the well-known Irish orphan girls, as the first shipload of workhouse girls would not arrive in Sydney for another two years.[25] He can only have had in mind those Irish women, many of them single female domestic servants, who, like Anne Reilly, had arrived under the government-assisted bounty immigration system of 1836 to 1845. Between 1839 and 1845 some 25,800 Irish, men and women, had arrived in New South Wales in this way.[26]

At the Sydney meeting, subscription lists were opened and £300 was instantly collected for 'The Irish Relief Fund'. A similar fund was set up in Melbourne, while agents for the Sydney fund encouraged contributions in the Moreton Bay District (Brisbane). Local branches of the fund also appeared in many rural areas of New South Wales. The situation in South Australia and Tasmania, however, needs further research. However, it is likely that similar sums were raised in February 1847 when Revd Davis preached a 'Charity Sermon' in aid of the Irish Relief Fund.[27] Appealing for support, Fr Thomas Butler, priest at St Joseph's, Launceston, wrote:

> I take the liberty of asking the ministers of every denomination, both in town and country, to follow his noble and benevolent example. Subscriptions will be thankfully received at each of the Banks and most cheerfully by your humble etc., Thomas Butler.[28]

Later, in April the *Cornwall Chronicle* published an interesting subscription list of those who had given to what was then being called 'The Scotch and Irish Relief Fund' right across the main settlements of northern Van Dieman's Land. Of particular interest is the long list of not insignificant donations from individuals with Irish-sounding names from the small Westbury settlement.

On the mainland the *Sydney Morning Herald* kept up the printing, on its front page, of subscription lists to the relief fund from all over New South Wales. The early lists from Sydney, contained familiar names of colonial worthies, mainly but not exclusively of Irish birth or connection – the Governor, Sir Charles Augustus Fitzroy; the Anglican Lord Bishop of Australia, William Charles Wentworth; Fr John McEncroe; Justice Roger Therry; John Hubert Plunkett (the Attorney General) and Sir Maurice O'Connell. Scrutinisers of the columns would have been amused or moved, no doubt, by contributions from 'Biddy the Orangewoman', 'For the Irish poor, with prayer', 'a widow and family', 'twenty six labourers in the blue metal quarry', 'a Liberal Protestant', 'a friend', 'from Edward Delaney remitting his charge from the use of the Market Shed', a 'Connaughtman', a 'Widow's Mite', a 'Jewess', and, most wonderful of all, *2s 6d* from Mundhalay, an Aborigine living in Braidwood! In addition, as he went 'on his rounds', the English Benedictine, Dr Henry Gregory, temporarily in charge of the Sydney Catholic archdiocese, was reported to have collected £20 in 'sundry small subscriptions'.[29] Meetings to promote the fund were held outside Sydney at Maitland, Yass, Windsor and other locations, so that by mid-September 1846 the *Herald* was printing subscription lists from the bush.[30] One interesting donation came from Sydney's Victoria Theatre whose management donated the takings from the whole of one night's performances to the 'Irish Relief Fund'. The bill of fare on this occasion had a distinctly Hibernian flavour:

> This evening September 17, 1846, will be presented (by particular desire, and for the last time this season) the original tragedy in five arts entitled 'The Hibernian Father'. Walter Lynch (to be played by) Mr. Nesbitt; Oscar Lynch, Mr. Arabin; Alonzo de Velasquez, Mr. Spencer; Rupert D'Arcy, Mr Hambleton; Gerald, Mr. Griffiths; Anastasia, Mrs. Guerin; Morna, Mrs, Ximenes. The popular song of 'Molly Bawn' by Mr. F. Howson. The favourite jig from the 'Green Bushes', by Mr and Madame Torning. Mr. J. Howson will sing, for the first time, a song of 'Liberty for Old

> Ireland', composed by H Russell. To conclude with the popular farce of 'The Irish Tutor'. Charles (played by) Mr. J. Howson; Terry O'Rourke, Mr. Hambleton; Rosa, Mrs Ximenes; Mary, Madame Torning.[31]

It is important to highlight that the whole issue of Australian charitable response to the situation in Ireland between 1845 and 1850 needs more research before some satisfactory conclusions can be drawn as to its extent, in comparison to other countries, and its nature in general.[32] What we do know is that around £4,000, in different instalments, was remitted to Ireland from that initial 'Irish Relief Fund' and that, on 22 May 1847, the Catholic newspaper, the *Sydney Chronicle*, reported that the last instalment of money raised, £200, had been sent 'home'.[33] Those who had used the fund to send small sums to their families could rest easy that it had been delivered to them. On 31 July 1847 the *Chronicle* published a letter from the Catholic Archbishop of Dublin, Daniel Murray, which read in part:

> The sums sent by your colonists for their poor relatives have, of course, been set apart from the charity fund; and no diligence is spared in seeking out the individuals for whom, respectively, these sums were intended. Many of them have already received their portions, and the search throughout the different parts of Ireland continues for the rest.[34]

It would be fascinating to know just who received help from their Australian kith and kin during the Famine years. One who might have done was Margaret Kane (*née* Spencer), who arrived in Sydney as an assisted immigrant on the *Coldstream* in January 1863.[35] She was nominated for a passage by her brother, Philip Spencer, living in Boorowa, who arrived as a 'bounty' immigrant on the *Glenswilly* in 1841.[36] What can be pieced together of Margaret's story provides a window into the reality of the landscape of Famine which surrounded Irish society between 1845 and 1850, and long thereafter. Indeed, long thereafter, because the material and social landscape in which the survivors of those years of hunger lived was greatly altered, and went on changing as the great waves of emigration persisted for the rest of the century. Margaret Kane came from Tipperary, a county which, during her lifetime, saw its population reduced by more than a half between 1841 and 1871.[37] Kane was born in Ballagh in 1794, in the parish of Clonoulty, in south central Tipperary, a few kilometres west of the Rock of Cashel.

The Famine devastated Clonoulty; the population declined by 54 per cent from 6,932 people in 1841 to just 3,219 in 1871.[38] Whatever Ballagh looked like in 1841, it was a very different place by the time Margaret left in 1863. Like many other townlands and parishes, people were on the move to America, Britain and, in relation to Ballagh, most significantly to Australia.[39] Margaret experienced the Famine at first hand in Clonoulty, as did her son, Michael Kane, who arrived in Sydney on the *Chance* in 1860, aged 22, also nominated by his uncle, Philip Spencer in Boorowa.[40] When the disaster struck in 1845, he would have been only 7 years of age.

Something of the effects of the Famine on Ballagh families can also be seen in the emigration to Boorowa, New South Wales, of the Dwyers. Edmund Dwyer, his wife Mary and seven of their eleven children (four died in Ireland), born between 1835 and 1857, arrived in Sydney on the *Queen Bee* in March 1861.[41] Land records show that Edmund was a blacksmith in Ballagh village in 1848.[42] Between 1848 and the late 1850s the village lost its teeming pre-Famine population, which was evidently bad news for a blacksmith. Although we have no particular proof, it is likely that by the end of a decade when his business could only have suffered, Edmund Dwyer decided to try the family's luck in New South Wales. In Boorowa, the family kept up the blacksmith tradition and indeed they became one of the most prominent Irish Catholic families in the area.[43] Clearly, here was a family the course of whose lives had been deeply touched by Famine and the changes it brought in its wake.

Almost certainly the Dwyers knew Margaret Kane and her young son Michael. A glimpse of the Kanes' lifestyle can be ascertained from the Poor Law house valuations of Ballagh townland undertaken in February 1848. Living in a cabin valued at £1 10*d* (there were no lower valuations), her cabin measured 3.81 metres long, by 3.81 metres in breadth, by 1.6 metres in height.[44] Bare statistics and a couple of nominal entries in land and emigration records give but a glimpse of a woman and her son living through the greatest social catastrophe in modern Ireland. That might be all but for a little line beneath Margaret Kane's valuation entry relating to nearby neighbouring cabins – 'Houses all down, and land given up to Col. Perceval'. This was Colonel Alexander Perceval, of Templehouse, County Sligo, who, in addition to his estates there and in Ulster, owned three townlands in Clonoulty – Piercetown, Kilmore and Ballagh.[45]

In Clonoulty, Perceval was an absentee landlord as he gave most of his time, when not at Templehouse, to his duties as an MP in London and then to his position as serjeant-at-arms in the House of Lords. Templehouse, near Ballymote in County Sligo, is today a fashionable guesthouse offering what is described on its website as the 'big house' experience. Revealingly, the website has this to say about the Famine years:

> At a time when many of the owners of the demesnes of Ireland lived in feudal splendour and extracted crippling rents from their unfortunate tenants, the Percevals distinguished themselves by their concern for the welfare of their poorer neighbours – a noble sentiment which was to end in tragedy. Jane Perceval [the Colonel's wife] used to visit the workers and tenantry with gifts of food and medicine. She died in the winter of 1847 of 'famine fever', the fate of many of those good people who had gone to the assistance of the starving peasantry. Her large portrait may be seen in the dining room. A touching letter of the time tells of her reminding those around her 'not to neglect the tenant families between my death and my funeral'.[46]

Such concern would have come as a surprise to Colonel Perceval's tenants in Ballagh in the 1840s. Perhaps his wife's death at the hands of the Famine, so to speak, hardened him for on 22 August 1850 he was caustically described as an 'Exterminator' in the *Freeman's Journal*:

> It will be seen that the lord of the soil, and of the bodies and souls of Ballaghers, is Col Perceval MP, who is, we believe, remarkable for the strength of his religious zeal, and for the sensitiveness for the sufferings of human beings. Of course, it was in this spirit of Christian fortitude that he has just 'chastised' those he loved.[47]

Percevals' chastisement involved the eviction from their homes of 148 residents of the townland of Ballagh for non-payment of rent amid what were described in the *Freeman's* as 'heart rending scenes' accompanied by 'wailings tears and curses'. Those who physically carried out the removal of the people and their meagre possessions from their cabins were labelled the 'crowbar brigade' and they did the job quickly from 'constant practice'. To ensure the residents did not reoccupy these miserable dwellings, the 'tumbling' began and twenty of the twenty-eight cabins were levelled. New occupants, in due course, probably then occupied the other eight. Perceval's agent, a Mr Warburton, supposedly fled after the first eviction and Perceval himself, the newspapers correspondent surmised, 'would have prided himself as much with this coup de main as on any of his military exploits through his brilliant career'. The reporter of all this, a local resident simply identified with the letters WTL, went on to say that those thrown from their homes spent nights, with their possessions, along the hedgerows. Remarkably, the *Freeman's Journal* printed the names, allowing us to identify who the Ballagh evictees were.

Perceval, it was argued, deserved the title 'Colonel Faugh a Ballagh' in honour of his victory at Ballagh and that, as a military man, the results of the 'storming' of the townland should be properly recorded. Among the names on the *Freeman's* list was that of Peggy Spencer; Margaret Kane's maiden name. With her in the house (one of those 'tumbled' by the crowbar brigade) was one other member of her family, most likely her son Michael, then aged 12. Interesting some of the other names on this list can be associated with Australian emigrant families of the period. These evictions were part of more than 248,000 people recorded by the Royal Irish Constabulary who were evicted from their homes across Ireland between 1849 and 1854. 1850 marked the high point of this process with 73,871 non-readmitted evictees.[48] It was all part of a period of consolidation and clearance of estates, in some cases already well under way before the Famine, whereby Irish landowners – and not always so-called Anglo-Irish landowners such as Perceval – were ridding their lands of surplus tenants incapable of paying rents. These events in Ballagh would have been a sensation in Clonoulty and not one likely to be forgotten by the hundreds of emigrants who left that place in the 1850s and 1860s for the Australian colonies. Such sights and experiences formed as much of the emigrant experience as the insides of workhouses, prisons, or convict ships so often associated with the movement to Australia at this point.

How Margaret and Michael Kane survived in those years between eviction from their cabin in Ballagh and their leaving for New South Wales, we do not know. Margaret died in 1876 at Naraallen Creek, near Boorowa, her funeral departing from Michael's home. The brief obituary described her as one 'deservedly esteemed for her many kindly qualities' who had been born in Clonoulty.[49] Michael went on to open an inn at Marengo, also near Burrowa, called the Dewdrop Inn. He died at Marengo in 1906 after a long illness, leaving a 'wife and grown up family to mourn their loss'.[50] One wonders if she ever shared with them his memories of the storming of Ballagh on 22 August 1850?

Irish-Australia's experience of the Great Famine is a complex one. It embraces the dramatic stories of convicts, male and female, sent to Van Dieman's Land, some of whom may have deliberately committed crimes which carried a sentence of transportation; of the wives and families of convicts who had served their time and were brought out at government expense during the Famine years; of young female workhouse orphans; of political exiles transported for their part in the failed 1848 rising; and of thousands who came to Australia paying their own way, with money sent to them for the fare or who received a government-assisted passage.

Today, there are two locations in Australia where the tragedy of the Famine has been given visual expression. Firstly, at that striking and indeed emotive Famine Rock Memorial at Williamstown in Victoria and at the elegant and challenging memorial at Hyde Park Barracks in Sydney. Both memorials state that they remember all those affected by the Great Hunger, but in reality in Sydney we are invited only to see the Australian connection with the Famine through the eyes of the workhouse orphan girls. The names of a handful of these girls can be seen etched beautifully into glass at the barracks. There can be no question that this story of the Famine orphans is worth commemorating and that their story is a central and appropriate one when considering how Irish-Australia might portray its relationship to the Great Hunger. However, a fuller accounting of that history, when it comes, will embrace Margaret and Michael Kane, Michael Tuohy, as well as those who agonised about their families in Ireland and tried to help them and a host of others. And it will tell of people like Peter and Anne Reilly and Mary Anne, their abandoned child at Ballyhaise. On 16 June 1854, the ship *Switzerland*, from Liverpool, dropped anchor in Sydney Cove with 242 assisted immigrants on board. Waiting to meet the ship, we can be sure, was Peter Reilly, now a builder of South Head Road, Sydney, for coming to land was his wife Anne Reilly and their daughter Mary Anne, aged 16.[51] This girl had experienced and survived five years of Famine in Ballyhaise and eventually her mother had gone back to Ireland to bring her away to a new country. Unfortunately, little else is known about her life during the Famine.

When Kevin Whelan wrote of the wide-ranging impact of the Famine on all levels of Irish society he left his final image, not to someone reporting the horrors of starvation, malnutrition and eviction, but to an American poet who observed the poor Irish streaming into New York. Walt Whitman wrote of those who had escaped that tragic country not in despair but instead looking to a new life away from a country that had failed them. His poem 'Old Ireland' is one of hope and Whelan called it his own tribute to the Famine emigrants. It is a worthy tribute to that emigrant generation, which included Australian-bound people like Michael Tuohy, Margaret Kane and Peter Reilly:

Far hence amid an isle of wondrous beauty,
Crouching over a grave an ancient sorrowful mother,
Once a queen, now lean and tatter'd seated on the ground,
Her old white hair drooping dishevel'd round her shoulders,
At her feet fallen an unused royal harp,
Long silent, she too long silent, mourning her shrouded hope and heir,
Of all the earth her heart most full of sorrow because most full of love.

Yet a word ancient mother,
You need crouch there no longer on the cold ground with forehead between your knees,
O you need not sit there veil'd in your old white hair so dishevel'd,
For know you the one you mourn is not in that grave,
It was an illusion, the son you love was not really dead,
The Lord is not dead, he is risen again young and strong in another country,
Even while you wept there by your fallen harp by the grave,
What you wept for was translated, pass'd from the grave,
The winds favor'd and the sea sail'd it,
And now with rosy and new blood,
Moves to-day in a new country.[52]

11

The Irish in Australia: Remembering and commemorating the Great Famine

Perry McIntyre

On the eve of the sesquicentenary commemoration of the Great Irish Famine in 1995, the Famine Museum at Strokestown Park House, County Roscommon, was opened to widespread acclaim. The Famine Museum incorporated the archive of the house itself and the experiences on the Mahon estate with an interpretation of the national tragedy of the Famine. Privately funded by the Westward Group, the Famine Museum, and the subsequent restoration of the gardens and recent work on the house, are a testament to private and public cooperation, and to the energy of Jim Callery and others. Strokestown Park House and the Irish National Famine Museum remains the most outstanding memorial to the Famine in Ireland.[1] The sesquicentenary also prompted people to create visual representations of the Famine in Ireland and indeed anywhere in the world where Irish people had settled. In Ireland, the first of a series of memorials was erected at Ennistymon, County Clare, opposite the site of the former workhouse. The memorial depicts the suffering of a young boy, Michael Rice, who sought admission to the workhouse during the worst months of the Famine. Other memorials followed during the commemorative period, including the now iconic Rowan Gillespie statues, erected in 1997 and which stand forlornly on Custom House Quay, Dublin, depicting the emaciated emigrant Irish before departure. In 2007, statues continuing this journey, by Gillespie, were unveiled in Toronto and suggest hope for the emigrants in their new home. This theme of emigration is replicated elsewhere, including in Sligo town where three statues depict a family group about to emigrate on the quayside (erected in 1997) and the Irish National Memorial situated at the foot of Ireland's holy mountain, Croagh Patrick, County Mayo. Sculpted by John Behan and erected in 1997, this piece depicts a coffin ship strewn with skeletal bodies. Indeed, all across Ireland plaques and memorials of all sizes were erected in the mid-1990s.[2] In addition, the intervening period has seen the establishment of museums at surviving workhouses including Carrick-on-Shannon, Portumna, Donaghmore and Dunfanaghy, all of which relate the story of the buildings' Famine past.[3]

There was also an outpouring of publications on the Famine, both national and local, during the commemorative period. Indeed, since the mid-1990s that trend has continued unabated. The publication and success of the voluminous *Atlas of the Great Irish Famine*, published in 2012, with over sixty contributors, is further evidence of this. Publications of local interest are particularly numerous and examine a number of important issues which have been neglected elsewhere, providing an in-depth analysis of how the Famine played itself out at a local level.[4] This new wave of Famine scholarship has also extended to the examination of emigration to America, Canada and Australia. While in the past much of the research was conducted outside of Ireland, recent studies have begun to reverse that trend.[5]

Famine memorialisation in Australia can be traced to when President Mary Robinson travelled to Sydney in 1995, following a visit to Grosse Île the previous year. Speaking in Sydney, President Robinson called on the Irish community to mark the memory of the Famine 'in a special way'. At that time there were many active Irish county organisations in Sydney, all involved in a number of activities, loosely co-ordinated by the Irish Communications Council, then headed by Mayo-born, Martin Coleman. In November 1995, the county associations met to discuss the idea sown by President Robinson and, by February 1996, a sub-committee of the Communications Council elected Clonmel-born Tom Power as the chairman to discuss a way to appropriately remember the Famine in Australia. At this time the Irish-Australian community had become aware of the story of the female workhouse emigrants, brought to Australia between 1848 and 1850, through the published work of the County Down-born academic, Trevor McClaughlin who was involved in discussions with Tom Power. In addition, a re-enactment, organised by Richard Reid and Cheryl Mongan, of the trek of over 100 workhouse orphans to the southern New South Wales town of Yass in 1850 under the care of the Surgeon Superintendent of the *Thomas Arbuthnot*, Charles Strutt, also contributed to the idea for a memorial.[6] Many ideas and potential sites were considered before the Immigration Barrack which housed the first workhouse orphan girls was eventually chosen as the most appropriate site. Subsequently, following a process of tender, the memorial sculpture by Hossein and Angela Valamanesh, with associated soundscape by Sam Carter, was selected in December 1997. Support from the Irish and Australian governments, Australian businesses and individuals, including descendants of the orphan girls, met the final cost of approximately $A300,000. On 28 August 1999, St Mary's Cathedral, situated beside the Hyde Park Barracks, was thronged with people brought together to remember an event in Ireland 150 years before. Thirty-two descendants of the orphans, representing each county of Ireland, officiated with the dean, the bishop and Catholic priests, supported by Presbyterian and Anglican ministers, for a modern memorial service of prayer and drama. The crowd then moved to the courtyard at the Barracks where the Governor-General of Australia, Sir William Deane, officially unveiled the monument. For Australia, this memorial to the Great Irish Famine represents the nation's Irish heritage and the names of some of the orphan girls from the workhouses etched on the glass panels of the sculpture represent all who suffered in the Famine.

White settlement of Australia began with the arrival of the first convicts from England in 1788. No convict ships sailed directly from Ireland until the *Queen* departed from Cork on 10 March 1791 but there were Irish-born convicts and Irish members of the military guard involved from the start.[7] Between then and the landing of the last convict ship in Western Australia in 1868, approximately 162,000 men and women arrived in the Australian colonies as convicts. Of this number an estimated one quarter were women, while about a third were Irish. A total of 30,231 Irish transportees, including 5,521 women had arrived in Sydney by 1849.[8] In addition to convicts, many Irish people chose to migrate to the Australian colonies. Besides those who fully paid their own passages, various assisted-immigration schemes operated from the 1830s, bringing skilled labourers and single women who were needed in the burgeoning colonies. Thousands arrived from Great Britain and Ireland during the nineteenth century; the British and colonial governments provided funds and encouraged skilled mechanics and their families, as well as young single women, to emigrate, facilitating the payment of a government bounty. The movement of selected groups of women commenced with a process devised by the Emigration Commissioners in 1831 and continued throughout the century. Initially, some women took up passages offered on female convict ships such as the *Palambam*, which brought fifty girls from the Foundling Hospital in Cork in 1831.[9] Under a separate scheme designed to reunite families with their reformed previously transported spouses, at least 1,795 Irish wives and families were given a free passage and successfully emigrated.[10] However, even under the 'assisted' schemes most immigrants were required to pay a portion of the fare and at times those eligible were provided with a 'bounty' which took the form of a subsidised passage; £20 for mechanics and their families and £8 for single women. However, this was not money paid to the immigrant. In the 1830s, because of a high demand from the colonies for eligible women, the commissioners organised the departure of two ships with women only: the *Red Rover* carrying 202 women from Cork to Sydney and the *Princess Royal* from London to Hobart with English women.[11] This proved successful and resulted in fourteen more ships carrying single young women from Britain and Ireland between 1833 and 1837, four of which brought young Irish women to Sydney.[12] Only a few emigrants, such as this latter group of women in the 1830s, did not contribute towards their own passages and were supported, in this case, by charitable groups. In total, only three groups of Irish emigrants travelled at no expense to themselves: the young females from the Irish workhouses, the previously mentioned wives and families of convicts and a group of children of 'bounty' emigrants whose parents were forced to leave them behind because of regulations at the time.

By 1844 the government and bounty schemes had ceased and in mid-1847 the Colonial Land and Emigration Commissioners (CLEC) began their work using colonial funds to select and bring suitable emigrants from Great Britain and Ireland to the Australian colonies. Under this scheme, potential immigrants had to apply, be selected and approved. The idea was to satisfy the labour needs in the colony; it was not designed to relieve distress in Great Britain or Ireland. Despite this stipulation, 43 per cent of the total number of Irish embarked between

1848 and 1850 would not have qualified under the commissioners' normal selection criteria but did so as workhouse orphans, convict families or 'children left behind'.[13] Early in 1848 the British Government, drawing on years of experience, began its organised emigration of young females from Irish workhouses. Irish Poor Law Commissioners sent circulars to the Board of Guardians of each Irish Poor Law Union asking if any young women 'between the ages of fourteen and eighteen' were willing and eligible for a passage to Australia. The commissioners had to be willing to pay for an outfit of clothing for each girl. For example, in February 1849, the Cashel Guardians' Minutes record the arrival of the Emigration Agent, Lieutenant Henry, to make a 'selection of inmates eligible to be sent to Australia'. Their outfits were to be provided and the matron was in charge of selecting and making them as quickly as possible. At Cashel, William Sooly's tender to make forty boxes (sea chests) for the emigrants (each to the specified dimensions, painted oak colour, at a cost of 4*s* 8*d* each) was accepted, as was John Comans' proposal to supply eighty pairs of shoes at 3*s* 10*d* a pair; 'the whole number to be furnished by Saturday 17th', giving him less than ten days to complete the order.[14]

The workhouse officers were obliged to seek character references, complete medical examinations and choose suitable young women before Lieutenant Henry arrived. The CLEC chartered the ships and arranged thee berths, food and supervision, while a surgeon superintendent was also appointed. These young workhouse women were a small part of renewed government-assisted emigration to the Australian colonies. The Famine orphans were viewed as young women, eligible for marriage who would bring a stabilising influence to the rough masculine colonial societies, while helping fill the need for female domestic servants. The Poor Law guardians provided an outfit of clothing to girls who had indicated they wanted to take advantage of the passages offered and, following inspection by Lieutenant Henry, they agreed to emigrate and their passage was paid from the workhouse to the port of departure in Ireland by the local Guardians. All twenty ships with workhouse orphans set sail from Plymouth, England. The Emigration Commissioners were responsible for their welfare and payment of passage to Plymouth and beyond to the colonies.[15] Despite the level of care, some Irish orphans were criticised in the Australian press as immoral dregs of the workhouse, and ignorant of the skills required of domestic servants. In truth that did not reflect reality. For example, the 105 women who sailed on the ship *Thomas Arbuthnot* and after arrival travelled with Charles Strutt, the Surgeon of that vessel, were widely welcomed on their settlement journey south from Sydney to Yass and Gundagai, where Strutt helped them find suitable employment.[16] However, ultimately, the opposition to the female orphan scheme was so strong that it ended within two years.

In total 4,114 single adolescent Irish females arrived to three Australian colonies, docking at Sydney, Port Phillip (Melbourne) and Adelaide. The first of these orphan ships was the *Earl Grey*, which sailed on 3 June 1848 to Sydney. Earl Grey, Secretary of State for the Colonies in Lord John Russell's Whig government, was the driving force behind the emigration of these young workhouse women, which is now often commonly referred to as the 'Earl Grey Scheme'. The selection of young girls was strictly adhered to and the lists, for example,reveal the youngest girls were aged 13 (five in total), all on the *Tippoo Saib*, the last ship to arrive in Sydney at the end of July 1850. The oldest women were recorded as aged 19, although Margaret Sullivan, perhaps the oldest of the orphans, who came from the Kenmare workhouse on the *John Knox* in April 1850 was recorded variously as 18 or 20. An analysis of the ages and backgrounds of these workhouse orphans as a total group is difficult because little is known about the 606 girls on the three ships to Adelaide. The *Elgin*, which sailed from Plymouth on 31 May 1849 to Adelaide, has the only surviving 'Certificate of Final Departure', which is simply a list of names and ages.[17] No such list survives for the other two Adelaide-bound ships, the *Roman Emperor* and the *Inconstant*, so these orphans' names can only be identified from other records such as the *South Australian Register* newspaper, documents in South Australia including gaol reports and detailed research by some descendants. The surviving Board of Guardian Minutes Books and Indoor Registers for some workhouses, held in the Public Record Office of Northern Ireland and local studies collections in counties in the Republic, occasionally augment details of individuals.[18]

Likewise, no details of parents or native place is provided for the six ships to Port Phillip (Melbourne) carrying 1,255 orphan girls. Therefore the comprehensive data for the native place and parents of the workhouse orphan girls is only readily available for the 2,253 who arrived on eleven ships to Sydney. For these ships we know that 25 per cent could read and write, 42 per cent were illiterate and the remainder could 'read only'. These numbers nonetheless debunk the idea that they were all illiterate. In addition, 72 per cent are recorded as 'true' orphans with both parents' dead, keeping in mind that the term 'orphan' in the nineteenth century could mean that one parent was still alive. Indeed, this was the case for almost 20 per cent of the Sydney arrivals, with just over 400 mothers and 135 fathers recorded on the shipping list as still alive. Moreover, thirty-six of the workhouse women sent to Sydney indicated that both parents were still alive.

Not surprisingly, many of the workhouse women who travelled to the Australian colonies as Famine survivors did so without family and arrived with only their shipmates as friends to offer support. The generic name of'orphan' arises from their destitution and residence in the workhouse and their genuine lack of parental support due to the Famine. The shipping lists reveal that 22% per cent of the Sydney arrivals had a relative already in the colony or they travelled with a sister or had a sister also arrive under this Irish workhouse emigration scheme: 140 stated they had a sister, brother, cousin, uncle, aunt or parent already in the colony. The evidence of family reunion and the resourcefulness of these survivors of the Famine are revealed in their family stories, which historians and descendants have been able to reconstruct. Their life stories are increasingly made available to all via the website of the Australian Famine Memorial and an integral part of the aim of the website is to commemorate and remember the Famine in general.[19] This website is constantly updated as material is gathered from primary research in Australia and Ireland, and is in part facilitated by grants from the Irish Government through the Emigrant Support Programme. The stories of the colonial lives of these women who left the workhouses as teenagers is their historical legacy, not only to their own families, but to the Australian nation and, in turn, back to their homeland. Local societies, workhouse museums and county libraries in Ireland are showing increasing interest in and awareness of these women, previously thought to have been lost during the Famine.

An examination of their stories reveals much about the fate of these Famine emigrants (and indeed earlier). Catherine Naughton, for example, from Tynagh, County Galway, left the Loughrea workhouse and sailed on the *Inchinnan* from Plymouth on 4 November 1848, bound for Sydney. The Immigration Board's list indicated that she had a father, Edward/Edmond Naughton, living in Sydney. Her sister, Mary, also arrived as a workhouse orphan a month later on the *Digby* with the father again noted, but as living in Goulburn. By this time their mother, Bridget, had died and further research reveals that the father had been transported for Whiteboy offences in 1832 under the Insurrection Act. His convict record noted that he was a widower with children.[20] He remarried to Anne Mary Broderick in Goulburn in August 1843 and, in 1853 he sponsored the passage of another daughter, Bridget, who arrived on the *Sabrina* on 10 July 1854.[21] This family were fortunate to have survived conviction, transportation and the Famine to be reunited in New South Wales by assisted immigration. As well as his three Irish-born daughters, Edward Naughton produced a new family of eight children in Goulburn, where he ran the Railway Inn, thriving until his death in 1877.[22]

The background to the Stephens sisters from County Wicklow is somewhat similar. Ruth and Jane Stephens, aged 15 and 14, arrived in Sydney on the *Thomas Arbuthnot* on 3 February 1850, simply recorded as natives of Wicklow. Both were members of the Church of England and house servants who could read and write; their parents, John and Eliza, were 'living in Sydney'.[23] Along with all 194 orphan girls on *Thomas Arbuthnot* the Stephens sisters spent five days at anchor on the ship, bringing their boxes from the hold and preparing to go ashore. Like most who landed in Sydney, they went to Immigration Depot at Hyde Park Barracks in Macquarie Street.[24] Both were hired after twenty-one days by the Bowermans of Macquarie Street. Ruth was indentured as a servant for three years at a wage of £6 a year; Jane, being younger, was indentured for four years at the same rate. Both received full board and lodgings as part of their indentured employment. Prior to their departure the Stephens sisters had been in Rathdrum workhouse in County Wicklow and the Poor Law Minute Book, uncharacteristically, provides a clue to their family details:

> Two letters were read from Lieutenant Henry, Government Emigration Officer in reference to the proposed Emigration from the Workhouse of Ruth and Jane Stephens, daughters of Eliza Stephens, who has been sent out to Australia as a sub-matron in one of the Government Emigration Vessels in August last.[25]

The Stephens' were escorted to Dublin by the schoolmaster of the workhouse who was going to Dublin on leave and was charged with seeing that the girls arrived safely on the steamer bound for Plymouth.[26] Their mother, Eliza, received a passage as a sub-matron on a previous orphan ship, the *Lismoyne*, which had left Plymouth on 22 August 1849[27] while John, a blacksmith, had arrived in Hobart on the *Tory* in March 1847, following a sentence of ten years transportation 'for stealing John Pearce's cows'. His physical description identifies him as 5ft 9ins, aged 34, fresh complexion, large head, brown hair, no whiskers, oval visage, high forehead, brown eyebrows, grey eyes, large nose, large wide mouth and medium chin.[28] His facial features resemble those depicted in the surviving photograph of his daughter, Ruth. When the Stephen sisters arrived on the *Thomas Arbuthnot* the authorities found that the parents were in Van Dieman's Land so the girls spent a short time in Sydney before being reunited with them, despite being given employment as indentured servants.[29] As they were free, all these orphan girls could voluntarily leave their employment and going to Van Diemen's Land with their mother to be reunited as a family group seems to have been acceptable.

The fate of other workhouse orphans was not as comfortable as that of Catherine Naughton or the Stephen sisters. A Select Committee Report into Irish Female Immigrants in 1859 provides an appendix listing 254 of these workhouse orphans indicating why their employment apprenticeships were cancelled. Offences range from unspecified 'bad conduct' and 'improper conduct' to 'absent without permission', 'general misconduct', 'refusing to work' and 'charges of ill-treatment'. In most instances the case was dismissed or the indentures were cancelled and the girl was sent to the country or returned to her employer on the condition she behaved.[30] Occasionally, the women brought charges against their employers. For example, Christiana Wynne, who had left the South Dublin Union Workhouse, made a charge against her master in Sydney. The case was dismissed but she was sent to far away Moreton Bay where, by mid-1850, she married William Darling and managed their farm on the banks of the Brisbane River, which, although initially granted to him, was transferred to her name and managed by her. She subsequently had eleven daughters and when she died in 1892 her estate was valued at £3,313.[31]

Mary McCarthy arrived in Sydney in February 1850, aged 18, with a mother still alive in County Galway. Miss J.A. Rossiter, a milliner, in Fort Street, Sydney, employed her at £8 a year but three months later McCarthy's indentures were cancelled for 'disobedience and neglect of duty, her wages ordered to be kept from her until she behaves better'.[32] Nothing further is confirmed but it seems she was sent to the country for employment and in August 1851 she married George Cooper at St Michael's Catholic church, Bathurst. The details of her private life are unrecorded, but it seems she had three children with him between 1853 and 1857 before he disappeared.[33] In 1858 Mary married Edward Jacob Young, also at Bathurst, with whom she had eleven children.[34]

In 1872, during a violent argument, Mary McCarthy, stabbed and killed her husband. She was sentenced at the Mudgee Quarter Sessions on 16 March 1872 to six months' imprisonment for manslaughter and sent to Darlinghurst Gaol in Sydney.[35] Following her release, she raised her children alone in Sydney. In 1887, aged 55, Mary Ann, now calling herself 'Edith', was discovered in a dying condition by her daughter, Mrs McNabb. An inquest took place and on 20 December the *Herald* reported that she had died from an overdose of chlorodyne, a widely available medicine used for treatment of insomnia, neuralgia and migraines.[36] Composed of a mixture of laudanum (an alcoholic solution of opium), cannabis and chloroform, it readily lived up to its claim of relieving pain, sedating and treating diarrhoea. Whether she took an overdose on purpose is unknown but her initial battle with authority, the disappearance of her first husband, and dealing with her violent second husband as she struggled to support her many children, perhaps hastened her decline. She is buried in Waverley Cemetery, not far from the memorial to the 1798 Irish Rebels. Today, Mary McCarthy is one of the 400 names etched in the glass panels of the Australian Famine Memorial in Sydney.

Like Mary McCarthy, Margaret Simmons (or Simons) has her named engraved on the Sydney memorial. The shipping list of the *Lismoyne*, which arrived in Sydney at the end of November 1849, shows she was aged 14, a Catholic, could read and write, and was the daughter of William and Johanna. Her native place was given as Manchester, England. Margaret was one of nineteen orphan emigrant girls who indicated their birth place was outside Ireland. She was one of nine born in England, four in Scotland, three in the USA, one in the Cape of Good Hope, one in Jamaica and one born in Van Diemen's Land. This of course reflected the fluidity with which the pre-Famine Irish travelled as seasonal workers. On arrival in Sydney, Margaret Simmons spent an unusually long 134 days in the immigrant depot at Hyde Park before being sent to Bathurst, 200 kilometres west of the city. There is no indication why her employment was so delayed.

Her stated skill as a 'needle woman' may well have been utilised in the Immigration Barracks and therefore there was no rush to find her employment elsewhere, but this is mere speculation. In Bathurst in 1852, she married John Smith in a Catholic ceremony, but she was soon widowed without offspring. The records are silent on her life until she married Australian-born James Whiley in 1861 in the same church as her first marriage. The couple lived at Canowindra some miles distant but in the same parish. She had nine children between 1862 and 1880, the births registered in various surrounding country districts, perhaps due to his occupation as a tradesman as stated in their marriage records. In October 1856, Margaret's two sisters, Agnes, aged 19, and Johanna, aged 14, arrived on the *Vocalist* after £5 was paid by Margaret as part of their passage under the Remittance Regulations. Their native place was given as Killmannock (obviously Kilmallock), County Limerick, a place where there was also a workhouse, so presumably it was from there that Margaret Simons began her journey to New South Wales in August 1849. It seems the Simons family spent time in Manchester before returning to Ireland before the Famine necessitated relief in the workhouse. Following their marriage in Bathurst, Margaret and James Whiley moved further west and selected land in the remote area of Condobolin where James died of pneumonia in 1890. Margaret's will, written a week before her death in February 1901, gives an insight to her life. She left her property, the Exchange Boarding House, its effects and two other properties in Condobolin, as well as 320 acres and cash to two daughters and a son, although all nine of her children were still living. She died at 'Molong House' in the wealthy Sydney suburb of Darlinghurst and was buried in the Catholic section of Rookwood Cemetery. Her story indicates a continued adherence to her Catholic faith as stated on the shipping list of the *Lismoyne* in 1849.

Another emigration case study linked to the workhouse emigrant women is that of Elizabeth Mackey (or McKay as she was later known), born in Van Diemen's Land. Elizabeth arrived to Sydney on the *John Knox* in April 1850 and was recorded as a member of the Church of England, aged 19 with parents Edmund and Ann, both dead. She could read only and travelling with her on the *John Knox* was her sister, Sarah, whose native place was noted as Stepney, near Cootehill, in County Cavan. According to Elizabeth's birth certificate, she was born on 7 March 1831 and baptised twenty days later. Her father,

Edward Mackey, was a sergeant in the 63rd regiment and her mother noted simply as Mary Mackey.[37] The 63rd (Suffolk) regiment was in Ireland, where Edward enlisted, from 1820 to 1826, but was stationed in Portugal from 1826 to 1828, and then Van Diemen's Land from 1829 to 1833. The family had also resided in India, where his wife Ann died in 1836. Two years later Edward was discharged but died at sea. His daughters, Elizabeth and Sarah, were apparently reared in the British Military Orphan Asylum in Madras, before returning to Ireland where they entered the Cootehill workhouse.

The aforementioned case studies highlight the variety of circumstances which the workhouse 'orphans' endured both before and after departure. Although the stories of these women have become better understood since the unveiling of the Famine Memorial at Hyde Park Barracks in 1999, undoubtedly more remains to be done and increasingly the memorial is recognised as a living symbol of historical upheaval in Ireland and a chilling reminder of similar suffering in the world today. This memorial was erected with the hope that the young Irish Famine orphans would be seen as representative of all such 'refugee' women who came, and indeed who still come, to Australia. Refugees in the broad sense of the word are people who leave their native lands through some form of persecution, whether it is as a result of natural disasters or political upheaval. Indeed, even as I write in 2015, Syrian migrants and others are forced from their homeland and scattered across the globe, just as the Irish were in the 1840s and 1850s. As Tom Power, chairman of the Great Irish Famine Commemoration Committee (GIFCC), remarked at the unveiling of this memorial in 1999, 'these workhouse orphan girls are a continual reminder of the many terrible realities, similar to the Great Famine of Ireland, occurring in the world today and which cry out for our compassion and concern'.[38]

Through the work on individual histories of Earl Grey's workhouse orphan girls and the outreach education programmes, the GIFCC is contributing to Irish-Australian history and, in a small way, to global peace and harmony.

12

'*Une voix d'Irlande*':[1] Integration, migration, and travelling nationalism between Famine Ireland and Quebec

Jason King

'Remember your soul and your liberty', enjoined James Quinn, a 45-year-old Irish emigrant from Lissonuffy, part of the Mahon estate in County Roscommon, to his two young sons Patrick (aged 12) and Thomas (aged 6), as he lay dying in the quarantine station on Grosse Île, Quebec, in late August 1847.[2] Sixty-four years later, his son, the Abbé Thomas Quinn, stood before the First Congress of the French Language in North America, on 25 June 1912, to express his gratitude to the people of French Canada for their 'untiring charity', which enabled 'my unfortunate parents … to sleep in peace with God, pardoning their enemies, and carrying with them the ineffable consolation of leaving their children in the care of French-Canadian priests'. The adoption of Irish orphans like Patrick and Thomas Quinn and Catherine and Daniel Tighe into French-Canadian families and communities in 1847 has long been remembered in Ireland and Quebec as a tragic historical event that nevertheless brought the French and Irish closer together.[3] At the 2014 National Famine Commemoration in Strokestown, County Roscommon, the Taoiseach Enda Kenny, TD, echoed Thomas Quinn when he unveiled a glass wall memorial to the 1,490 people who were assisted in emigration from the Mahon estate in 1847 on board some of the most notorious 'coffin ships'. Like Quinn, Kenny paid tribute to Quebec's 'priests and nuns … and especially … the French-Canadian Sisters of Charity … the Grey Nuns … and the quality of their mercy' for looking 'after 800 children whose parents had died on board the emigrant ships'.[4] Similarly, the return of the descendants of emigrant orphan Daniel Tighe from Quebec to Strokestown, in July 2013, provided another occasion for the commemoration of the Famine exodus, as a flagship event of The Gathering.[5]

These rituals of remembrance mark the symbolic reconnection between Famine emigrants and their Irish homeland as well as the generosity and hospitality they received in the Canadian host society. And yet, when Thomas Quinn delivered his '*Une voix d'Irlande*' address to the French Language Congress, he acknowledged a growing rift in 'the relationship between my original and my adopted race'.[6] In particular, the Irish clergy's support for Regulation 17 in Ontario, which was issued in July 1912, to restrict French language teaching in the province's public schools, had incensed French-Canadians and aggravated ethno-linguistic and religious tensions between them and the Irish. 'Why, in changing countries, do the noble, patient, chivalrous Irish people who have suffered oppression want to be oppressive in turn?' Quinn asked.

This chapter examines the ways in which Irish Famine orphans such as the Quinn brothers and Tighe siblings became perceived as figures of ethno-religious conciliation and models of integration in Ireland and English and French Canada. More specifically, it will argue that their ordination as priests made the Quinns into exponents of French-Canadian nationalism that brought them into conflict with their Irish Catholic co-religionists in the latter nineteenth and early twentieth centuries, which they hoped to resolve through personal reminiscences of past benevolence. As Irish Famine orphans who had travelled from Roscommon to Quebec and started new lives within the clergy, the Quinn brothers sought both to embody and reconcile the differences between the French-Canadian and Irish Catholic sides of their congregations, which struggled for control of the Church and its medium of instruction. As child migrants they became intermediaries between their divided communities. Their story provides a case study of contested acculturation and travelling nationalism between their home and host societies. In honouring their father's pledge to 'remember your soul and your liberty', they were confronted with their parishioners' split loyalties. More broadly, the Quinn brothers' struggle to reconcile the French and Irish sides of their congregations attests to shifting cultural fault lines and the gradual realignment of their ethno-religious identities into linguistic identities in the latter nineteenth and early twentieth centuries. Ultimately, their protestations of fidelity to their French-Canadian brethren were held in tension with their Irish ancestry.

Like Catherine and Daniel Tighe, the Quinn brothers were assisted in emigration from the Mahon estate in Roscommon to Liverpool and then to Quebec in May 1847 on board the *Naomi*, which was one of the worst of the 'coffin ships'. According to A.C. Buchanan's 'Return of Passenger Ships arrived at the Port of Quebec' recorded in the *British Parliamentary Papers*, the *Naomi* arrived in Quebec on 10 August 1847 after carrying 421 steerage passengers from Liverpool on a journey to Grosse Île that lasted forty-five days, of whom 196 or slightly under 50 per cent perished, including seventy-eight at sea, thirty-one at quarantine and a further eighty-seven in the quarantine hospital on the island.[7] Two days later, the *Virginius*, which also carried assisted emigrants from the Mahon estate, arrived at Grosse Île with an even higher mortality rate of over 50 per cent or 267 of the 467 steerage passengers on board. Even by the standards of 1847, the conditions on board the *Naomi* and *Virginius* were horrific and only obliquely recalled by the Quinn and Tighe children and their descendants in their subsequent recollections. In the words of Daniel's grandson Léo Tye, who was interviewed by Marianna O'Gallagher and met with Jim Callery, founder of the Irish National Famine Museum at Strokestown:

> In 1847, Mary, widow of Bernard Tighe, left Ireland with her five children and her younger brother ... The voyage was a long nightmare of eight weeks. Drinking water ran low and food was reduced to one meal a day. Comfort and hygiene were non-existent. Typhus broke out on board, and the ship was ordered to stop at Grosse Île. Of Mary Tighe's family, only two children survived: Daniel (12), and Catherine (9). When the children left the ship, they never saw the other family members again, nor did they have any word about them.[8]

Likewise, Thomas Quinn's recollection of his Famine voyage decades later was equally sketchy: 'In the designs of Providence, we were cast upon the shores of Grosse-Ile after a stormy passage of two months at sea. A malady ... – the famine fever – came to add its untold terrors to so much other suffering and misery', he declared at the French

Language Congress in 1912.[9] The voyage of the Quinn family was also recalled in the *Roscommon Herald* in 1931:

> During the Famine of Black '47, a family named Quinn were driven out of their home near Strokestown by the cruel and wicked Major Mahon, whose infamous boast was that he would make Strokestown a Cattle Walk, and Elphin a Sheep Pen. He had the peasantry of a large district driven out and deported on the Coffin Ships [whose] … victims were flung out on the banks of the St. Lawrence, near Montreal… There were, however, some survivors, and two have been traced.[10]

In fact, both the Quinn and Tighe children were evacuated from the quarantine station at Grosse Île in August and September of 1847 into the care of the Catholic Orphanage run by the 'Charitable Ladies of Quebec' and, after 1849, the Grey Nuns, who presided over their adoptions into French-Canadian and Irish Catholic families. As Léo Tye recounted:

> On 8 August 1847, Daniel and Catherine along with several other immigrants left Grosse Île on a sail boat which brought them to … the General Hospital [in Quebec] where they were very well treated. Then one morning, the pastor of Lotbinière, Fr. Edouard Faucher, came to get Daniel and Catherine and eleven other Irish children. He loaded them into his horse drawn 'express wagon' [and] during the long trek, held one of the smaller children on his knees.[11]

Léo Tye also recalled how his grandfather Daniel and his sister Catherine were adopted by the French-Canadian Coulomb family who decided to keep the children together after they:

> cried so hard at the idea of being separated that they were inconsolable … The Coulombs proved to be good parents to these two orphans … Upon the parents death, Daniel inherited their farm, which since then, has been handed on from father to son.

Like the Tighe orphans, Patrick and Thomas Quinn were also escorted by clergy from Grosse Île to Quebec and then adopted into a French-Canadian family. According to the *Annals of Richmond County* in Quebec's Eastern Townships:

> Previous to his appointment at Richmond Fr. [Luc] Trahan had worked at Grosse Isle Quarantine Station in 1847... [He] took under his protection two orphaned boys, Patrick and Thomas Quinn whose father James Quinn and mother, Margaret Lyons, of Strakestown, [sic] Co. Roscommon, Ireland, had died of the fever. Through his efforts, the two boys were adopted by a French-Canadian family named Bourque, at Nicolet. They completed their education at the Seminary at Nicolet and both entered the priesthood. Fr. Patrick Quinn [the elder brother] succeeded his benefactor Fr. Trahan as Pastor at ... Richmond [where he remained parish priest for 50 years until his retirement in 1914].[12]

The adoption of the Quinn and Tighe Famine orphan siblings into French-Canadian families thus symbolises a wider story of social acceptance and the upward mobility of model immigrants who became thoroughly integrated into the agrarian and ecclesiastical institutions of Quebec's host society. As parish priests and proprietors of the family farm, they left behind the Famine-afflicted Mahon estate and typhus-infested *Naomi*'s steerage and Grosse Île fever sheds to start new lives ascending social ladders they could never have gained a foothold on in Ireland.

At the heart of this story is the generosity of the French-Canadian clergy and families who not only took in Famine orphans but also allowed them to keep their Irish surnames. According to Marianna O'Gallagher and Rose Masson Dompierre, in Quebec 'today names like Tye, Kelly, O'Connor, [and] Ryan ... bear witness to the families that had the heart to help their adopted children remember their Irish heritage'.[13] Through the retention of their native surnames, the Famine orphans became conduits for the transmission of their Irish ancestry and living memorials of the catastrophe they had overcome. Perhaps the most poignant expression of Irish gratitude came from Thomas Quinn himself, who 'was ever grateful to the French Canadian people and [for whom] it was an honor ... to proclaim it publicly when the occasion arose'.[14]

> According to the unpublished Hayes papers held by the Richmond County Historical Society: Fr Thomas Quinn, often related with emotion how, before leaving Grosse Île, the admirable ecclesiastic who cared for his parents led him to the bedside of his father, who, when he recognized them exclaimed with his dying breath the old Irish slogan: 'Remember your Soul and Liberty'. The incident remained deeply graven in his memory.

Indeed, Quinn equated his paternal injunction of remembrance with a pledge to preserve not only his French-Canadian parishioners' Catholic faith but also their cultural identity.

The emphasis on the orphans' retention of their Irish surnames and rescue by French-Canadian clergy in posthumous fulfilment of their parents' wishes provide recurring motifs in the transmission of Famine memory between Ireland and Quebec.[15] As Famine orphans who were not only raised by French-Canadians families but became priests themselves, the Quinn brothers provide a case study of Irish integration into Quebec's French-speaking host communities. Indeed, they appear to be exemplary immigrants and mythic figures who not only embodied but endeavoured to reconcile the distinct cultural traditions and linguistic identities of their divided host society. The most detailed account of their Famine voyage from Roscommon and arrival in Quebec can be found in the Hayes papers:

> Fr. Patrick Quinn was born February 20, 1836 at Strakestown [*sic*], County Roscommon, Ireland. He was the son of [James] Quinn and Mary Lyons, his wife. In common with countless others, his parents emigrated from Ireland in the dark days of 1847, hoping to better their fortunes in Canada, only to find a grave at Grosse Isle, where under the shadow of the recently erected Celtic Cross [in 1909], they lie buried, victims of the dread typhus which carried off the parents and three small children of a family of five. In the annals of the Irish Migration with its harrowing record of sorrow and death, there is no more pathetic incident than that of the Quinn family. The survivors, Thomas and Patrick, aged six and eleven respectively were adopted by generous French-Canadian families at the insistence of Rev. Mr. Trahan and Robson, then in charge of the unfortunate orphans. Under the friendly guidance of Rev. Fr. Fortier … at Nicolet, whither he was sent with twenty others, Thomas Quinn fell into the charitable hands of Mr. George Bourque, where he slowly recovered from the effects of the illness which had brought him nigh death while yet at sea. Meanwhile Patrick Quinn at Grosse Isle was slowly convalescing only to find himself bereft of his parents: death had claimed both of them and the two little girls. Patrick was later sent to Nicolet and adopted by the family of Mr. Joseph Geoffroy. Separated and amongst strangers at six and eleven years of age, respectively! Such was their plight when the generosity of Mr. Bourque prompted him to adopt Patrick and thus bring the disconsolate boys together. Both were placed at Nicolet Seminary where they received the full collegiate education of that institution.[16]

Like Catherine and Daniel Tighe, the Quinn brothers were initially separated from one another after losing their families and then were only reunited because of the compassion of their French-Canadian benefactors who adopted more children than they had originally intended.

Under their care, the Quinn brothers became emblematic figures of French-Canadian piety and patriotism during the period of the Catholic Revival after the arrival of the Famine influx and the 1837 rebellion in Quebec a decade earlier. The rebellion had been instigated by the Patriote movement, led by the French-Canadian Louis Joseph Papineau and his Irish deputy Edmund Bailey O'Callaghan, who had created an Irish-French alliance to overthrow British colonial rule. Its failure consolidated the Church's authority in Quebec and redefined relations between its French and Irish Catholic inhabitants. More specifically, the figure of the French-Canadian was transformed in the Irish imagination from being a political compatriot to a Catholic co-religionist, as reflected in Quebec's Irish press. Indeed, the very ideal of French and Irish political co-operation had been largely supplanted after the rebellion by a new type of cultural nationalism, closely aligned with the Catholic Revival's ultramontane political and social conservatism, which had the effect of accentuating cultural differences between Quebec's French-Canadian and Irish communities.[17] Whereas before the rebellion the Patriote newspaper *The Vindicator* had championed the political alliance between 'Pat and Jean Baptiste' who both served '*mon pays avant tout* … the simple emblems – the Shamrock and the Maple Leaf',[18] after the Famine the *True Witness and Catholic Chronicle* repudiated such 'rebellious sentiment' and any 'attempt to kindle anew in our mixed community the scarce extinguished embers of religious and national discord'.[19] Expressions of political discontent were condemned as 'directly opposed to the teachings of the Catholic Clergy of Canada, who are now, as they were in '37 and '38, the preacher of dutiful obedience to lawfully constituted authority'.[20]

The cleric Thomas Quinn was one such 'preacher of dutiful obedience', though he was adopted by a former Patriote rebel. In his eulogy delivered in 1923, Elzear Bellemere recalled that:

> Fr. Thomas Quinn had the … benefit of being raised by a sincere patriot. George Bourque had in good faith taken part in the disturbances of 1837, and he was even forced to emigrate to save his life and spend some time in the United States. This good man was like George-Etienne Cartier

> and others mistaken in the impulses of his patriotism. But he deeply loved his country and he even shed blood for it; he thought well of his countrymen. This noble patriotic sentiment … he transmitted into the souls and hearts of his adopted children. These orphans clung tightly to their protectors in particular, and in general to the people of French Canada whom they have always regarded as fellow countrymen sharing their own nationality, without, however, setting aside the affection they owed to their mother country.[21]

Bellemere makes clear that the Quinn brothers inherited their benefactor's sense of patriotism, but repudiated his youthful impulse to political violence. Indeed, he emphasises that:

> Fr. Thomas Quinn had the feelings of a strong and enlightened patriot. Although he was a native of Ireland, no one could say with more conviction and truth those words expressed from the heart of a famous patriot! 'O Canada, my country, my love'. He vigorously condemned the Fenian invasion in 1866, which he considered unfair to Canada and unnecessary for the cause of Ireland. He condemned with the same energy the campaign organized by a number of his countrymen against the existence and rights of the French language.

Thus, Thomas Quinn channelled his patriotism into his pastoral role as a defender not only of the Catholic faith but also French-Canadian culture. As an ultramontane adherent of the Catholic Revival, Quinn's rejection of Fenianism was less remarkable than his renunciation of 'his countrymen' opposed to the 'rights of the French language'. Indeed, his affection for his 'mother country' did not extend to their ethno-religious rivalry.

Nevertheless, as they rose through the ranks of the clergy, the Quinn brothers endeavoured to create institutions that would bring together their French and Irish parishioners. The most important of these was the St Patrick's Society of Richmond, Quebec, founded by Patrick Quinn in 1877. In his recent study entitled *Irish Settlement and National Identity in the Lower St. Francis Valley* (2012), Peter Southam notes that 'the experience of the Richmond Irish Catholic community's future pastors, the brothers Patrick and Thomas Quinn, became a legendary part of the Richmond area's collective consciousness … Through their teaching, both brothers ensured that their parishioners in the Lower

Saint Francis Valley did not forget the lessons of the Famine'.[22] Perhaps the most vital lesson was the need to create institutions that would safeguard not only the spiritual but also the material wellbeing of their parishioners. The establishment of St Patrick's Society in the nearby town of Sherbrooke earlier in 1873 had inspired French-Canadians to found their own Société Saint-Jean-Baptiste shortly thereafter. Patrick Quinn played a pivotal role in mobilising French-Canadian and Irish Catholic support through his creation of similar fraternal associations in Richmond four years later. According to Southam:

> From Quinn's perspective, the organizing of a local St. Patrick's Society had more than patriotic value. Its establishment, along with that of a local Société Saint-Jean-Baptiste three years later, promised to strengthen parish ties and, through Quinn's office of chaplain of both societies, reinforce his pastoral oversight. He no doubt understood that such organizations could serve the parish in material ways.[23]

Indeed, through these offices Quinn raised sufficient funds to establish and refurbish all of the town's Catholic ecclesiastical and social institutions which 'came into existence under his administration and fostering care'.[24] Even today, 'Richmond's two most inspiring buildings – Sainte-Bibiane Church and what was once *le couvent Mont Saint-Patrice* – pay silent tribute to the man whose energy and vision led to their construction more than a century ago'.[25]

Patrick Quinn's legacy of institution building was inspired by his father's injunction to safeguard the souls and the liberty of his French-Canadian and Irish parishioners. More broadly, the remembrance of Irish Famine orphans in Quebec tended to be evoked in a spirit of French and Irish fraternal association, especially to alleviate tension when relations between them became increasingly fraught in the latter nineteenth century. As I have argued elsewhere, the popular memory of the Famine orphans took shape a generation after their migration in the 1860s, during a moment of heightened ethno-religious conflict and social friction between Quebec's French-Canadian and Irish Catholic communities.[26] Even in 1847, the Canadian-Irish *Pilot* newspaper acknowledged 'the humane and Christian dispositions of our [French-] Canadian brethren' who adopted 'these poor destitute little orphans' in spite 'of the calumny which imputes to them hostility to the Irish race'.[27] A letter published in Montreal's *True*

Witness from an 'English Catholic' in the Eastern Townships in 1859 similarly recalled those 'French-Canadian protectors' who adopted Famine orphans to question received wisdom about their ostensible 'aversion and antipathy towards the Irish'.[28] The letter alluded in particular to 'another Irish boy, an orphan' who became a notary as proof 'he must have received a good education, and have been well cared for by his French Canadian benefactor. Is this, too, an example of aversion, hostility, and antipathy on the part of French Canadians towards Europeans and Irishmen?' the author asked. Apprehensions of French-Canadian aversion, hostility and antipathy towards the Irish were assuaged by the orphans' conspicuous success under the auspices of French-Canadian protectors.

Nevertheless, in the decades that followed the Famine migration, an increasing sense of rivalry did begin to escalate between French-Canadian and Irish Catholic clergy and members of the laity, especially in Montreal, for control of the Church and the social institutions it administered. In particular, the establishment of St Patrick's Orphan Asylum in Montreal in 1851 became a symbol of Irish communal resilience and self-reliance that gradually supplanted the memory of French-Canadian compassion and benevolence.

Elsewhere I have suggested that it was, in fact, Montreal Bishop Ignace Bourget's plan to subdivide his parish in 1866 that mobilised the city's Irish clerical and lay leadership, such as Fr Patrick Dowd and Thomas D'Arcy McGee, to struggle to preserve their social institutions, especially St Patrick's Orphan Asylum, from French-Canadian ecclesiastical encroachment.[29] In a pastoral letter, Bishop Bourget all but accused the Irish of ingratitude, questioning if they had forgotten 'when the ravages of the typhus left the children of your countrymen by hundreds, orphans on our shores, did we did not make an appeal to all our Diocese, to obtain for them other fathers and mothers, who as you know, reared them and cherished them as their own?'[30] His insinuation that the Irish were forgetful and ungrateful for the sacrifice made by French-Canadians in caring for the Famine orphans two decades beforehand incensed Fr Dowd and D'Arcy McGee, who took the unusual step of publishing a couple of pamphlets that acknowledged French-Canadian generosity, but also accused the Bishop of now imperilling their welfare and 'bringing back to their memory that they were once before driven from their native land, as if it were not their home'.[31] They proclaimed St Patrick's Asylum to be a specifically Irish 'institution which we, strangers here, have built out of the sweat of our brow to save the orphan children of our own race from vice and heresy'. Indeed, when the Governor General Lord Dufferin paid a vice-regal visit to St Patrick's Orphan Asylum in 1873, he was informed that 'the children are now rarely given to be adopted into families. That system was tried and did not work well … permitting them to be adopted by strangers'.[32]

The legacy of Famine orphan adoptions had acquired disparate meanings for French Canadians and Irish Catholics in Montreal in the latter nineteenth century. The memory of French-Canadian generosity in taking in orphaned children like the Quinn and Tighe siblings contrasted sharply with that of their compatriots who had provided an impetus for Irish institution building in Montreal and the consciousness of communal resilience and self-reliance it engendered.

These conflicting legacies of French-Canadian and Irish familial and institutional adoption became conflated and embodied in the figure of Fr Thomas Quinn, a Famine orphan himself, who sought to reconcile both sides of his heritage as he stood before the First Congress of the French Language in Quebec City on 25 June 1912. The Congress was held to defend the rights of French speakers not only in Quebec but across Canada which were perceived to be increasingly under threat since the controversy surrounding the Manitoba Schools Question had emerged a decade earlier. Its speakers, including former Canadian Prime Minister, Wilfred Laurier, and Quebec intellectual and founding editor of *Le Devoir*, Henri Bourassa, were particularly incensed by the role that Irish Catholic clergy had played in clamouring to restrict the teaching of French in public schools in Manitoba and especially Ontario, which led to the passage of the infamous Regulation 17 in July 1912. It was the Irish Catholic Bishop Michael Fallon, of London, Ontario, who led a commission of inquiry that called for the extreme curtailing of French language education in Ontario public schools that was implemented in Regulation 17. 'To the disappointment of French Canadians, the Catholics bishops of Ontario, most of whom were of Irish ancestry, supported the government's position', notes Garth Stevenson.[33] In his classic study entitled *Language and Religion: A History of English-French Conflict in Ontario* (1975), Robert Choquette claims that Fallon 'was an extremist and the foremost agitator in the conflicts' that ensued from the implementation of Regulation 17.[34] Mark McGowan offers a more nuanced interpretation that 'although Bishop Fallon has frequently been singled out as the "bête noir" in the assault against the French', he was actually espousing views that were widespread amongst Ontario's English-speaking Catholic clergy, for whom he was initially 'acting as the spokesperson, or perhaps "fall guy"'.[35] In fact, Fallon was hardly alone in contending that French should not feature any more prominently in the curriculum than other languages, such as 'Italian or Polish or Irish … for, I assure you', he claimed in January 1912, 'that I can organize in very short order a province-wide demand for the teaching of Gaelic in the schools'.[36] The same point was made more brutally by Toronto's Bishop Lynch, who observed that 'little did Irish children suspect when they were whipped in school for not knowing the English lesson that God destined the English language in their mouths to spread the true faith of his Divine Son throughout the greater part of the world'.[37] Indeed, one of the strongest defenders of Regulation 17 was Robert Sellar, author of *Ulster and Home Rule: A Canadian Parallel* (1912), *The Tragedy of Quebec: The Expulsion of its Protestant Farmers* (1907) and his fictionalised account of Irish Famine orphan Gerald Keegan *The Summer of Sorrow* (1895), which provided the source text for Ireland's best-seller *Famine Diary* (1991).[38] In *The Tragedy of Quebec*, Sellar noted approvingly that 'a considerable number of French-Canadians saddle the blame [for Regulation 17] on Bishop Fallon and the Irish Catholics', whom he regarded as fellow travellers in resisting the predations of Quebec's French clergy.[39]

Throughout the Regulation 17 controversy, 'the only English-speaking clerical support of the French Canadians seems to have come from an obscure priest Fr. Thomas Quinn', observes Choquette.[40] As an Irish Famine orphan who was no less a member of Quebec's French-speaking clergy, Quinn struggled to reconcile his Irish ancestry with his pastoral duties as he addressed the First Congress of the French Language in 1912:

> I do not belong by birth to the French family … The language of my childhood is a foreign language, and if I am afforded the great honour to speak before this patriotic gathering, then it is as an adopted child and son of Ireland … But, ladies and gentlemen the adoption was a complete success and I claim my place at the paternal table. The French language, it is mine as it is yours … It is still the tongue of old, and it is in this language that I am here today to recognize the people of French Canada who adopted and took in an Irish son.[41]

Fr Quinn then took it upon himself to denounce the 'cruel irony' and 'deplorable contradiction' that put him in a position of seemingly having to choose between the land of his birth and that of his adoption.

However, he left his audience in no doubt about where his loyalty belonged. Of his Irish compatriots in Canada, he asked why after having suffered oppression they 'want to be oppressive in turn? And that in circumstances marked by the blackest and most revolting ingratitude?'[42] In the face of such ingratitude, Fr Quinn sought to placate his audience by paying tribute to the generosity of the French-Canadian clergy and family that adopted him six decades years earlier. As he recalled:

> It was in 1847. A famine … threatened the Irish people with total extinction. The most astonishing part of the awful spectacle was, not to see the people die, but to see them live through such great distress … Like walking skeletons they went, in tears, seeking hospitality from more favoured lands.

After recounting the hardships his family, like the Tighes, had experienced for weeks on end during their voyage on the *Naomi* and in quarantine at Grosse Île, Fr Quinn recalled how the French-Canadian priests were 'stirred with compassion' and in 'braving the epidemic contended for glory in rushing to their relief'. 'Sixty-six years have passed since then', he avowed, 'but my soul belongs to the French-Canadian people, and my spirit jealously guards their rights and freedoms'.

In paying tribute to his clerical predecessors on behalf of his parents, Fr Quinn was not simply expressing a personal debt of gratitude. He was also implicitly contrasting their generosity and open mindedness with the bigotry of his fellow English-speaking clergy in Ontario. To underscore this point, Quinn noted that not only did his adoptive parents allow him to keep his Irish surname, but:

> They also enrolled me in an English school, run by two old women, who were imbued with a sense of narrow bigotry. One day when the procession of the Blessed Sacrament passed in the street, led by a priest, I wanted to kneel, following the Catholic custom. My mistress reacted violently with an expression I will not repeat. I was forced to obey her, but never returned to the school. My education in English was over. It was not the language of my soul or my freedom!

Nobody listening to Fr Quinn could have been in any doubt that his personal experience of linguistic and religious suppression was being imposed on a much larger scale on French children in Ontario. Not only did Fr Quinn proclaim his solidarity with his French-speaking brethren, however, he also likened their condition to his own. 'The people of French Canada, too, were once abandoned by their mother country, and so they became an orphan', he declared, alluding to the British conquest of Quebec. 'They had imposed on them a foreign language, unknown, and said: "It is not the language of our soul or our freedom"'. In his remembrance of his father's dying utterance, Quinn identified his French parishioners' vulnerability with his own. Just as he was taken in as a helpless orphan by the French-Canadian people, he would now champion their linguistic and religious freedom in turn. 'Dear descendant, God thank you', he avowed, 'for your fathers cared for those starving and shivering with fever, and you are now seeking the right to speak your language, in the name and under the guise of religion, not to have imposed on you a foreign idiom! … These attacks will succeed only in strengthening your national feeling and love of your mother tongue'. Finally, just as his adoptive parents had taught him 'to preserve his heritage and freedom', Fr Quinn implored his audience to 'struggle without fear, like O'Connell and Redmond, because your cause is right and just and like theirs cannot perish'.[43] He thus equated Ireland's demand for Home Rule with the French-Canadian struggle for 'la survivance'. His reclamation of Irish ancestry was inspired by feelings of solidarity with his French-Canadian more than Irish parishioners.

In conclusion, with Fr Quinn's address to the French Language Congress in 1912, the myth of the Famine orphans had come full circle. His struggle to reconcile his Irish ancestry with his parochial duties epitomised a larger conflict between the memory of French-Canadian generosity in adopting Famine orphans and the Irish communal impulse to build institutions like St Patrick's Asylum for their care. By the later nineteenth century, the localised tensions between French-Canadian and Irish Catholic clergy surrounding the creation of the asylum had escalated and spread to the western provinces of Canada in the form of the Manitoba Schools Question and especially Regulation 17 in Ontario, which divided the loyalties of Quinn. As a Famine orphan and French-Canadian priest, he was forced to choose between his Irish compatriots and his French congregation, the land of his nativity and his adoption. He endeavoured to alleviate this tension by alluding to his own life story as a parable of conciliation in which his acceptance by a French-Canadian congregation led him to become their paterfamilias in turn. His story thus helped give shape to the myth of the Famine orphans that emphasised French and Irish affinity to alleviate their deepening sense of rivalry.

The recently unveiled glass wall memorial at the Irish National Famine Museum in Strokestown not only commemorates the 1,490 people like the Quinns and Tighes who were assisted in emigration from the Mahon estate in 1847, it also marks a campaign to trace them and their descendants.[44] There can be little doubt that the Quinn brothers, who left extensive archival records, created much of the cultural and built-up physical heritage in towns like Nicolet and Richmond, Quebec, and who figure proudly in the pantheon of French-Canadian nationalism, should feature prominently in the public memory and help put a face on the so-called '1490'. Much more ephemeral are the archival remains of Famine orphans like James Flood, whom Colin McMahon has tracked on his lonely journey from Strokestown and Liverpool on the *Virginius* to Grosse Île and Montreal in 1847, where he found himself alone and bereft of his family, to be given refuge by the Grey Nuns before becoming a labourer near the city's docks until he disappears entirely from public records in 1875.[45] More uplifting was the return of the descendants of Famine orphan Daniel Tighe during 'the Gathering' festivities in Strokestown in 2013, where they were reunited with their distant cousins and given 'a heroes' welcome' in their 'ancestral home' 166 years after the Famine exodus.[46] Richard Tye, however, was not the first member of the 1,490 Famine cohort to make an emotional return journey to his homeland. Indeed, in 1887, Fr Patrick Quinn himself 'was able to realise the cherished dream of his life and to see once again his native land of Ireland, whence he had gone many years before under such trying conditions'.[47] According to the Hayes papers, 'in Ireland it was his good fortune to find members of his family still living, in the persons of several nieces and nephews. One of them, Mary Quinn accompanied him on his return to Canada and remained with him until his death'. On this occasion, according to the *Roscommon Herald*, the Quinn brothers actually travelled together: 'About 1889, they returned to Ireland and stayed at Duffy's Hotel, Strokestown, from which they visited the track of their birthplace in Kilmacnanny, parish of Curraghroe, Co. Roscommon'.[48]

No doubt there are still descendants of the Quinn families on both sides of the Atlantic who remain to be reunited like the Tyes. Furthermore, although the Quinn brothers, unlike Daniel Tighe, did not leave any offspring themselves, their parishioners regarded themselves as their 'spiritual children' within 'an Irish and French-Canadian family' that is a cultural and institutional legacy of the Famine emigrants. Indeed, the still thriving St Patrick's Society in Richmond, Quebec, is no less an institutional descendant of the Strokestown Famine cohort of 1847 than the progeny of the Tighe family. Likewise, one of the most poignant cultural artefacts from the Strokestown Famine exodus is the little, light brown jacket worn by 6-year-old Thomas Quinn when he arrived in Nicolet from Grosse Île, which is now housed in the town's Archives du Séminaire, and was put on display for the 'Being Irish O'Quebec' exhibit at Montreal's McCord Museum in 2009.[49] As a material cultural artefact, its miniature size confronts viewers with a palpable reminder of the absolute vulnerability of the Irish orphaned children like the Tighe and Quinn siblings who arrived in Quebec and the great distance they travelled not only geographically but also socially to start new lives overseas. Together these cultural, familial, institutional and memorial artefacts and traces comprise much of the legacy of the households and orphaned children who emigrated from Strokestown to Quebec in 1847. The recovery of their legacy has now begun in earnest.

13

Languages of memory: Jeremiah Gallagher and the Grosse Île Famine Monument

Michael Quigley[1]

> Standing on Telegraph Hill, the most elevated point on the island, where it occupies a site of 150 feet square, and overlooking the graves of the Irish dead near its western shore, the monument, which is composed of grey Stanstead granite, rises to a further height of 46 feet 6 inches, so that its total altitude above the level of the river is 140 feet, making it a most conspicuous and striking object … visible for miles up and down the river.[2]

On Sunday 15 August 1909, the Feast of the Assumption, some 9,000 people gathered at Grosse Île – a small island in the middle of the St Lawrence River, 30km downstream from Quebec City – to unveil a memorial to the dead of the Great Irish Famine. The officiates and dignitaries included: Mgr Antonio Sbaretti, the Papal Legate to Canada; Louis Nazaire Bégin, Catholic Archbishop of Quebec; federal and provincial cabinet members, including Charles Murphy, Secretary of State for the Dominion of Canada and Charles Devlin, Quebec Minister of Colonisation and Mines, Sir Charles Fitzpatrick, the Chief Justice of Canada's Supreme Court; Canadian and American leaders in the Ancient Order of Hibernians (AOH) – Matthew Cummings, US National President; Charles J. Foy, Canadian National Director, and Major Edward T. McCrystal, New York. The monument consists of a high Celtic cross, occupying a parcel of land granted, quite extraordinarily, by the Canadian Government to the AOH. The cross was designed and built by Jeremiah Gallagher, County President of the AOH in Quebec. For over a hundred years, from 1832 to 1937, Grosse Île was the quarantine station for arriving immigrants. However, during that period, two years in particular stand out: 1832, the year of the cholera epidemic, and 1847, the year of starvation, typhoid and ship fever, when the medical and administrative facilities of the station were overwhelmed by the flood of Famine emigrants from Ireland. Thousands died, on the ships and on the island – in the late nineteenth century, Quebec historians put the death toll at 12,000.[3]

The four faces of the base of the cross bear inscriptions in English, French and Irish. The rear panel, facing west towards Quebec City and Canada, lists the names of forty-five Catholic priests who ministered to the Famine refugees in 1847, on Grosse Île and elsewhere (including Bishop Michael Power of Toronto and Fr Hugh Paisley in Quebec City), noting those who contracted fever and recovered and those who died 'martyrs to their charity and zeal'.[4] The north and south panels bear similar inscriptions in English and French:

> Sacred to the memory of thousands of Irish emigrants who,
> to preserve the faith, suffered hunger and exile in 1847-48 and,
> stricken with fever, ended here their sorrowful pilgrimage.
> Erected by the Ancient Order of Hibernians in America,
> and dedicated Feast of the Assumption, 1909.

> À la pieuse mémoire de milliers d'émigrés irlandais qui,
> pour garder la foi, souffrirent la faim et l'exil et, victims de la fièvre,
> finirent ici leur douloureux pélérinage, consolés et fortifiés par
> le prêtre canadien.
> Ceux qui sèment dans les larmes moissonneront dans la joie – Ps. XXV, 5.

The Irish inscription, facing east, towards the Atlantic Ocean and Ireland, tells a different story altogether:

> Cailleadh Clann na nGaedhael ina míltibh ar an Oileán
> so ar dteicheadh dhóibh ó dlíghthibh na dtíoránach ngallda
> agus ó ghorta tréarach isna bliadhantaibh 1847-48.
> Beannacht dílis Dé orra.
> Bíodh an leacht so i gcomhartha garma agus onóra dhóibh ó

Ghaedhealaibh Americá.
Go saoraigh Dia Éire.

Translated this reads:

> Children of the Gael died in their thousands on this island,
> fleeing from the laws of foreign tyrants and an artificial famine in the years 1847-48.
> God's blessing on them.
> Let this monument be a token to their name and honour from the Gaels of America.
> God Save Ireland.

In a letter to the AOH convention in Boston in 1900, Gallagher explained the origins and intent of the monument:

> In 1897, mindful of the sad fate of so many of our kindred, and it being the 50th anniversary, our Division of the AOH organized a pilgrimage to the Island. Service for the dead was held and a sermon appropriate to the occasion was preached by the Rev Rector of St. Patrick's Church Quebec. There was a large gathering of our people and the proceedings were most solemn and impressive. However, the desolate and neglected aspect of the particular portion of the Island allotted for the resting place of so many of our blood and our faith seemed to strike us with reproach. After careful consideration of the matter in division meetings we have concluded that it is our duty to see that this hallowed spot where so many thousands of our country people are buried should be reclaimed, be becomingly enclosed and have a befitting monument, with suitable inscriptions (in Gaelic, in Latin, French and English) not only 'in memoriam' of the unhappy Irish exiles but also as protest against the misgovernment of which they were the victims.[5]

The AOH concurred and voted that $5,000, as well as a levy of 10 cents per member, should be granted for the project. The monument was designed – in pencil sketches on his kitchen wall – by Jeremiah Gallagher. His son, Dermot, recalled that his ambitions for the cross expanded as the money flowed in. Curiously, in her definitive history of Grosse Île, Jeremiah's granddaughter, the island's foremost historian, Marianna O'Gallagher, declared that 'the inscriptions on three sides offer the same message, in Gaelic, in English and in French'.[6] Clearly, for reasons of diplomacy or otherwise, this statement is misleading, for it elides the strikingly different message in the Irish text. Three elements in the Irish inscription unmistakably identify its Fenian origins and intentions: 'laws of foreign tyrants', 'artificial famine' and the slogan adopted after the execution of the Manchester Martyrs in 1867, 'God save Ireland'.

To use an anachronism, Gallagher's Irish inscription can be described as 'speaking truth to power', and in this case, it is plain that he understood that the truth – his rendering of Mitchel's dictum that God sent the blight, but the English made the Famine – needed to be disguised in Irish. Bearing this in mind, Peter Toner wrote, 'Gallagher demands some attention'.[7] Born in Macroom, County Cork, in 1837, Jeremiah and his brother Francis (always known, apparently, as Jerry and Frank), left Ireland for North America around 1858. They both spent some time in the USA – in Jeremiah's case perhaps only a few months, because Marianna reports that his first job in Canada was as a time-keeper on the construction site for the Victoria Bridge in Montreal in 1859. It was while digging the foundations for the bridge that the workers on the site uncovered the mass graves of the Famine victims at Point Saint Charles, and they prevailed upon the contractors to create the monument which is still there – a huge black boulder dredged up from the St Lawrence riverbed, inscribed:

> To Preserve From Desecration The Remains of 6,000 Immigrants A.D. 1847-48 This Stone Is Erected By The Workers Messrs Peto Brassey And Betts Employed In The Construction Of The Victoria Bridge A.D. 1859

Did Jeremiah Gallagher play some role in this development? Although Marianna was unable to find his face in the (very few) photographs of the occasion of the unveiling of the monument, reading backward from the rest of his career suggests that he would have been involved.

In the early 1860s, Frank Gallagher was already established in Quebec City, teaching at the Sillery Academy. Jeremiah joined him on the staff at the academy and furthered his own education at the Séminaire de Québec and the Ste-Anne-de-la-Pocatière college, where he took degrees in engineering and surveying. He also taught at the college (English, mathematics and Irish). On the face of it, one might be tempted to see a contradiction between the Catholic piety and republican militancy reflected in the inscriptions on the Celtic cross. A closer look at the central character dispels this notion. That Jeremiah Gallagher was both a devout Catholic and a committed republican cannot be doubted; his energy and capacity for work were exemplary; and finally, his diplomacy must have been remarkable. Both facets of his character – as displayed on the cross at Grosse Île – are amply embodied in his life and work. For forty years, from 1869 to the unveiling of the cross at Grosse Île, Gallagher balanced full-time employment as a highly regarded waterworks engineer and surveyor for the City of Quebec with unremitting organisation and agitation for physical force nationalism in a long series of Irish organisations in the city. All the while, he was an active member of his parish, and a trustee and accountant on the management committee overseeing St Brigid's Orphanage. Later in life, he joined the St Patrick's Total Abstinence Society and his parochial League of the Sacred Heart of Jesus. Finally, 'as a member of the Quebec Catholic School Commission he was instrumental in having St. Mary's Academy built for the growing Irish population'.[8]

Among the Irish organisations in Quebec in which Jeremiah and his brother Frank played leading roles, several can, with some confidence, be identified with the Fenians. This most certainly applies to the Hibernian Benevolent Society in which they held executive positions from the mid-1860s into the 1880s. Toner reports that Frank Gallagher was 'the most likely candidate for having been Centre of the Quebec Fenian Circle in 1865'.[9] It is very probable that the St Patrick's Literary Institute and Debating Club was at least a Fenian front. The Emmet Skirmishing Club – the name speaks for itself – fundraising for O'Donovan Rossa in the Quebec suburb of Sillery in 1876, left no records but it is probably safe to assume that the Gallaghers had a hand in it. They also organised two 'constitutional' bodies with the clear intention of steering them along physical force lines. In 1881, Jeremiah was busy, and it seems comfortable, with the New Departure. On 7 July, for example, Fanny Parnell (Charles Stewarts' sister) visited Quebec 'and was received by the Irish with an address of welcome composed and read by Jeremiah Gallagher'.[10] Indeed, he was a member of the Quebec delegation to meetings with Parnell himself in Montreal. In November 1881, as vice president of the Quebec branch of the Land League, he attended the concurrent conventions in Chicago of the Land League and the United Brotherhood (Clan na Gael's underground organisation), at which he was named District Member (Officer Commanding) for Canada.[11] The Brotherhood's directive to its members was plain:

> When Land Leagues are formed ... no pains should be spared to secure control of these movements or organizations by members of the UB. A few of our good men working in concert can always manage to secure this control. Lest these organizations may at any time prove dangerous rather than assistants to our work, we should so secure the control of their managements as to be able to disband them if that ever became necessary.[12]

It is certain that neither Frank nor Jeremiah needed instruction in this tactic – a decade earlier, in 1873, the Quebec Hibernian Benevolent Society (of which Jeremiah was corresponding secretary), created a branch of the Home Rule League, ostensibly in support of Isaac Butt and the Irish Party. Toner puts the case tactfully: 'It is probable that the Quebec Hibernians preferred to control any branch of the Home Rule League in their city rather than allow moderates to organize and control one'.[13]

A British spy at the United Brotherhood convention in 1881 reported that Jeremiah Gallagher was 'a violent Fenian' who had knowledge of dynamite activities in Montreal.[14] Presumably, this refers back to the Emmet Skirmishing Club. In 1888, another British spy reported that Gallagher had sent $1,000 to Clan na Gael 'to be used for the "appliances of civilization", i.e explosion and outrages'.[15] As to the violence, however, an anecdote by Marianna O'Gallagher belies the suggestion:

> One story, mysterious because of one pronoun, illustrates the kind of man he was. At some point in the Irish Republican Brotherhood history Jeremiah had received a message to go to Levis and meet a certain man, evidently a spy sent to report on Quebec activities. Jeremiah was to 'deal with him'. According to [his son] Dermot, Jeremiah recognized the person in question, followed him onto the Levis ferry, stood beside him at the rail and contemplated his next move. 'He was to throw him overboard, but he thought of his eternal soul and he could not do it'. Since the story was told in the third person, I cannot determine whether Grandfather Jeremiah was thinking of his own soul, or that of the spy he was supposed to deal with.[16]

On the other hand, there is no doubt whatever that Jeremiah Gallagher was a physical force nationalist. As his son Dermot told Peter Toner, while Jeremiah was prepared to work with the moderate Home Rulers for Irish freedom, he 'was convinced that only armed rebellion could achieve that end'.[17] And Marianna added a qualification: 'Jeremiah believed that only force could ever remove the British from Ireland, but that violence on this side of the ocean was pointless and out of place' – that is, the lesson drawn by all the Canadian Fenians from the failures of John O'Neill's incursions into Canada between 1866 and 1870.[18]

In the 1880s, after the demise of the Land League, Jeremiah Gallagher was connected to two more explicitly Fenian organisations: he was on the executive of the Irish National Association in 1883, and the Canadian delegate to the Irish National Brotherhood's convention in 1887. Rounding up this list is the Quebec branch of the Ancient Order of Hibernians – founded by Jeremiah Gallagher in 1895 and directed by him thereafter. Why did Jeremiah Gallagher initiate and lead the AOH in Quebec – an organisation which, in Ireland at least, was a rival of the Fenian Irish Republican Brotherhood? For the same reason he founded and led all the other Irish and Catholic bodies he was involved in – to forward the republican project. An illumination of this can be found in *Devoy's Post Bag*, in a letter from Robert Johnston of Belfast, a Fenian leader and member of the IRB's Supreme Council, to John Devoy in New York, urging the latter to encourage the American AOH to support their counterparts in Ireland:

> A considerable number of our friends throughout the country have lately joined these divisions, with the object of leading them in the right direction, and the support and approval therefore of the Order in American would be an encouragement to them in their efforts.[19]

Indeed, the AOH conceded this point too: 'At the same time, the militant Fenian Brotherhood began to infiltrate the AOH and run their people for top AOH offices.'[20] The AOH in Quebec City was Jeremiah Gallagher's last Fenian nest.

While Marianna O'Gallagher may have been discreet in her book, in biographical notes on her grandfather for the Vancouver Irish Memorial website and in the speech to the AOH in 2009, she was more forthright:

> The Gaelic inscription was written by Jeremiah, but he called upon a well-known scholar of the day, Major McCrystal of the 69th Regiment of New York, the Fighting 69th, to read it and comment. In their letters Jeremiah insists on the term artificial famine, to describe the situation of 1847. From the letters one can gather that these men were in touch with people in Dublin too, over the inscription.[21]

On the occasion of the inauguration of the monument, Jeremiah Gallagher, accompanied by his wife Marianne (Corrigan) and his children, Mary and Dermot, remained silent. In his stead, three luminaries of the AOH spoke: Charles J. Foy, National Director for Canada, Matthew Cummings, National President (from the US) and Gallagher's correspondent and collaborator, Major Edward T. McCrystal, who spoke in Irish. Foy's remarks elaborated the English and French inscriptions:

> Suffice it to say that we assemble here today for the purpose of showing our respect to the dead who died for Ireland; also to show our appreciation for the devotion which they had to Faith and Fatherland ... Never did Ireland draw a sword unjustly, but solely in the defence of the highest, holiest and best of causes – the Altar of God and the Altar of the Nation.[22]

Matthew Cummings was made of sterner stuff, but he too stayed close to the party line:

> Today we are assembled to unveil and dedicate this magnificent Celtic cross to the memory of those poor Irish immigrants who were hunted like wild beasts from their native land, and who died victims of pestilence and fever on this bleak island, far from the land they loved, far from friends and relatives, their only comfort, their religion, and sight of the brave and saintly Catholic priest bringing the last sacraments of the Church to them.[23]

The last word, however, went to McCrystal, and to Fenianism:

> Before the majority of us were born, more than twelve thousand people perished and were buried here ... They were fleeing from the laws of tyrants, from famine, and from plague ... They were destroyed by England but we are hopeful – no, we are certain – that they found

> peace with God in heaven. Our native country is in bondage still and our people are ruined. But I say to you, and listen to me, as certain as we are here, as certain that there is the memorial above our poor destroyed dead, the Gaels will not forget what the Englishman did to us and the day will come – the day of the revenge of God – and on that day, some of us will be ready to strike a blow for Ireland and her cause.[24]

Jeremiah Gallagher died in Quebec City in August 1914, two years before the blow was struck in Dublin at Easter 1916. But his legacy remained – physically in the monument he created, but also in the continuation in subsequent commemorations of both faces of his personality, Catholic and republican. Having inaugurated the pilgrimage to the island in 1897, Gallagher's section of the AOH continued to organise regular visits to the island. Marianna O'Gallagher told the AOH centennial pilgrimage in 2009 that:

> Through the 1920s and 1930s there was a pilgrimage to Grosse Île from Quebec City almost every summer. The exceptions occurred when a ship came in with contagion on board. Grosse Île remained an active quarantine station until 1935. If the island happened to be in full use for quarantine the Irish of Quebec were asked to cancel their pilgrimage.[25]

At the end of the shipping season in 1937, the quarantine station on the island was finally closed after 105 years. From 1939 until 1957, Grosse Île was transferred from Public Works to the Department of National Defence as an animal disease and bacteriological warfare research station. In 1957, jurisdiction changed hands again, passing to the Department of Agriculture. In response to the growing demand among Canadian farmers for improved cattle and sheep stock lines, the island became a quarantine station again, this time for four-legged immigrants. The commemorative plaque on the island records that 'the exotic animal disease research laboratory and training centre, opened following the 1952 foot-and-mouth epidemic, remained in use until 1988'. For all of this period, access to the island was prohibited under the Official Secrets Act. Grosse Île's modern incarnation began with the closure of the animal quarantine station, and the island's identification by the National Monuments and Sites Board as a National Historic Site in 1974. The driving force behind the earliest campaign to preserve the island's history was Jeremiah's granddaughter, Marianna, who first visited the island in 1972, when she found the mass burial ground completely overgrown with shrubs and brambles. But even after the proclamation of the National Historic Site and the transfer of jurisdiction to Parks Canada, access remained restricted.

In the 1980s, after a brief contest with the Canadian Government, the Irish organisations in Montreal, including the AOH, revived the tradition of the annual summer pilgrimage to Grosse Île. A key figure in the revival was another republican from County Cork, Denis Leyne, a banker from Youghal. In 1989, to mark the eightieth anniversary of the inauguration of the Celtic Cross, the pilgrimage featured an address by Dr Edward J. Brennan, Irish Ambassador to Canada, who recalled the Famine in words which captured both contemporary and modern Irish understanding of the Great Hunger, and echo O'Gallagher's inscription:

> During the years 1845–47, with the failure of the potato crop, which was their principal means of sustenance, the Great Famine struck the people of Ireland. As an immediate consequence over a million people were to perish from hunger, disease and lethal fever ... The Great Famine was Ireland's holocaust, and the slow-sailing vessels ... became coffin ships in which many would-be emigrants died a lingering and painful death. The Great Famine condemned the Irish to be the first boat people of modern Europe.[26]

Five years later, in August 1994, Mary Robinson, then President of Ireland, made a state visit to Canada. In a striking diplomatic gesture, her first engagement was to visit Grosse Île. Echoing Dr Brennan, she stressed that while the failure of the potato was a 'natural disaster' across Europe, 'in Ireland it took place in a political, economic and social framework that was oppressive and unjust'. A keynote of her address was a lyrical tribute to the island:

> Islands possess their own particular beauty and Grosse Île is no exception. But Grosse Île – Oileán na nGael / l'île des irlandais – is special. I believe that even those coming to this beautiful island, knowing nothing of the tragedy which occurred here, would sense its difference. I am certain that no one knowing the story could remain unaffected. This is a hallowed place.[27]

The lyricism was tempered by harsh reality. Robinson continued:

> We are not here to honour an island, however beautiful, but to recall a human tragedy of appalling dimensions. The relics of this tragedy are all too visible. The mass graves marked with the small white crosses assume an added poignancy in their obvious anonymity. And yet we know that each one represents not just the untimely death but the collapse of dreams, not of one person, but of many.[28]

President Robinson reiterated the recognition of the 'debt of gratitude' owed by the Irish community to all those who succoured the Famine victims in 1847, and especially the very many Québecois families, most of them Francophone, who gave homes to the estimated 1,600 children orphaned that summer. In this, she again recalled the original unveiling ceremony, echoing the note struck by Fr Edward Maguire, AOH chaplain, in 1909, when he had called forward an elderly lady, Madame Roberge – one of those orphans. In keeping with the tenor of her presidency, President Robinson also emphasised that:

> What is particularly Irish about this occasion is not simply the nationality of those who died here. It is also our sense, as a people who suffered and survived, that our history does not entitle us to a merely private catalogue of memories. Instead, it challenges us to consider, not just little Ellen Keane, the four year old child who was the first to die here in 1847, but the reality that children are usually the first victims of famine and displacement.[29]

The Irish Government's continued interest in and commitment to Grosse Île brought the next President of Ireland, Mary McAleese, to the island as the Canadian Government's guest of honour at the inauguration, in 1998, of a new monument commissioned by Parks Canada – a stylised, roofless passage tomb, surrounded by glass panels inscribed with names of the identifiable dead of 1847 (and subsequent years). Shortly before Marianna O'Gallagher died in May 2010, President McAleese wrote to her:

> *Il n'y a pas de mots pour décrire la dette immense et la gratitude que le peuple irlandais et tous ceux de descendance irlandaise ont envers vous. Vous nous avez apporté honneur et une grande fierté par votre engagement extraordinaire envers la cause de Grosse-Île.* [There are no words to describe the immense debt

> of gratitude that the people of Ireland and all those of Irish descent owe to you. You have brought great honour and pride to us by your extraordinary devotion to the cause of Grosse Île].[30]

Irish-Canadian collaboration continues and in May 2009 Eamon Ó'Cuiv, TD, then Minister for Community, Rural and Gaeltacht Affairs, visited Grosse Île to mark the centenary of the cross by opening a permanent display in the Lazaretto, a restored hospital shed, the only building remaining from 1847.

However, it was not all plain sailing and the example of Grosse Île highlighted that commemoration can be a stormy sea. When, for example, in 1992, Parks Canada published a *Development Concept* for Grosse Île, they made the tactless mistake of referring to the Famine refugees as 'British immigrants', and declared:

> It is also felt that there should not be too much emphasis on the tragic aspects of the history of Grosse Île. On the contrary, the painful events of 1832 and 1847, which have often been overemphasized in the past, need to be put back into perspective, without robbing them of their importance.[31]

Within weeks, Denis Leyne and this writer co-founded Action Grosse Île in Toronto to galvanise and co-ordinate Irish-Canadian (and subsequently, broader Irish diaspora) response to this proposal. It rapidly became clear that there was widespread opposition to what was viewed as a denial or even betrayal of Jeremiah Gallagher's Irish-language vision. Gallagher's monument featured centrally in the campaign – the cross itself as the committee's logo and the Irish language plaque as the face of a protest postcard addressed to the Canadian Prime Minister. In particular, the campaign focused explicitly on the Irish inscription, favouring its secular message over the more religious version in English and French. During the course of public hearings, stretching from Charlottetown, Prince Edward Island in the east through Montreal and Toronto, where the uproar was so loud as to demand three days of hearings, to Vancouver on the west coast, hundreds of Irish organisations, large and small, GAA clubs, county associations, charitable and community groups, were joined by municipalities, MPs and provincial legislators, in a parade of opposition. In virtual unanimity, more than 200 activists called on Parks Canada to withdraw the offending words – and the implication behind them. The campaign included a television documentary, 'Hunger's Children', aired several times by the CBC, Canada's national broadcaster, petitions, letter-writing and three successful fundraising concerts. In March 1994, the Action Grosse Île committee was honoured as one of *Irish America* magazine's 'top ten' influential bodies. The result – after a campaign lasting four years – was the announcement on St Patrick's Day 1996 by Minister of Canadian Heritage, Sheila Copps, MP, that the island would henceforth be known as 'Grosse Île and the Irish Memorial'. Looking back to their progenitor, Jeremiah Gallagher, Action Grosse Île declared this a vindication of a century-long struggle to assert the importance of Grosse Île as the most important Great Famine site outside of Ireland.[32]

The campaign had included several organised visits to Grosse Île. The first involved close collaboration with the Irish Ambassador, Antóin MacUmfraigh, in planning for Mary Robinson's visit. The trip to the island was preceded by a two-day Famine Walk of 40km, from Quebec City to Berthier-sur-Mer, modelled on the pattern established in Ireland by Don Mullan, executive director of Concern Worldwide. In Berthier, the civic reception of the walkers underlined that '*l'île des irlandais*' was the local appellation, Parks Canada's resistance notwithstanding. On the island, Mullan posed a crucial question:

> Why aren't there Italian, Portuguese, Maltese, Norwegian pilgrimages to Grosse Île? Why haven't the presidents of other nations visited Grosse Île on the first day of their visits to Canada? The answer is simple. It's because to no other Canadian community does Grosse Île have the same evocative memory as Grosse Île has to the Irish.[33]

Action Grosse Île mobilised over 400 supporters to travel to the island, including several families of direct descendants of those who had survived passage through quarantine in the summer of 1847.

In 1997, as both a celebration of the Canadian Government's decision of the previous year, and a demonstration of the strength of the movement behind the political campaign, Action Grosse Île and the AOH combined their efforts to bring an unprecedented number of visitors to the island. More than 2,000 people, travelling on cruise ships chartered from Quebec City, attended two days of events marking the 150th anniversary of 1847 and the centenary of Jeremiah Gallagher's original initiative. The events on the island included a series of talks at the important sites (the cross, the Lazaretto, and the mass graveyard);

an ecumenical service for the repose of the souls of the dead, concelebrated by Mgr. André Gaumont, Catholic Archbishop of Sherbrooke and the Revd Bruce Stavert, Anglican Bishop of Quebec; the laying of wreaths at the cross by the AOH, Comhaltas Ceoltóiri Èireann and the GAA, among others, and the planting of a living memorial – an oak tree – in honour of those buried on the island. Next day, after the dedication of a plaque to the Irish in Quebec at Old St Patrick's church, organised by Marianna O'Gallagher, the participants marched in formation to the Basilica of Notre Dame de Québec to High Mass celebrated by Mgr. Fortier, former Archbishop of Sherbrooke. The final event was a secular celebration of thanksgiving to the people of Quebec for their succour of the Irish of 1847, hosted by Action Grosse Île.

Annual pilgrimages to the island continue to be organised by the Montreal division of the AOH. Their most recent large-scale effort was held to mark the centenary of the inauguration of Gallagher's Celtic cross in 2009. On that occasion, two commemorations were held. The AOH ceremony included an open-air Mass and the rededication of the cross at the summit of Telegraph Hill, with speeches from Victor Boyle, president of the Montreal branch of the AOH, who organised the commemoration, and Declan Kelly, the Ambassador of Ireland to Canada. A week later, the Irish Protestant Benevolent Society of Montreal held its own ceremony, to rededicate the Anglican chapel on Grosse Île, recently restored by the society.[34]

Although Action Grosse Île declared a victory in 1996, the island remains a contested zone. It is certainly, in Mary Robinson's words, 'a hallowed place' to the Irish communities in Canada and the USA, but in two vital respects Parks Canada remains obdurate. Their guides are evidently directed to maintain a very explicit, conservative commitment to the number of 5,424 as the Irish death toll from 1847 – this being the number inscribed by Dr George Douglas, Medical Director in 1847, on the monument he erected to the four doctors who died working with him in that year. The number is carved in stone, but is almost certainly an underestimate, by perhaps as many as several thousand. And while the guides accurately describe the appalling conditions on the island and the coffin ships, and the inadequate and ill-informed medical care, not a word of the background and source of the tragedy, in Ireland, is permitted. Neither John Mitchel's dictum nor Jeremiah Gallagher's version are entertained. One is led to ask: does the opinion of the mother country still hold sway?

Notes

CHAPTER 1

1 David Fitzpatrick, 'Irish emigration in the later nineteenth century' in *Irish Historical Studies*, xxii, no. 86 (Sept. 1980), p. 137.

2 See Gerard Moran, *Sending Out Ireland's Poor: Assisted Emigration to North America in the Nineteenth Century* (Dublin, 2004).

3 *Report from the Select Committee on Colonization; Together with the Minutes of Evidence*, HC 1890 (354), xli, p. 352, q. 5680.

4 Peter Gray, *The Making of the Poor Law in Ireland, 1815-43* (Manchester, 2009), pp. 38, 48–9. For the overall debate on the merits for and against assisted emigration before the Famine see Moran, *Sending out Ireland's Poor*, pp. 17–34.

5 *Report of George Nicholls esp to his Majesty's Principal Secretary of State for the Home Department on Poor Laws, Ireland*, HC 1837 (69), li, p.32; Sir G. Nicholls, *A History of the Irish Poor Law* (London, 1856), pp. 185–6.

6 Nicholls, *History of the Irish Poor Law*, pp. 226–7 and Christine Kinealy, *This Great Calamity: The Irish Famine 1845-52* (1995), pp. 307–8.

7 Moran, *Sending Out Ireland's Poor*, pp. 125–6 and Gerard O'Brien, 'The new Irish poor law in pre-famine Ireland: a case study' in *Irish Economic and Social History*, xii (1985), pp. 41–3. Between 1832 and 1836 nearly 3,000 girls, most of them Irish were sent to Australia, with the cost incurred by the colonial authorities from the proceeds of the sale of Crown lands in the colony. For more see Malcolm Campbell, *Ireland's New Worlds: Immigrants, Politics and Society in the United States and Australia, 1815-1922* (Madison, Wisconsin, 2008), p. 17.

8 *A Return of the Number of Persons who have Emigrated at the Expense of the Different Poor Law Unions in Ireland, in the Years 1844, 1845 and 1846*, HC 1847 (255), lvi, p.1; Trevor Parkhill, '"Permanent deadweight": Ulster female emigration' in *Ulster Local Studies*, 10:1 (1988), p.20; idem, '"Permanent deadweight": emigration from Ulster workhouses during the famine' in E. Margaret Crawford (ed.), *The Hungry Stream* (Belfast, 1997), p. 68–9.

9 *Return on Number of Persons who Emigrated at the Expense of the Different Poor Law Unions*, p.1.

10 *Fourth Report from the Select Committee of the House of Lord appointed to Inquire into the Operation of the Irish Poor Law, and the Expedience of Making Amendments to its Enactment, together with the Minutes of Evidence*, HC 1849 (365), xvi, q. 764, qs 7861-2.

11 *Third Report from the Select Committee on the Poor Law (Ireland)*, HC 1849 (93), xv, p. 81, q. 1808.

12 *Tuam Herald*, 11 November 1848.

13 *Eight Report from the Select Committee on the Poor Law (Ireland)*, HC 1849 (237), xv, p. 74, q. 6985.

14 *Nation*, 1 August 1846.

15 Nicholls, *History of the Irish Poor Law*, p. 341.

16 See Moran, *Sending Out Ireland's Poor*, especially chapter three.

17 *Eight Report from the Select Committee on the Poor Law* (Ireland), HC 1849 (237), pp. 73-4, qs 6979-80; *Report of the Select Committee of the House of Lords on Colonization from Ireland, together with the Minutes of Evidence*, HC 1847 (737), vi, p. 192, qs 1885-7.

18 *Limerick Reporter and Tipperary Vindicator*, 31 October & 14 November 1851.

19 *Seventh Report of the Select Committee on the Poor Laws (Ireland)*, HC 1849 (194), pp. 32-3, q. 5328.

20 Joseph Robbins, 'Emigration of workhouse children to Australia' in John O'Brien and Pauric Travers (eds), *The Irish Emigrant experience in Australia* (Dublin, 1991), p.34. See also Parkhill, 'Famine emigration from Ulster', p.44.

21 Moran, *Sending out Ireland's Poor*, p.138.

22 Michelle O'Mahony, *Famine in Cork City: Famine life in Cork Union Workhouse* (Cork, 2005), p. 105.

23 *Limerick and Clare Examiner*, 15 November 1848.

24 *Mayo Telegraph*, 7 May 1851.

25 For more on the experience at Grosse Île see Marianna O'Gallagher & Rose Masson Dompierre, *Eyewitness Grosse Île, 1847* (Quebec, 1995).

26 *Report of the Select Committee on the Poor Law (Ireland)*, HC 1861 (408), x, p. 215, q. 4368.

27 O'Mahony, *Famine in Cork City*, pp. 41-2, 52 and Daniel Grace, *The Great Famine in Nenagh Poor Law Union, Co. Tipperary* (Nenagh, 2000), p. 125.

28 *Fourth Report from the Select Committee of the House of Lords Appointed to Inquire into the Operation of the Irish Poor Law, and the Expediency of Making any Amendments to its Enactment, together with the Minutes of Evidence*, HC 1849 (365), xvi, pp. 754-5, q. 7793.

29 *Tuam Herald*, 11 November 1848.

30 *Tipperary Vindicator*, 15 January 1848.

31 Moran, *Sending Out Ireland's Poor*, p.140.

32 Minutes for the week ending 16 June 1849 (Galway County Library, Galway Poor Law Minute book, November 1848-August 1849). In Cahirciveen workhouse the female inmates were also employed making fishing nets as it was argued it would help in the development of the local fishing industry, *Fourth Report from the Select Committee of the House of Lords appointed to Inquire into the Operation of the Irish Poor Law*, HC 1849 (365), xvi, p. 727, q. 7512.

33 Minute book for the week ending 27 March 1852 (Galway County Library, Galway Poor Law Minute book, January-July 1852).

34 *Tipperary Vindicator*, 5 February, 15 November & 20 December 1848; *Tuam Herald*, 11 March 1848 and *Galway Vindicator*, 29 September 1849.

35 Between 1848 and 1854 fifty-five riots have been catalogued in the workhouses resulting in the military and constabulary having to be called in to restore order, see Gerard Moran, 'Disorderly conduct: riots and insubordination in the workhouses during the Famine' in John Cunningham and Niall Ó Ciosáin (eds), *Society, Culture and Politics in Ireland since 1750: Tributes to Gearóid Ó Tuathaigh* (forthcoming, Dublin, 2015). See also Virginia Crossman, *The Irish Poor Law in Ireland, 1838-1948* (Dundalk, 2006), pp. 32-3.

36 Ó'Murchadha, *Sable Wings over the Land: Ennis, County Clare and its Wider Community during the Great Famine* (Ennis, 1998), p. 186.

37 *Report of the Select Committee on the Poor Law (Ireland)*, HC, 1861 (408), x, p.215, q. 4368.

38 See Moran, *Sending Out Ireland's Poor*, pp. 123-6.

39 James Buchanan to Lord Monteagle, 10 November 1833 (NLI, Monteagle papers, Ms 13,400/2/1).

40 *Report from the Select Committee of the House of Lords on Colonization from Ireland*, p. 314, q. 3041.

41 *Seventh Report of the Select Committee on the Poor Laws (Ireland)*, HC 1849 (194), xv, pp. 31-2, q. 5325.

42 For the Peter Robinson scheme see, Moran, *Sending Out Ireland's Poor*, pp. 21-9 and Wendy Cameron, 'Selecting Peter Robinson's emigrants' in *Histoire Sociale/Social History*, 9:17 (May, 1976).

43 See Richard Reid, *Farewell My Children: Irish Assisted Emigration to Australia, 1848-70* (New South Wales, 2011), pp. 141-52.

44 *Fourth Report from the Select Committee of the House of Lords appointed to Inquire into the Operation of the Irish Poor Law, and the Expediency of Making any Amendment to its Enactment, together with the Minutes of Evidence*, HC 1849 (365), p. 764, qs 7808-9; p. 765, qs. 7871-2.

45 *Limerick and Clare Examiner*, 3 June 1848; *Galway Vindicator*, 7 June 1848; *Sligo Journal*, 5 May 1848; *Tipperary Vindicator*, 9 September 1848. It was alleged that the New Ross vice-guardians put the most attractive girls on the list in the hope they would get marriage parrtners, but they were not necessarily the best candidates for emigration, see *Galway Vindicator*, 26 September 1849.

46 Thomas Reddington to Lord Claredon, 9 December 1848 (Bodlien Library, box 24, Irish department, Clarendon papers).

47 See Patrick Duffy, 'Emigration and the estate office in the mid-nineteenth century: a compassionate relationship, in E. Margaret Crawford (ed.), *The Hungry Stream: Essays on Emigration and Famine* (Belfast, 1997) and Moran, *Sending Out Ireland's Poor*, pp. 58-9.

48 *Limerick Reporter*, 9 June 1854. See also *Leinster Express*, 26 January 1850.

49 O'Murchadha, *Sable Wings over the Land*, p. 224 and Kilrush Poor Law Guardians Minute Book, 7 February 1852 (Clare County Library).

50 *Ninth Report from the Select Committee on the Poor Laws (Ireland)*, HC 1849 (259), xv, p. 87, qs 8381-4

51 *Seventh Report from the Select Committee on the Poor Laws (Ireland)*, HC 1849 (194), xv, p, 89, q. 5674.

52 *Limerick Reporter and Tipperary Vindicator*, 8 January 1850.

53 S.C. O'Mahony, 'Emigration from the workhouses of Limerick, 1848-1859' in Liam Irwin, Gearóid Ó Tuathaigh and Matthew Dottern (eds), *Limerick History and Society* (Dublin, 2009), p. 444.

54 *Ennintymon Union, Minutes of Board Meetings, 1839-1850*, book 9, meeting of 1 May 1850 (Ennistymon, 1992), p. 59.

55 *Limerick Reporter and Tipperary Vindicator*, 4 March 1850. The only evidence of Poor Law engagement in emigration to Argentina came in the late 1880s when twenty-eight female orphans were sent from Ballymahon workhouse.

56 *Nation*, 9 February 1850.

57 Anne Lannigan, 'Tipperary workhouse children and the Famine' in *The Tipperary Historical Journal* (1995), p. 71.

58 Grace, *Great Famine in Nenagh Poor Law Union*, p. 198 and Chris O'Mahony, 'Emigration from the Tippeary workhouses, 1848-58' in *Tipperary Historical Journal* (1994), p. 105.

59 O'Murchadha, *Sable Wings over the Land*, p. 224.

60 Stephen de Vere to Monteagle, dated 23 December 1847 (NLI, Monteagle papers, Ms13,400/11/47). For the landlord emigration schemes during the Famine see Moran, *Sending Out Ireland's Poor*, p, p 35-69.

61 R.A. Duncan to A.C. Buchanan, 28 April 1852 in *Papers Relative to Emigration to the North American Colonies*, HC 1852-3 (1650), xlviii, p. 24.

62 Ibid., dated 10 June & 25 August 1852, p. 25, 27.

63 See the correspondence between A.C. Buchanan and W.P. O'Brien in ibid., p. 29. *Tuam Herald*, 24 July 1852. The issue of assisting the orphans had first been raised in Roscommon Union by the guardian, Mr West, in February 1850 who argued it would be a major saving for the union as it would cost only £4 per person. See *Nation*, 23 February 1850.

64 *Nation*, 6 March 1852.

65 *Tuam Herald*, 9 April 1853.

66 A.C. Buchanan to Earl of Elgin and Kincardine, 31 December 1851 in *Papers Relative to Emigration to the North American Colonies*, HC 1851 (1474), xxxiii, p. 21; *Limerick Reporter and Tipperary Vindicator*, 24 February 1852.

67 *Limerick Reporter and Tipperary Vindicator*, 30 June 1854.

68 See Judy Collingwood, 'Irish workhouse children in Australia' in O'Brien and Travers, *Irish Emigrant Experience in Australia*, pp. 47–50; Reid, *Farewell my Children*, pp. 46–61.

69 Dympna McLoughlin, 'Superflous and unwanted deadweight: the emigration of nineteenth-century Irish pauper women' in Patrick O'Sullivan (ed.), *The Irish Worldwide: Irish Women and Irish Migration*, iv (London, 1995), p. 80.

70 For an example of the negative reaction of the Canadian authorities to the appearance of the emigrants from the Palmerston estate see Adam Gerrie to Lord Gray, 1 December 1847 in *Papers Relative to Emigration to the British Provinces in North America*, HC 1847–8 (932), xlvii, p.36. See also Thomas Power, 'The Palmerston estate in County Sligo: improvements and emigration before 1850' in Patrick Duffy and Gerard Moran (eds), *To and from Ireland: Planned Migration Schemes, c 1600-2000* (Dublin, 2004), pp. 127–30.

71 McLoughlin, 'Superflous and unwanted deadweight', p. 79.

72 South Dublin Poor Law Union minute book, January – December 1854 (NAI). Janette Butler was eventually employed to travel with the girls.

73 *Papers Relative to Emigration to the North American Colonies*, HC 1852–3 (1650) lxviii, p. 22.

74 M.H. Perley to the Hon. John R. Parlelow in *Copies or Extracts of any Despatches Relative to Emigration to British North America,* HC 1851 (1474), xxxiii, p. 33. See also *Nation*, 19 July 1851.

75 Gerard Moran, 'Shovelling out the permanent deadweight: the Cork workhouse paupers sent to New Brunswick during the Great Famine' (*Canadian Journal of Irish Studies*, forthcoming).

76 *Report from the Select Committee on the Poor Law (Ireland); Together with the Proceedings of the Committee, Minutes of Evidence and Appendix*, HC 1861 (408), x, p. 214, q. 4364.

77 *Copies of Extracts of Despatches Relative to Emigration to the North American Colonies*, HC 1860 (606), xliv, p. 5.

78 Dympna McLoughlin, 'Workhouses and Irish female paupers, 1840–1870' in Maria Luddy and Cliona Murphy (eds), *Women Surviving: Studies in Irish Women's History in the Nineteenth and Twentieth Centuries* (Dublin, 1990), pp. 120–1.

79 *Copies or Extracts of Despatches relative to Emigration to the North American Colonies*, HC 1861 (186), xl, p.7.

CHAPTER 2

1 Allen Levine, 'Bawlf, Nicholas' in Ramsay Cook and Jean Hamelin (eds), *Dictionary of Canadian Biography* (22 vols, Toronto, 2003), xiv, pp. 39–40.

2 Ibid.

3 Ontario Canada Catholic Church Records [Drouin Collection] 1747–1967 available at www.ancestry.ca [accessed 15 July 2013].

4 Levine, 'Bawlf, Nicholas', p. 39.

5 A.G. Levine, 'The Bawlf Family: a vanished legend in the Winnipeg grain trade' in *Manitoba Business*, 6, vii (1984), pp. 33–8.

6 Levine, 'Bawlf, Nicholas', p. 39.

7 Patrick Duffy, 'Disencumbering our crowded places: theory and practice of estate emigration schemes in mid-nineteenth century Ireland' in *To and from Ireland: Planned Migration Schemes c. 1600-2000* (Dublin, 2004), pp. 79–104.

8 *Nation*, 6 November 1847. For an in-depth study of the Mahon estate see Ciarán Reilly, *Strokestown and the Great Irish Famine* (Dublin, 2014).

9 Tyler Anbinder, 'From Famine to Five Points: Lord Lansdowne's Irish tenants encounter America's most notorious slum' in *The American Historical Review*, cii (2002), pp. 351–87; p. 360.

10 It was not until 1867 that the name Canada was applied to the country with the passing of the British North American Act of that year. For the purposes of this article I will refer to the country as Canada throughout.

11 The third Earl Fitzwilliam had married Lady Anne Wentworth in 1744 but died prematurely in 1756 at the age of 37. Thus, with the death of Charles Watson-Wentworth, Anne's brother in 1782, the Wentworth estates, which were located in Ireland and England, passed to the couple's eldest son, William, who became the fourth earl. See Charles Mosley (ed.), *Burke's Peerage, Baronetage and Knightage* (105th edition, London, 1975), p. 1021.

12 Jim Rees, *Surplus People from Wicklow to Canada* (Cork, 2014), p. 6.

13 Terence Dooley, *The Big Houses and Landed Estates of Ireland: A Research Guide* (Dublin, 2007), p. 20.

14 Rees, *Surplus People*, p. 7.

15 Asa Briggs, *The Age of Improvement: 1783-1867* (2nd ed., Essex, 2000), p. 10.

16 William Nolan, 'Land and landscape in County Wicklow *c.* 1840' in Ken Hannigan and William Nolan (eds), *Wicklow History and Society: Interdisciplinary Essays on the History of an Irish County* (Dublin, 1994), pp. 649-93; p. 657.

17 John Bateman, *The Great Landowners of Great Britain and Ireland* (4th edition, New York, 1970), p. 168.

18 Nolan, 'Land and landscape in County Wicklow *c.* 1840', p. 657.

19 Charles Taylor, *The Literary and Panorama and National Register: Comprising Interesting Intelligence from the Various Districts of the United Kingdom; the British Connections in and from all Parts of the World* (7 vols, London, 1818), p. 686.

20 Mr Symme to Earl Fitzwilliam, 16 October 1817 (SA, WWM/F/79/68).

21 William Haigh, Malton to Earl Fitzwilliam, 27 October 1822 (SA, WWM/F/79/149).

22 See for example Rental account books, 1835-6 (SA, WWM/A/924) which gives details of tenants leaving that year.

23 *The Times*, 19 December 1825; 20 March 1826.

24 'Household and other expenses of the Earl Fitzwilliam in connection with his estate in County Wicklow, 1831-33' (NLI, Fitzwilliam papers, MS 4963).

25 Rees, *Surplus People*, p. 25.

26 'The McCabe List: the early Irish in the Ottawa valley, 5 February 1829' at www.dippam.ac.uk/ied/records/22293.pdf [accessed 12 July 2014].

27 Ibid.

28 Ibid., entry 233.

29 'Memoranda dealing with tenancies on the estate of Earl Fitzwilliam in County Wicklow, 1796-1841' (NLI, Fitzwilliam papers, MS 4,948).

30 'Maps of the Shillelagh estate of the Right Hon. Earl Fitzwilliam by Rogers and Smith, 1842' (NLI, Fitzwilliam Papers, Mss. 22,020-1).

31 Ibid.

32 *Evidence taken before Her Majesty's Commissioners of Inquiry into the state of the law and practice in respect to the occupation of land in Ireland, part III,* p. 533, HC 1845 (657), item 5, 6 and 14.

33 Ibid.

34 Ibid.

35 Ibid.

36 Fitzwilliam Irish estate rentals, 1836-37 (SA, WWM/A/925, entries 211-31).

37 Ibid., 1837-38 (SA, WWM/A/926, entries 186 and 188).

38 Ibid., 1838–39, (SA, WWM/A/927, entry 198).

39 Ibid., 1839–40, (SA, WWM/A/928, entries 260, 267 and 268).

40 Ibid., 1841–42, (SA, WWM/A/930 entry, 264).

41 Gerard Moran, *Sending Out Ireland's Poor: Assisted Emigration to North America in the Nineteenth Century* (Dublin, 2004), p. 65.

42 Rees, *Surplus People*, p. 33.

43 Letter-book of Robert Chaloner, agent of the Fitzwilliam estate March 1842–January 1853 (NLI, Fitzwilliam papers, MS 3987, entry dated 12 March 1846).

44 Rees, *Surplus People*, pp. 34–5.

45 'Emigration books in respect of the estate of Earl Fitzwilliam in County Wicklow' (NLI, Fitzwilliam papers, Mss. 4974–5).

46 Ibid.

47 Ibid., 1848, entry 44.

48 Ibid., 1849, entry 61.

49 Ibid. See entries for 1848 (38); 1851 (22); 1856 (2) and 1847 (198).

50 Ibid. See entries for 1851 (63 & 69).

51 Ibid. See for example entries for 1847 (111–116). In these cases property and land amounted to a cabin and a kitchen garden, and in the rare instance a few acres.

52 Rees, *Surplus People*, p. 125.

53 Fitzwilliam Irish estate rental, 1846–47 (SA, WWM/A/935).

54 Rees, *Surplus People*, p. 127.

55 Ibid.

56 'Emigration books in respect of the estate of Earl Fitzwilliam in County Wicklow' (NLI, Fitzwilliam papers, Mss. 4974–5, entry 1854:49). See also Rees, *Surplus People*, pp. 124–5.

57 Ibid.

58 General correspondence of Charles Wentworth Fitzwilliam, Fifth Earl, dated March 1849 (SA, WWM/G/83/519).

59 1861 Census of Canada East, West, New Brunswick & Nova Scotia, Frontenac Co. Pittsburgh Township, ON, available at www.ancestry.co.uk [accessed 5 March 2015].

60 'Emigration books in respect of the estate of Earl Fitzwilliam in County Wicklow' (NLI, Fitzwilliam papers, Mss. 4974–5, entry 1849:86).

61 1851 Census of Canada East, West, New Brunswick & Nova Scotia, Huron Co., ON, Canada West, p. 19 available at www.ancestry.co.uk [accessed 5 March 2015].

62 1861 Census of Canada East, West, New Brunswick & Nova Scotia, Huron Co., ON, Canada West, p. 9 available at www.ancestry.co.uk [accessed 5 March 2015].

On 25 August 1870, the couple's ninth child Ellen Jane Redmond died aged 8 years. Her cause of death was listed as 'amputation of limb'. See 1871 Census of Canada, Schedule No. 2, p. 1.

63 Ibid., see Schedule no. 3 p. 1 for information on real estate and agricultural machinery.

64 'Emigration books in respect of the estate of Earl Fitzwilliam in County Wicklow' (NLI, Fitzwilliam papers, Mss. 4974–5, entry 1852:4).

65 See '1861 Census of Canada East, West, New Brunswick & Nova Scotia, Enumeration District 1, Barrie, Simcoe Co., ON, p. 9' available at www.ancestry.co.uk [accessed 5 March 2015].

66 'Emigration books in respect of the estate of Earl Fitzwilliam in County Wicklow' (NLI, Fitzwilliam papers, Mss. 4974–5, entry 1847:10, 24, 62, 33).

67 *Brandon Daily Sun*, 27 January 1915.

68 Ibid.

69 Cormac Ó Gráda, *The Great Irish Famine* (Cambridge, 1995), p. 8.

CHAPTER 3

1 William Murphy, 'Conceiving Irish diasporas: Irish migration and migrant communities in the modern period' in Leeann Lane, Mary McAuliffe and Katherine O'Donnell (eds), *Palgrave Advances Irish History* (Hampshire, 2009), p. 127.

2 'Guide to the Public Records of Tasmania Section Three. Convict Department: Archives Office of Tasmania.' www.linc.tas.gov.au/tasmaniasheritage/popular/convicts/convictdept/appendix-d [accessed 12 February 2012].

3 Hamish Maxwell-Stewart, *Closing Hell's Gates: The Death of a Convict Station* (New South Wales, 2008), p. 76. See also David Kent and Norma Townsend, *The Convicts of the Eleanor: Protest in Rural England, New Lives in Australia.* (London, 2002), p. 155.

4 Rena Lohan, 'The treatment of women sentenced to transportation and penal servitude 1790–1898' (Unpublished M. Litt Thesis, Trinity College Dublin, 1990), p. 65.

5 John Williams, *Ordered to the Island: Irish Convicts & Van Diemen's Land* (Sydney, 1994), p. 168.

6 Peter King, 'Decision makers and decision making in the English criminal law, 1750–1800' in *The Historical Journal*, no. 1 (1984), p. 42.

7 David Meredith and Deborah Oxley, 'Condemned to the colonies: penal transportation as the solution to Britain's law and order problems' in *Leidschrift*, vol 22, no. 1. (2007), p. 31. See also Hamish Maxwell-Stewart 'Convict transportation from Britain and Ireland 1615–1870' in *History Compass*, 8 (2010), p. 11.

8 Robert Hughes, *The Fatal Shore: A History of the Transportation of Convicts to Australia, 1787-1868* (London, 2003), pp. 68–9.

9 Charles Bateson, *The Convict Ships* (Glasgow, 1969), pp. 393–4.

10 L.L. Robson, *The Convict Settlers of Australia: An Enquiry into the Origin and Character of Convicts Transported to New South Wales and Van Diemen's Land 1787-1852* (Melbourne, 1965), p. 65.

11 Bláthnaid Nolan, 'Power, Punishment and Penance: An archival analysis of the transportation of women from Grangegorman in Dublin to Hobart Town in Van Diemen's Land (Tasmania) 1844–1853' (Unpublished PhD Thesis, UCD, 2013), p. 191.

12 Deborah Oxley, 'Living standards of women in pre-Famine Ireland' in *Social Science History*, 28, no. 2 (2004), pp. 271–95.

13 Catherine Fleming, *The Transportation of Women from Kildare to Van Diemen's Land in 1849* (Dublin, 2012), p. 18.

14 Convict Reference File, CON41/1/14, image 16 (Archives of Tasmania). See also CON15/1/4, images 136–137.

15 Fleming, *The Transportation of Women from Kildare*, pp. 18–9. Placing any children in a workhouse seems an expensive decision for the authorities. Had they all been allowed to travel with her, it may have been financially beneficial for the colony to place them in the Orphan Schools in order to have them apprenticed out.

16 Ibid., p. 18.

17 MFS 59/38, Convict Reference File 1847 B3, p. 4 (NAI).

18 Ibid.

19 Correspondence on the subject of convict discipline and transportation (785), *Parliamentary Papers* (Great Britain) 1847, p. 58. See also Kirsty Reid, *Gender, Crime and Empire* (Manchester & New York, 2007), p. 208. Byron's husband Peter was also transported for this crime, embarking on the *Blenheim* in 1849, as the transportation of all male convicts had been suspended for two years from late 1846 to 1848.

20 Convict Reference File, CON41/1/14, image 16 (Archives of Tasmania).

21 Ibid.

22 Kay Daniels, *Convict Women* (Sydney, 1998), p. 71.

23 Tony Rayner, 'Historical survey of the female factory: Historic site cascades Hobart' in *National Parks and Wildlife Service, Tasmania: Occasional Papers*, no. 3, (1981), p. 25.

24 Daniels, *Convict Women*, p. 116.

25 Convict Reference File, CON41/1/14, image 16 (Archives of Tasmania).

26 Joyce Purtscher, *Children in Queen's Orphanage, Hobart Town, 1828-1863* (Hobart, 1993).

27 *Leinster Express*, 3 April 1847. Quoted in Fleming, *The Transportation of Women from Kildare*, p. 31.

28 MFS 59/38, CRF 1847 C101, p. 1 (NAI).

29 Ibid.

30 Ibid.

31 Ibid.

32 John Braithwaite, 'Crime in a convict Republic' in *Modern Law Review* 64, no. 1 (2003), p. 33.

33 Convict Reference Files, CON41/1/14, image 30 (Archives of Tasmania).

34 Ibid.

35 Ian Duffield, 'Stated This Offence': High-Density Convict Micro-Narratives' in Lucy Frost & Hamish Maxwell Stewart (eds), *Chain Letters. Narrating Convict Lives* (Melbourne, 2001), p. 135.

36 Convict Reference Files, CON41/1/14, image 30 (Archives of Tasmania).

37 Ibid. Oatlands, situated in central Van Diemen's Land, is north of Hobart and almost halfway between Hobart and Launceston. Instructions such as 'to be assigned to the interior' or 'not to be allowed enter service in Hobart' appear frequently in the *Conduct Registers* of the women.

38 Convict Reference Files, CON41/1/14, image 30 (Archives of Tasmania).

39 MFS 59/12, CRF 1844 C 38, p. 1 (NAI).

40 Ibid.

41 Ibid.

42 King, 'Decision makers and decision making in the English criminal law, 1750-1800' in *The Historical Journal*, no. 1 (1984), p. 46.

43 MFS 59/12, CRF 1844 C 38, p. 1 (NAI).

44 Ibid.

45 Mary Cullen, 'Breadwinners and Providers: Women in the Household Economy of Labouring Families 1835-1836' in Maria Luddy & Cliona Murphy (eds), *Women Surviving: Studies in Irish Women's History in the 19th and 20th Centuries* (Dublin, 1990), p. 99.

46 If there is a case in which the judge is not in effect the final arbiter, that would demand some scrutiny as it would be very much be an exception to the rule.

47 MFS 59/12, CRF 1844 C 38, p. 2 (NAI)

48 Ibid.

49 Convict Reference Files, CON41/1/5, image 19 (Archives of Tasmania).

50 Ibid. Obviously delivery of illegitimate children was not limited to the 18 to 34-year-olds.

51 Along with 119 other women, and their twenty-eight children, she embarked on board the barque, the *Greenlaw*, from Kingstown on 5 March 1844 for Van Diemen's Land.

52 MFS 59/27, CRF 1843 L16, p. 1 (NAI).

53 Convict Reference Files, ADM101/30/3, Surgeon's Report, *Greenlaw* (Archives of Tasmania).

54 Convict Reference Files, CON41/1/2, image 70 (Archives of Tasmania).

55 Ibid.

56 Convict Reference Files, CON41/1/33, image 164 (Archives of Tasmania).

57 Dympna McLoughlin, 'Superfluous and unwanted deadweight: the emigration of nineteenth-century Irish pauper women' in Patrick O'Sullivan (ed.) Irish Women and Irish Migration (London & New York, 1995), p. 74.

58 Convict Reference Files, CON41/1/33, image 164 (Archives of Tasmania).

59 Ibid.

CHAPTER 4

1 *Boston Bee*, 17 April 1847.

2 In what follows, I will survey the various narrative motifs individually, with the understanding that the characteristics of more than one narrative might appear in a single story, and with the recognition that many of the themes in these narratives overlap and merge in their attempt to offer a comprehensive account of the Famine in Ireland.

3 *New Hampshire Sentinel*, 24 September 1845. Almost all the newspapers of the period were four-page publications, with a significant portion of column space devoted to advertising and official notices. I have refrained, then, from including page numbers, as most of the stories of Ireland and the Famine are easily found by identifying the section devoted to foreign news.

4 *Barre Patriot*, 26 September 1845; *The Times Picayune*, 30 September 1845. Steamship traffic from Liverpool and Queenstown to an American port (usually Boston or New York via Halifax) normally took between eighteen and twenty-one days, and thus news from Ireland was reported in America about three weeks after events occurred.

5 *Tri-Weekly Ohio Statesman*, 8 October 1845.

6 *Berkshire County Whig*, 27 November 1845.

7 *Pittsfield Sun*, 27 November 1845.

8 *Baltimore Sun*, 5 November 1845.

9 *Boston Daily Atlas*, 24 November 1845.

10 *Baltimore Sun*, 7 November 1845 & *Barre Patriot*, 7 November 1845.

11 *Southern Patriot*, 25 November 1845. See also *New Hampshire Sentinel*, 26 November 1845.

12 This point is made clear by comparison of the stories about Ireland with stories in American newspapers from a year earlier that reported on the outbreak of the potato blight in the USA. Those stories, common between September and December 1844, remarked on the potato failure as a scientific mystery, an agricultural loss, and an economic setback, but never as a threatened human tragedy. While the 'calamity' was one 'of sufficient importance to claim the attention of scientific men,' (*New Hampshire Sentinel*, 18 September 1844) it was nowhere reported as the precursor to a famine. For other stories on the 1844 potato blight in the USA, see for example: *Barre Gazette*, 20 September 1844; *Southern Patriot*, 27 September 1844; *Boston Daily Atlas*, 1 October 1844; *Vermont Gazette*, 8 October 1844; *Pittsfield Sun*, 10 October 1844 and *New York Herald*, 13 November 1844.

13 *Baltimore Sun*, 8 December 1845 (italics in the original). Scepticism about the reports from Ireland of a pending famine was not uncommon. See for example, *The Boston Atlas* of 7 January 1846. The *Sun* later addressed the concerns about exaggeration directly. On 7 March 1846, quoting from the *London Times* of 6 February, they wrote: 'There appears to be no longer a doubt that an almost universal famine is about to visit Ireland. Such is the dire reality which has been looming upon us through the midst of Irish rumour and English incredulity these four or five months, and which is now too distinct and too palpable to be any longer denied'. See also *Southern Patriot*, 9 March 1846; *New Hampshire Sentinel*, 11 March 1846; *Wisconsin Democrat*, 4 April 1846 & *Farmer's Cabinet*, 25 June 1846.

14 *Ohio Statesman*, 10 December 1845, (emphasis in the original).

15 *Emancipator*, 7 January 1846 (italics in the original).

16 *Vermont Watchman and State Journal*, 10 June 1847.

17 *New York Tribune*, 12 February 1847.

18 *New Hampshire Sentinel*, 10 February 1847.

19 *Wisconsin Democrat*, 20 March 1847.

20 *Constitution*, 24 February 1847.

21 *Friends' Review*, 6 November 1847. The quoted scripture passage is Romans 11:33.

22 *Christian Secretary*, 9 April 1847.

23 *New York Evangelist*, 20 May 1847.

24 *Christian Inquirer*, 3 July 1847. The scripture passage is Jeremiah 10:33. See also Psalm 127:1.

25 *Boston Transcript*, 3 October 1846. See Genesis 47:15.

26 *Albion*, 20 February 1847.

27 *Barre Patriot*, 12 February 1847.

28 *Boston Times*, 23 April 1847.

29 Sean Ryder, 'Reading Lessons: Famine and the *Nation* 1845-1849' in Christopher Morash and Richard Hayes (eds), *Fearful Realities: New Perspectives on the Famine* (Dublin, 1996), p.158.

30 The personification of famine and pestilence draws on biblical images familiar from 2 Samuel 24:15-17, and 1 Chronicles 21:9-13.

31 *Baltimore Sun*, 26 November 1846.

32 Ibid., 27 November 1845.

33 *Southern Patriot*, 18 December 1845.

34 George Potter, *To the Golden Door: The Story of the Irish in Ireland and America* (Boston, 1960), pp. 454-5.

35 *Trenton State Gazette*, 1 March 1847.

36 *Baltimore Sun*, 17 February 1847.

37 *Barre Patriot*, 12 March 1847. See also *New York Herald*, 11 February 1847; *Wisconsin Democrat*, 22 May 1847 & *United Brethren's Missionary Intelligencer*, (annual) 1847.

38 *Southern Patriot*, 17 February 1847.

39 *Farmer's Cabinet*, 4 March 1847. See also *Boston Evening Transcript*, 18 February 1847 & *Charleston Mercury*, 27 May 1847. Boston papers, in particular, also gave extensive coverage to the voyage of the *Jamestown*, and the gratitude of the Irish for the relief sent in that vessel by the citizens of Boston. See for example the *Boston Daily Times*, 6 May 1847 and *Boston Evening Transcript*, 7 & 8 May 1847. An account of the *Jamestown* voyage is contained in Edward Laxton, *The Famine Ships: The Irish Exodus to America* (New York, 1998), pp. 49-60.

40 *New Hampshire Sentinel*, 30 December 1845.

41 *Berkshire Whig*, 16 April 1846.

42 *Times Picayune*, 26 August 1848.

43 *Wisconsin Democrat*, 1 May 1847. See also *Boston Emancipator*, 6 January 1846; *Catholic Telegraph*, 2 April 1846; *New Englander*, April 1847 & *National Era*, 6 May 1847.

44 *Farmer's Cabinet*, 4 March 1847.

45 *Saturday Rambler*, 27 February 1847.

46 *Barre Patriot*, 26 March 1847. See also the *Wisconsin Democrat*, 26 June 1847.

47 *New Hampshire Sentinel*, 8 April 1847.

48 *Baltimore Sun*, 12 November 1847.

49 *Boston Atlas*, 18 November 1846.

50 *Ohio Statesman*, 11 November 1847.

51 *New Hampshire Sentinel*, 10 June 1847. See also *Boston Atlas*, 11 November & 7 December 1846.

52 *New York Tribune*, 19 February 1847.

53 *Christian Advocate, and Journal*, 20 December 1849.

54 *Zion's Herald and Wesleyan Journal*, 14 April 1847.

55 *Christian Observer*, 8 January 1848.

56 *Friends' Review*, 22 December 1849.

57 *Farmer's Cabinet*, 4 March 1847. See also *The Independent*, 7 June 1849.

58 *Barre Patriot*, 12 March 1847.

59 *New Hampshire Gazette*, 25 May 1847. See also *Christian Observer*, 29 January 1847; *Baltimore Sun*, 30 January 1847; *Trenton State Gazette*, 8 February 1847; *Morning News*, 12 February 1847; *New London Morning News*, 17 February 1847; *Wisconsin Democrat*, 23 March 1847; *Pennsylvania Freeman*, 25 March 1847; *Emancipator*, 31 March 1847; *National Era*, 1 April 1847 & *Constitution*, 11 August 1847.

60 *Boston Evening Transcript*, 2 February 1847.

61 See Sean Ryder, 'Reading Lessons: Famine and the *Nation* 1845–1849' in Christopher Morash and Richard Hayes (eds), *Fearful Realities: New Perspectives on the Famine* (Dublin, 1996), p. 161.

62 *Baltimore Sun*, 25 February 1847.

63 *Boston Evening Transcript*, 29 January 1847. The account by Cummins, from a letter he sent to the Duke of Wellington, is among the most well-known testimonies of the gruesome effects of the Famine, along with the reports of Dr. Daniel Donovan, and those of Revd Elihu Burritt.

64 'Speech of Henry Clay at New Orleans', as reported in the *Hudson River Chronicle*, 23 February 1847.

65 Clark was referring to writing about American slavery. See Elizabeth Clark, '"The sacred rights of the weak": Pain, sympathy, and the culture of individual rights in Antebellum America' in *Journal of American History*, 82 (1995), p. 465.

66 *Boston Transcript*, 31 July 1847.

67 *New York Tribune*, 19 August 1847. See also *Weekly Ohio State Journal*, 4 June 1847; *Trenton State Gazette*, 20 August 1847 & *Southern Patriot*, 23 August 1847.

68 To gather data on the waning interest in the Famine as a news story, I searched the database of 'America's Historical Newspapers' (see www.readex.com/content/americas-historical-newspapers) using the terms 'Ireland' and 'Famine'. In the period of 1 January 1845 to 31 December 1847, there were 691 articles returned, of which 351, more than half, were published

between January and August 1847 (more than half of those, 179, appeared between January and March 1847, a national rate of publication for that period of almost two stories per day). From 1 September 1847 to the end of that year, there were only sixty-seven articles on the Famine, a national rate of publication that had dropped to about one story every two days. For the entire year of 1848, there were 176 articles on the Irish Famine, continuing the publication rate of roughly one story every two days. In 1849, the number of stories dropped to 104 for the entire year.

69 *New London Morning News*, 26 January 1847. See also *Boston Evening Transcript*, 25 January 1847.

70 *Emancipator*, 9 June 1847.

71 *Farmer's Cabinet*, 4 March 1847.

72 Ibid., 1 April 1847.

73 *New Hampshire Sentinel*, 1 July 1847.

74 *Trenton State Gazette*, 19 July 1847.

75 *Boston Bee*, 20 February 1847.

76 *Trenton State Gazette*, 10 June 1847.

77 *Boston Bee*, 9 January 1847.

78 *Boston Evening Transcript*, 10 June 1847.

79 Ibid., 21 June 1847.

80 Ibid., 26 June 1847.

CHAPTER 5

1 James Driscoll Dependent Mother's Pension File, WC 29,468 (National Archives and Records Administration, Washington, DC *Civil War 'Widow's Pension' Applications*, Records of the Department of Veterans Affairs, Record Group 15). [Hereafter cited as NAR *'Widow's Pension'* Applications].

2 Susannah J. Ural, *The Harp and the Eagle: Irish-American Volunteers and the Union Army, 1861-1865* (New York, 2006), p. 2; David T. Gleeson, *The Green and the Gray: The Irish in the Confederate States of America* (Chapel Hill, 2013), p. 60. The figure of 150,000 for the Irish in Northern armies is almost certainly too low, as it excludes Irish in branches of the service such as the navy and regular army. A comprehensive new analysis of these figures is required.

3 Campbell Gibson and Emily Lennon, 'Tech Paper 29: Table 4. Region and Country or Area of Birth of the Foreign-Born Population, With Geographic Detail Shown in Decennial Census Publications of 1930 or Earlier: 1850 to 1930 and 1960 to 1990' available at www.census.gov/population/www/documentation/twps0029/tab04.html [accessed 14 June 2014].

4 See for example Christian G. Samito, *Becoming American under Fire: Irish Americans, African Americans, and the Politics of Citizenship during the Civil War Era* (Ithaca, 2011); Susannah J. Ural, *The Harp and the Eagle: Irish-American Volunteers and the Union Army, 1861-1865* (New York, 2006); William L. Burton, *Melting Pot Soldiers: The Union Ethnic Regiments* (New York, 1998) & Gleeson, *The Green and the Gray.*

5 Maris A. Vinovskis, 'Have Social Historians Lost the Civil War? Some Preliminary Demographic Speculations' in M.A. Vinovskis (ed.), *Toward a Social History of the American Civil War: Exploratory Essays* (Cambridge, 1990), p. 22. It should be noted that this and subsequent acts applied only to those in Union service. Former Confederates and their families would not become entitled to Federal pensions until 1958, although many would receive pensions through the state in which they lived.

6 Megan J. McClintock, 'Civil War Pensions and the reconstruction of Union families' in *The Journal of American History*, 83, 2 (1996), pp. 456-80.

7 Vinovskis, 'Have social historians lost the Civil War?, pp. 26-7.

8 Amy E. Holmes, 'Such is the price we pay: American Widows and the Civil War Pension system' in Vinovskis (ed.), *Toward a Social History of the American Civil War*, p. 174. This figure is based on the long-held number of *c.*618,000 dead from the conflict. Recent work by J. David Hacker has suggested the actual figures could be as high as 750,000. See J. David Hacker, 'A Census-Based Count of the Civil War Dead' in *Civil War History*, 57, 4 (2011), pp. 307-48.

9 Holmes, 'Such is the price we pay', p. 174.

10 Ibid., p. 172.

11 McClintock, 'Civil War Pensions and the Reconstruction of Union Families', p. 463.

12 Holmes, 'Such is the price we pay', p. 172.

13 Ibid., p. 173.

14 McClintock, 'Civil War Pensions and the Reconstruction of Union Families', p. 468.

15 Holmes, 'Such is the price we pay', p. 173.

16 Richard O'Neill Widow's Pension File, WC 36,780 (NARA *'Widow's Pension'* Applications).

17 Ibid., Michael Sullivan Widow's Pension File, WC 119,143.

18 Ibid., John Murphy Widow's Pension File, WC 4,653.

19 Ibid., Richard Cochran Widow's Pension File, WC 14,220.

20 Ibid., Patrick Scanlan Widow's Pension File, WC 83,473.

21 Ibid., Colin Cairns Widow's Pension File, WC 112,001.

22 Ibid., Patrick Martin Widow's Pension File, WC 60,522.

23 Ibid., James Butler Widow's Pension File, WC 90,849.

24 Ibid., John Daly Widow's Pension File, WC 126,148.

25 Ibid., John D. Murray Widow's Pension File, WC 22,113.

26 McClintock, 'Civil War Pensions and the Reconstruction of Union Families', p. 467.

27 Patrick O'Dea Dependent Mother's Pension File, WC 92,882 (NARA, 'Dependent Mother's' Applications).

28 Ibid., Denis Horan Dependent Mother's Pension File, WC 123,532.

29 Ibid., John Sheehan Dependent Mother's Pension File, WC 34,550.

30 Ibid., Matthew Henry Dependent Mother's Pension File, WC 109,272.

31 Ibid., Jeremiah Durick Dependent Father's Pension File, WC 109,831.

32 Ibid., Daniel Divver Dependent Mother's Pension, WC 11,048.

33 Ibid., Patrick Kelley Dependent Mother's Pension File, WC 22,521 (NARA, 'Dependent Mother's Applications').

34 Patrick Finan Dependent Father's Naval Certificate, File 2867 (NARA, 'Dependent Father's Applications').

35 1860 US Census Population Schedule (NARA, M653). They had four children, all born in America–Anthony, aged 15; Mary aged 12; Ann aged 6 and 4 year old Charles. Catherine Doyle, aged 10 also lived with the family.

36 New York State, *Annual Report of the Adjutant General of the State of New York for the Year 1897* (Albany, 1898).

37 Alfred Seelye Roe, *The Ninth New York Heavy Artillery* (Worcester, 1899), pp. 181–2.

38 New York State, *Annual Report of the Adjutant General of the State of New York for the Year 1897*.

39 Charles O'Reilly Widow's Pension File, WC 82,767 (NARA, 'Widow's Pension Applications').

40 *Auburn Daily Bulletin*, 7 March 1873.

CHAPTER 6

1 'Baptismal Certificate of Patrick A. Collins, Parish of Fermoy, Ireland' (Boston College Archives, (BCA), Collins Collection, Box Four, No. 20).

2 Patrick A. Collins, 'Autobiography', (BCA, Collins Collection, Box Four, No. 11). This relatively short document consists of a handwritten account on sheets and scraps of brown paper and was prepared by Collins for a newspaper in the 1890s. They were later used by the *Boston Globe* at the time of his death in September 1905. There are no page numbers.

3 Ibid.

4 Thomas Gallagher, *Paddy's Lament: Ireland, 1846-1847* (New York, 1982), pp. 223-9. The length of the journey may have seemed interminable. For example, the *Boston Pilot* reported that 'after a tedious passage of 20½ days' one such Famine-era vessel, *The Hibernia*, arrived in Boston. See *Boston Pilot*, 1 January 1848.

5 Lemuel Shattuck, *Report to the Committee of the City Council appointed to obtain the Census of Boston for the Year 1845* (Boston, 1846), p. 157. See also Oscar Handlin, *Boston's Immigrants: A study in acculturation* (revised edition, New York, 1975), p. 88.

6 Report of the Committee on the Expediency of Providing Better Tenements for the Poor (Boston, 1846), 6. For more on the city's development at this time see Lawrence W. Kennedy, *Planning the City upon a Hill: Boston since 1630* (Amherst, 1992), pp. 53-60.

7 Handlin, *Boston's Immigrants*, p. 88.

8 Collins, 'Autobiography'.

9 Thomas H. O'Connor, *The Hub: Boston Past and Present* (Boston, 2001), pp. 150-6.

10 *Boston Pilot*, 17 July 1847.

11 John R. Mulkern, *The Know-Nothing Party in Massachusetts: The Rise and Fall of a People's Movement* (Boston, 1990), p. 76.

12 Thomas H. O'Connor, *The Boston Irish* (Boston, 1995), pp. 69-70.

13 Thomas H. O'Connor, *Fitzpatrick's Boston: 1846-1866* (Boston, 1984), pp. 145-8 and Robert H. Lord, John E. Sexton, and Edward T. Harrington, *History of the Archdiocese of Boston*, (3 vols, New York, 1944), ii, pp. 669- 72.

14 *Boston Pilot*, 13 May 1854.

15 Ibid.

16 Ibid.

17 Collins, 'Autobiography'.

18 Ibid.

19 Ibid.

20 Ibid.

21 Ibid.

22 Thomas H. O'Connor, *South Boston, My Home Town: The History of an Ethnic Neighbourhood* (Boston, 1988), pp. 36-7 & pp. 61-3.

23 Collins, 'Autobiography'.

24 Alvin Jackson, *Ireland: 1798-1998* (Malden, 1999), p. 93.

25 R.V. Comerford, *The Fenians in Context: Irish Politics and Society 1848-1882* (Dublin, 1985), p. 48.

26 R.V. Comerford, 'Conspiring Brotherhoods and Contending Elites, 1857-63' in W.E. Vaughan (ed.), *A New History of Ireland V: Ireland Under the Union I, 1801-1870* (Oxford, 1989), p. 419.

27 Kevin Kenny, *The American Irish: A History* (New York, 2000), p. 128.

28 T.W. Moody, 'Fenianism, Home Rule and the Land War, 1850-1891' in W. Moody, F.X. Martin, and Dermot Keogh, with Patrick Kiely (eds), *The Course of Irish History* (5th edition, Lanham, 2012), p. 243.

29 Eileen Reilly, 'Modern Ireland: An Introductory Survey' in J.J. Lee and Marion R. Casey (eds), *Making the Irish American: History and Heritage of the Irish in the United States* (New York, 2006), p. 97.

30 Ibid.

31 See Iver Bernstein's *The New York City Draft Riots: Their Significance for American Society and Politics in the Age of the Civil War* (Oxford, 1990), especially pp. 23-34.

32 *Boston Pilot*, 18 July 1863.

33 Jack Tager, *Boston Riots: Three Centuries of Social Violence* (Boston, 2001), pp. 135-45.

34 E.R.R. Green 'The Beginnings of Fenianism' in T.W. Moody (ed.), *The Fenian Movement* (Cork, 1968), p. 20.

35 William D'Arcy, *The Fenian Movement in the United States: 1858-1886* (Washington DC, 1947), p. 36.

36 Ibid., p. 47.

37 Collins, 'Autobiography'.

38 Sister M. Jeanne d'Arc O'Hare, CSJ, 'The Public Career of Patrick Andrew Collins' (Unpublished Ph.D. thesis, Boston College, 1959), p. 36.

39 *Irish-American*, 17 June 1865.

40 *Boston Pilot*, 18 March 1865.

41 Ibid., 25 March 1865.

42 Ibid., 11 March 1865.

43 Ibid.

44 *Irish American*, 15 April 1865.

45 *Boston Pilot*, 3 June 1865.

46 O'Connor, *Fitzpatrick's Boston*, pp. 92-4 and James Hennessey, SJ, *American Catholics: A History of the Roman Catholic Community in the United States* (New York, 1981), p. 164.

47 Michael P. Curran, *Life of Collins with some of his most Notable Public Addresses* (Massachusetts, 1906), pp. 21-2.

48 D'Arcy, *The Fenian Movement in the United States*, p. 35.

49 Reilly, 'Modern Ireland', p. 98.

50 D'Arcy, *The Fenian Movement in the United States*, p. 81.

51 *Boston Post*, 18 October 1865.

52 D'Arcy, *The Fenian Movement in the United States*, p. 81.

53 O'Hare, 'Career of Patrick Andrew Collins', pp. 54–5.

54 Ibid., p. 58.

55 Kenny, *The American Irish*, p. 129.

56 Thomas N. Brown, *Irish-American Nationalism, 1870-1890* (Philadelphia, 1966), p. 40.

57 Kerby A. Miller, *Emigrants and Exiles: Ireland and the Irish exodus to North America* (Oxford, 1985), p. 337. Miller revisited his words in 2008: 'Middle-class Irish Americans usually explained nationalist aspirations in bourgeois and assimilationist terms … For instance, nationalist spokesmen such as Young Irelander Thomas Francis Meagher and Fenian leader Patrick Collins … used the reputation and followings created through their championship of Ireland's "sacred cause" to advance their own political careers'. See Kerby Miller, *Ireland and Irish America: Culture, Class, and Transatlantic Migration* (Dublin, 2008), p. 269.

58 Collins, 'Autobiography'.

59 Ibid.

60 F.S.L. Lyons, *Charles Stewart Parnell* (Dublin, 2005), p. 298. Collins had been appointed Brigadier General – Judge Advocate General in the Massachusetts State Militia in 1875 and thereafter was referred to as General Collins. According to his friend and biographer he 'never relished the title'. See Curran, *Life of Collins*, p. 36.

61 Curran, *Life of Collins*, p. 64.

62 Collins, 'Autobiography'.

CHAPTER 7

1 Kieran Furey, *The History House* (Roscommon, 2008), p. 11.

2 Robert James Scally, *The End of Hidden Ireland: Rebellion, Famine & Emigration* (New York, 1996).

3 Charles Orser Jr. (ed) *Unearthing Hidden Ireland: Historical Archaeology at Ballykilcline, County Roscommon* (Bray, 2006).

4 For more information on the society see www.ballykilcline.com.

5 Furey, *The History House*, p. 11.

6 Scally, *The End of Hidden Ireland*, pp. 102–3.

7 Ibid., pp. 9–22, 63–105 and Mary Lee Dunn, *Ballykilcline Rising: From Famine Ireland to Immigrant America* (Amherst, 2008), pp. 21–35. See also Ciarán Reilly, *Strokestown and the Great Irish Famine* (Dublin, 2014), p. 24.

8 Dunn, *Ballykilcline Rising*, p. 23.

9 Scally, *The End of Hidden Ireland*, p. 124.

10 Ibid.

11 Scally, *The End of Hidden Ireland*, p. 125.

12 Ibid., p. 126.

13 Ibid., pp. 125–127.

14 Charles E. Orser Jr., 'Seeking hidden Ireland: history, meaning, and material culture', in Orser, *Unearthing hidden Ireland*, pp. 219–20.

15 Ibid., p. 35.

16 Ibid., pp. 18, 36.

17 Katherine L. Hull, 'Forget me not: the role of women in Ballykilcline', in Orser, *Unearthing Hidden Ireland*, p. 159.

18 Ibid., pp. 150–3.

19 Ibid., pp. 154–8.

20 Ibid., p 158.

21 Ibid., p. 159.

22 Quoted in Ann Coleman, *Riotous Roscommon: Social Unrest in the 1840s* (Dublin, 1999), p. 11.

23 Quoted in Margaret Lynch-Brennan, *The Irish Bridget: Irish Immigrant Women in Domestic Service in America, 1840-1930* (Syracuse, 2009), p. xvii.

24 US Census Return 1850 (NARA). The US census returns can also be accessed through www.ancestry.com.

25 Cormac Ó Gráda, 'The New York Irish in the 1850s: Locked in by Poverty?' in Centre for Economic Research Working Papers (University College Dublin, 2005). See www.ucs.ie/economics/research/papers/2005/WP05.17.pdf [accessed November, 2013].

26 Various communications with independent scholar William Powers (2002–2004).

27 US census returns for Rutland, Vermont, 1850 and 1860 (NARA).

28 Various communications with Roger Lamson, a descendant of Kelly emigrants from Ballykilcline (2002– 2004).

29 Annual reports to Rutland summarised the aid given to the local poor, naming the recipients and giving the amount of aid dispensed. A number of dedicated local historians and family genealogists transcribed the reports and posted them on the Rutland Rootsweb list-serv where I accessed them. See http://resources.rootsweb.ancestry.com/USA/VT/Rutland [accessed 12 September 2015].

30 Dunn, *Ballykilcline Rising*, p. 143.

31 Vincent E. Feeney, *Finnigans, Slaters and Stonepeggers: A History of the Irish in Vermont* (Bennington, Vermont, 2009), p. 114.

32 See Reilly, *Strokestown and the Great Irish Famine*.

33 John Burke to [no name given], 17 Feb. 1848 (NAI, Quit Rent Office, 67/06/07).

34 Dunn, *Ballykilcline Rising*, p. 62.

35 Fortunately for this study, the pastor recorded the maiden names of his congregation.

36 William Powers' communication. Also various communications with Anne Marie Bell, descendant of John and Sabina Brennan Hanley, Ballykilcline immigrants in Rutland (1999-2004).

37 Various communications with Thomas Breedlove about his extended family from Kilglass and Rutland, (2002-2004).

38 Communications with William Stewart regarding his wife's adoptive family, the Caveneys of Ballykilcline (2008).

39 Feeney, *A History of the Irish in Vermont*, pp. 115-7.

40 Hasia R. Diner, *Erin's Daughters in America: Irish Immigrant Women in the Nineteenth Century*, (Baltimore, 1983), pp. xiv, xv.

41 Ibid., p. xvi.

42 Communications with Patricia Padian (2003-2006); the author's own research, primarily 1988-2014, on her Riley family who were immigrants from Kilglass in Rhode Island and Connecticut.

43 Communications with Margaret Alberts, descendant of Mullera emigrants from Ballykilcline who settled in the American Midwest (2002-2004).

44 Various communications with Lynne Sisk, descendant of McCormicks and McDonnells of the Strokestown-Kilglass area whose descendants settled in Albany, New York (1999-2004).

45 1880 US census for Minnetonka, Minnesota (NARA).

46 Various communications with Thomas Breedlove (2002-2008).

47 Ciarán Reilly has identified a similar pattern in relation to the Strokestown emigrants, including a Mrs Tarpey who lived to be 107 years old in Long Island, New Jersey.

48 Communication with Kathleen Madden, a descendant of the McDermotts from Ballykilcline (various dates, 2001-2003).

49 This process involved clusters of people from a root country who follow each other to the same place where they can find advice and friends to help them relocate and integrate in a community that provides congenial relationships.

50 Diner, *Erin's Daughters in America*, p. 52.

51 Charles Mackay, 'Forty Years Recollections of Life, Literature and Public Affairs' in J. Gordon Read (ed.), *Through Liverpool to North America 1830-1907: A Selection of Emigrant Narratives* (Liverpool, Merseyside Maritime Museum, n.d.), pp. 22, 23.

52 *Report from the Select Committee of the House of Lords on Colonization from Ireland with Minutes of Evidence, Appendix and Index; Emigration 4.*

53 Peter D'Amico, descendant of emigrants from Ballykilcline, donated three hand-drawn family trees (sources not identified) of lines which began in Kilglass and whose descendants went to Rutland and Dorset, Vermont. After 'spot' verification of the data, copies were donated by the Ballykilcline Society to repositories in Rutland, Kilglass, Roscommon Town and Boston.

54 Diner, *Erin's Daughters in America*, p. xvi.

55 For a report on death of Mary Featherstone Prendergast see *Providence Journal*, 30 December 1943. My thanks to Ann Helen Riley and Helene Riley Damore for alerting me to this source.

56 Sarah Palin's lineage was posted on the internet by September 2008, soon after she became a candidate for vice president of the USA. Some well-known genealogists had posted some of her familial line on the internet, showing that her great-great grandfather, Michael Sheeran had indeed been born in Vermont. See http://freepagesgenealogy.rootsweb.ancestry.com/~battle/palin.htm [accessed 14 September 2008].

57 Michael may have had a brother named James in Rutland as well since a James Sheeran was listed along with an Ann Sheeran in the 1857 census of St Bridget's parish in West Rutland.

58 Personal communications between the author and the late Joseph Sheeran of Minnesota (2009-2010).

59 Not to slight Kilglass men here, Edward Sheeran, a Kilglass native who became a banking executive, was a Grand Marshal of New York City's St. Patrick's Day Parade in 1990, one of three Kilglass natives so honoured between 1987, when New York City labour leader John Lawe led the parade, and 1998 when Ireland's former Taoiseach Albert Reynolds T.D. stepped out as the parade marshal. This is a remarkable record for a single parish in rural Roscommon.

60 Again, for more on these individuals, see Reilly, *Strokestown and the Great Irish Famine*.

61 See for example several issues of *The Bonfire*, newsletter of the Ballykilcline Society (Alfred, Maine, Fall 2010, Fall 2011, Fall 2013, respectively). The *Burlington Free Press* in Vermont has covered developments in the case as events have warranted.

CHAPTER 8

1 Harvey Scribner, *Memoirs of Lucas County and the city of Toledo, from the earliest historical times down to the present* (Madison, 1910), p. 211.

2 Thomas J. Archdeacon, *Becoming American: An Ethnic History* (New York, 1983), p. xi.

3 Kathy Charmaz, *Constructing Grounded Theory: A Practical Guide through Qualitative Analysis* (London, 2006), p. 23. See also Clive Opie (ed.), *Doing Educational Research: A Guide to First-Time Researchers* (London, 2004), p. 93.

4 'US Federal Census Schedules for Toledo, Ohio, 1850'. See www.ancestry.com [accessed 1 June 2014].

5 David Ward, *Cities and Immigrants: A Geography of Change in Nineteenth-Century America* (New York, 1971), pp. 105–25; Kathleen Neils-Conzen, 'Immigrants, immigrant neighbourhoods and ethnic identity: historical issues' in *The Journal of American History*, lxvi (1979), pp. 603–15 & Howard P. Chudacoff, 'A new look at ethnic neighbourhoods: residential dispersion and the concept of visibility in a medium sized city' in *The Journal of American History*, lx (1973), pp. 76–93.

6 David Emmons, *The Butte Irish: Class and Ethnicity in an American Mining Town, 1875-1925* (Chicago, 1990), p. 73 & Tyler Anbinder, *Five Points: The 19th Century Neighbourhood that Invented Tap Dance, Stole Elections and became the World's Most Notorious Slum* (New York, 2001), pp. 72–105.

7 Timothy J. Meagher, *Inventing Irish American: Generation, Class and Ethnic Identity in a New England City, 1880-1928* (Notre Dame, 2001), pp. 123–31 & Joseph P. Blanchette, *The View from Shanty Pond: An Irish Immigrant's Look at Life in a New England Mill Town, 1875-1938* (Charlotte, 1999), pp. 25–34.

8 US Federal Census Abstract 1850–1900 for Toledo, Ohio. See www.census.gov/prod2/decennial [accessed 1 June 2014].

9 Ibid.

10 Ibid.

11 Ibid.

12 Ibid.

13 Ibid.

14 Ibid.

15 Ibid.

16 Ibid.

17 Scribner, *Memoirs of Lucas County and the city of Toledo*, p. 131.

18 Ibid., p. 132.

19 Ibid.

20 Ibid., p. 423.

21 Ibid.

22 'US Federal Census Schedules for Toledo, Ohio, 1900'.

23 Ibid.

24 Stephen J. Bartha, 'A history of immigrant groups in Toledo' (Unpublished MA thesis, Ohio State University, 1945), p. 23.

25 Dorothy Stafford, *The Men who made Toledo: A Series of Articles which Appeared in the Toledo Blade 1949-52* (Toledo, 1952), p. 49.

26 Laura Duffy Crank, 'Father Edward Hannin', in Seamus Metress and Molly Scheiver (eds), *The Irish in Toledo* (Toledo, 2005), pp. 92–9.

27 Ibid.

28 Seamus Metress and Molly Schiever (eds), *The Irish in Toledo* (Toledo, 2005), p. 47.

29 Crank, 'Father Edward Hannin,', p. 94.

30 Ibid., p. 95.

31 Ibid., p. 47.

32 Ibid., p. 97.

33 Ibid., p. 48.

34 'Passenger List for SS Winchester, 28 Sep. 1853', see www.ancestry.com [accessed 1 June 2014].

35 *New York Herald*, 26 October 1853.

36 1860 US Federal Census Record for Hugh Duffy and family, Napoleon, Henry Co. Ohio, see www.ancestrycom [accessed 1 June 2014].

37 1870 US Federal Census Record for the Ursuline Convent, Cherry St, Toledo, Ohio (www.ancestry.com) [accessed 1 June 2014].

38 Ibid., 1880 US Federal Census Record for the Ursuline Convent.

39 Ibid., 1900.

CHAPTER 9

1 A phrase used by Thomas Francis Meagher, see footnote 49. Thomas Francis Meagher to Kevin O'Doherty, Nov. 1849 (NYPL, Madigan Collection).

2 This argument was made by John Saville, *1848: The British State and the Chartist Movement* (Cambridge, 1990) and Christine Kinealy, *Repeal and Revolution: 1848 in Ireland* (Manchester, 2009).

3 The Treason Felony Act 1848 (11 & 12 Vict. c. 12).

4 The fact that all Catholics had been excluded from Mitchel's jury was noted in the Irish press and discussed in the British House of Commons. See *Nation*, 2 June 1848.

5 *Freeman's Journal*, 26 September 1848.

6 *Inverness Courier*, 3 October 1848.

7 *Freeman's Journal*, 24 October 1848. Other Young Irelanders, including Maurice Leyne, Denis Tyne, Thomas Stack, and James Orchard, were not found guilty of High Treason.

8 Ibid., 26 October 1848.

9 Richard D'Alton Williams, the more senior of the editors of the *Tribune*, was not transported. One of the charges was that the paper had referred to its 'war department' – interpreted as signaling they intended to wage war against the Queen. See *Nation*, 14 July 1848.

10 *Spectator*, 21 October 1848.

11 *Times*, 2 November 1848.

12 Ibid., 8 & 10 August 1848.

13 *Mercury* (Hobart), 5 October 1914.

14 *Launceston Examiner* (Tasmania), 22 May 1850.

15 During the voyage, O'Donoghue kept a journal, extracts of which were reported widely in the British and Irish press. See for example, *Reading Mercury*, 29 December 1849. John Martin and Kevin O'Doherty, who had both been sentenced to ten years transportation but had remained in Dublin jails, were sent to Van Diemen's Land at the same time, but on board the *Mount Stewart Elphinstone*, a convict ship. The ship stopped at Cork to pick up Martin and O'Doherty. It carried 232 male convicts. For more see www.historyaustralia.org.au/twconvic/Mount+Stewart+Elphinstone+1849 [accessed 12 May 2014].

16 Carmel Heaney, 'William Smith O'Brien in Van Diemen's Land' in *History Ireland* (Autumn, 1998), p. 29.

17 John Mitchel, *Jail Journal, or Five Years in British Prisons* (Dublin, 1914), p. 270.

18 *Launceston Examiner*, 25 September 1850.

19 Mitchel, *Jail Journal*, p. 268.

20 *Nation*, 18 January 1851.

21 Quoted in Kiernan, *Exiles*, pp. 53–5.

22 Heaney, 'William Smith O'Brien in Van Diemen's Land', p. 30.

23 *Freeman's Journal*, 1 May 1851.

24 O'Brien to William Dunne, 15 March 1851 (NLI, MS 10,515).

25 When he escaped, he left his shaggy dog, Brian, in Meagher's care, the two men becoming friends in captivity. See Mitchel, *Jail Journal*, p.273.

26 The latter included a poem entitled, 'To My Country', which he asked should not be made public until after his death: 'When foes upon me lour, In exiles darkest hour, Whilst I defy their power, Still pines my heart for thee. In loneliest solitude, by dastard spite pursued, Silenced but not subdued, Still pines my heart for thee' (NLI, Smith O'Brien Collection MS, 10515).

27 This new body was one-third nominated by the Crown and two-thirds elected.

28 Mitchel, *Jail Journal*, pp. 110–11.

29 Ibid., p. 157.

30 *Freeman's Journal*, 14 December 1849. See also Reports on Cape Town Anti-Convict Movement, BPP, 1849, xliii, (217) p.22.

31 See *Jail Journal*, p.190 & 195.

32 Ibid., pp. 176–7.

33 Ibid., p. 180.

34 Ibid., pp. 217–18.

35 A.F. Hattersley, *The Convict Crisis and the Growth of Unity* (Natal, 1965), p. 89.

36 Mitchel, *Jail Journal*, p.221.

37 George Grey, London, to Lord Clarendon, December 1849 (Bodleian Library, Clarendon Papers, Irish box 34).

38 *Irishman*, 19 May 1849.

39 Ibid.

40 Mitchell, *Jail Journal*, p. 259.

41 Ibid., p. 136. Mitchel admitted he had no money.

42 O'Donoghue to O'Doherty, 9 Nov. 1849, reprinted in T.J. Kiernan, *The Irish Exiles in Australia* (Dublin, 1954), p. 66.

43 *National Library of Australia News* (August, 2006).

44 Kiernan, *Exiles,* pp. 26–7.

45 Mitchel, *Jail Journal*, p. 274.

46 Meagher to O'Doherty, 14 July 1851 (NYPL, Madigan Collection).

47 Ibid. See also Meagher to O'Doherty [possibly December 1849] and 10 January 1850.

48 Ibid., Meagher to O'Doherty, November 1849.

49 Quoted in *Nation*, 25 January 1851.

50 Meagher to O'Doherty, 14 July 1851 (NYPL, Madigan Collection).

51 Ibid.

52 Ibid., [n.d. – early 1851].

53 Ibid.

54 Ibid. The ceremony was performed by the Revd Robert Willson, the first Catholic Bishop of Hobart. John Mitchel marked the occasion by creating a pencil drawing of the house in which the newly-weds were to live. In 1932, descendants of Katherine presented this picture to the National Museum in Dublin. See *Freeman's Journal* (Sydney), 15 November 1932.

55 Meagher to O'Doherty, 12 December 1849 (NYPL, Madigan Collection).

56 Ibid., 15 August 1851.

57 Meagher to O'Brien, 11 May 1850 (NLI, Smith O'Brien Papers, MS 4444 f. 2690).

58 Meagher to O'Doherty, 15 August 1851 (NYPL, Madigan Collection).

59 See Paul R. Wylie, *The Irish General: Thomas Francis Meagher* (Oklahoma, 2011), pp. 79–82.

60 O'Doherty to O'Brien, 27 May 1850 (NYPL, Madigan Collection).

61 Mitchel, *Jail Journal*, p. 249.

62 O'Brien to O'Doherty, 11 October 1852, Ibid., 29 December 1852; Ibid., O'Brien to Dunne, 15 March 1851 (NLI, Smith O'Brien Letters, MS 10515 (3).

63 Mitchel, *Jail Journal*, p. 254.

64 O'Doherty to O'Brien, 27 May 1850 (NLI, Smith O'Brien Papers, f.2691).

65 Meagher to O'Doherty, 12 December 1849 (NYPL, Madigan Collection).

66 Ibid., 30 June 1851.

67 *Reynolds's Newspaper*, 18 May 1851.

68 Blanche M. Touhill, *William Smith O'Brien and his Irish Revolutionary Companions in Penal Exile* (Missouri, 1981).

69 Meagher to O'Doherty [nd - early 1851?] (NYPL, Madigan Collection).

70 *Inverness Courier,* 26 September 1848.

71 Touhill, *William Smith O'Brien,* p. 124.

72 His surname was spelled in a number of ways, including O'Donoghoe and O'Donohoe.

73 *Leeds Intelligencer*, 21 October 1848.

74 *Northern Star*, 28 July 1849.

75 O'Donoghue to O'Brien, 2 May 1848 (NLI, Smith O'Brien Letters, MS 442, f.2430).

76 Mitchel, *Jail Journal*, p. 227.

77 *Nation*, 31 August 1850.

78 Lindsay, 'Fanatic Heart'.

79 Davis, *Young Ireland*, p. 204.

80 In this case, working on a treadmill. See O'Donoghoe [*sic*] Papers, NLI, MS 770.

81 *Manchester Courier and Lancashire General Advertiser*, 16 July 1853.

82 *Stamford Mercury*, 19 August 1853.

83 The *Herald*'s account was, in turn, reprinted in British papers, including *Reynolds's Newspaper*, 14 August 1853. Throughout, his name is rendered as 'O'Donoghue'.

84 *Stamford Mercury*, 19 August 1853.

85 *New York Times*, 1 February 1854.

86 Ibid.

87 Also given as McManus.

88 Ibid., 3 April 1861.

89 Ibid.

90 Ibid., 15 September 1861.

91 Louis Bisceglia, 'The Fenian Funeral of Terence Bellew McManus' in *Éire-Ireland*, vol. 14, no. 3 (Fall, 1979), pp. 54–5.

92 *New York Times*, 19 October 1861.

93 Ibid.

94 Ibid., 21 November 1861.

95 In July 1854, he received $45 for an article published in the *Australasian*. See Meagher to Mr Didd, 3 July 1855 (NYPL, Madigan Collection).

96 Ibid., Meagher to John Fresner, 22 December 1853 (NYPL, Madigan Collection).

97 *New York Times*, 5 September 1855.

98 Dillon, *Life of Mitchel*, pp. 50–51.

99 *Leeds Times*, 29 October 1853.

100 *Mercury* (Hobart), 19 May 1937.

101 *Cork Examiner*, 9 November 1853.

102 Wylie, *The Irish General*, pp. 90–91.

103 *Leeds Times*, 29 October 1853.

104 Wylie, *The Irish General*, pp. 96–7. They had no children. Meagher's second son lived with his parents in Ireland. Following Meagher's death, Elizabeth brought him to America.

105 W.F. Lyons, *Brigadier General T.F. Meagher; His Political and Military Career, with Selections from his Speeches and Writings* (Glasgow, 1871), p. 58.

106 Ibid., p. 80.

107 Ibid., p. 82.

108 Ibid., pp. 32–5.

109 Meagher, Virginia City, Montana, to his father, 15 June 1867 (NYPL, Madigan Collection).

110 Ibid.

111 *New York Sun*, 4 July 1867.

112 *New York Times*, 8 July 1867.

113 *Irish People*, 13 July 1867.

114 Ibid., 20 July, 3 August 1867.

115 *Cork Examiner*, 28 August 1867.

116 J. Mitchel, *Shamrock*, vol. 4 (July 1867).

117 For example, on 19 October 1867 he commenced publishing the *Irish Citizen*,

of which he was both proprietor and editor.

118 The *Citizen*, 9 September 1854.

119 *Cork Examiner*, 6 February 1854.

120 *New York Times*, 2 January 1855.

121 John Mitchel to Horace Greeley, 22 October 1858 (NYPL, Horace Greeley Papers).

122 *New York Times*, 24 May 1875.

123 Griffith, preface to 1914 edition of Mitchel, *Jail Journal*, p. 370.

124 For more on the New York Directory see Kinealy, *Repeal and Revolution*.

125 Martin to Eva, 25 September 1862 (NLI, MS 10,520).

126 *New York Times*, 17 March 1867.

127 P.A. Sillard, *The Life of John Mitchel* (Dublin, 1908), pp. 258–60.

128 *New York Times*, 5 April 1875.

129 'Women of Young Ireland', pp. 46–7 (NLI, MS 10,906).

130 *New York Times*, 21 April 1875.

131 Ibid., 24 May 1875.

132 John Mitchel, *The Last Conquest of Ireland (Perhaps)* (Glasgow, 1882), pp. xxvi-xxvii.

133 *Morning News*, 2 October 1863.

134 *New York Times*, 25 May 1859.

135 Ibid., 6 May 1859.

136 *New York Times*, 8 December 1859.

137 Ibid., 4 November 1861.

138 O'Brien to Peel, 22 February 1862 (Trinity College Dublin, Dillon Papers, MS 6457 (f.337)).

139 Ibid., O'Brien to Dillon, (f. 338), 28 February 1862.

140 *Dublin Evening Mail*, 25 June 1864.

141 *New York Times*, 3 July 1864.

142 *Liverpool Mercury*, 22 June 1864.

143 *Dublin Evening Mail*, 25 June 1864.

144 *Cork Examiner*, 10 December 1864.

145 *New York Times*, 17 November 1869.

146 Martin to Eva, 18 September 1865 (NLI, MS 10,520).

147 Ibid., Martin to Eva, 25 September 1852.

148 William Dillon, *Life of John Mitchel*, 2 vols (London, 1888), ii, p.267.

149 *New York Times*, 17 November 1869.

150 *Sheffield Daily Telegraph*, 19 March 1868.

151 Charles Gavan Duffy, *Four Years of Irish History, 1845-1849* (London and Melbourne, 1883), p. 250.

152 Michael Hurst 'Ireland and Ballot Act of 1872' in *The Historical Journal*, vol. 8, no. 3 (1965), pp. 326–35.

153 *South Australian Advertiser* (Adelaide), 29 June 1885.

154 *Brisbane Courier*, 7 January 1886.

155 *Freeman's Journal* (Sydney), 28 November 1886.

156 See www.slwa.wa.gov.au/find/eresources/a2z/A/australian_dictionary_of_biography [accessed 10 October 2012].

157 *Freeman's Journal* (Sydney), 22 July 1905.

158 Michael Cavanagh, *Memoirs of Gen. Thomas Francis Meagher: Comprising the Leading Events of His Career Chronologically Arranged, with Selections from His Speeches, Lectures and Miscellaneous Writings, Including Personal Reminiscences* (Worcester, 1892), p. 164.

CHAPTER 10

1 Kevin Whelan, 'Pre and post-Famine landscape change' in Cathal Póirtóir (ed.), *The Great Irish Famine (The Thomas Davis Lecture Series)* (Cork, 1995), pp. 19–34.

2 'Board's Immigrant List', *Thetis*, arrived Sydney 20 May 1850 (State Records of New South Wales, 4/4919).

3 See *Ballan Times* (Victoria), 30 September 1915.

4 For details of the assisted passage system to mid-nineteenth-century New South Wales, see Richard E. Reid, *Farewell my Children: Irish Assisted Emigration to Australia, 1848-1870* (Spit Junction, 2011).

5 Quoted in *Clare Champion*, 4 August 2006.

6 *Limerick Chronicle*, 6 January 1847.

7 *Evening Packet*, 4 June 1849.

8 Quoted in C.H. Currey, *The Irish at Eureka* (Sydney, 1954), p.57.

9 *Ballan Times* (Victoria), 30 September 1915.

10 For the Donegal Relief Fund see Reid, *Farewell my Children*, pp. 172–96.

11 For an outline of Irish/Australian support of causes back in Ireland between 1870 and First World War see Patrick O'Farrell, *The Irish in Australia* (Sydney, 1987), pp. 221–51.

12 Census of New South Wales, 1846, in *Supplement to the New South Swales Government Gazette*, 3 November 1846, p.54.

13 *Sydney Gazette and Colonial Advertiser*, 5 March 1840.

14 'Entitlement Certificates', Peter and Anne Reilly, *Margaret*, arrived Sydney 28 March 1842 (State Records of New South Wales, 4/4875).

15 *Sydney Morning Herald*, 25 July 1846.

16 Peter Reilly's letter in published pamphlet, *Emigration and Transportation Relatively Considered, in a Letter Dedicated by Permission, to Earl Grey, by Mrs Chisholm* (London, 1847), pp. 44-6.

17 Margaret Kiddle, *Caroline Chisholm* (Melbourne, 1969).

18 Interestingly, Peter's child was recorded by Chisholm as a 'son'. See 'Roll of Immigrants who have left Children in Europe through their inability to pay for their Passage', attached to letter, Caroline Chisholm to the Colonial Secretary, New South Wales, 18 February 1846, 46/1457 (State Records of New South Wales, 4/2929).

19 *Morning Chronicle*, 8 April 1846.

20 *Emigration and Transportation Relatively Considered*, p.45.

21 Joseph Fowles described the sheds in George Street as follows: 'The market sheds on the opposite side of the street, were erected about seventeen years since, they consist of four separate buildings, each about two hundred feet long, by thirty in width, and divided into stalls for the sale of the various kinds of produce; the first in York-street is used for the sale of meat, poultry, eggs, butter, cheese, etc., and the next for fruit and vegetables, those on the side of George–street, for wholesale dealers.' See John Fowles, Sydney in 1848 (Sydney, 1848), p.68.

22 *Bells Life in Sydney and Sporting Review*, 5 September 1846. For Henry McDermott see entry in *Australian Dictionary of Biography*, vol. 2 (Melbourne, 1979), pp. 161-2.

23 For Fr John McEncroe see entry in *Australian Dictionary of Biography*, vol. 2 (Melbourne, 1979), pp.165-6.

24 *Bell's Life in Sydney and Sporting Review*, 5 September 1846.

25 Between 1848 and 1850, 4,114 orphan girls from workhouses all over Ireland went as 'assisted emigrants' to Australia. For this story see Trevor McClaughlin, *Barefoot and Pregnant? Irish Famine Orphans in Australia* (Melbourne, 1991) and Richard Reid and Cheryl Mongan, '*A Decent Set of Girls': The Irish Famine Orphans of the Thomas Arbuthnot, 1849-1850* (Yass, 1996).

26 R.B. Madgwick, *Immigration into Eastern Australia, 1788-1851* (Sydney, 1969), p.234.

27 *Cornwell Chronicle* (Launceston), 10 February 1847.

28 *Launceston Examiner*, 10 February 1847.

29 *Sydney Morning Herald*, 10 September 1846.

30 See for example amount collected from named individuals in Braidwood, New South Wales, see *Sydney Morning Herald*, 25 September 1846.

31 Ibid., 17 September 1846.

32 See Patrick O'Farrell, 'Lost in Transit: Australian reaction to the Irish and Scots Famines, 1845–1850' in Patrick O'Sullivan (ed.), *The Meaning of the Famine*, vol. 6 in *The Irish World Wide* series (London and Washington, 1997), pp. 126–40. This was a pioneering essay on this topic and deserves to be better known.

33 *Sydney Chronicle*, 22 May 1847.

34 Ibid., 31 July 1847.

35 'Board's Immigrant List', *Coldstream*, arrived Sydney 18 January 1863 (State Records of New South Wales, 4/4982).

36 'Entitlement Certificate', Philip Spencer, *Glenswilly*, arrived Sydney 11 March 1841 (State Records of New South Wales, 4/4869).

37 See W.E. Vaughan and A.J. Fitzpatrick (eds), *Irish Historical Statistics* (Dublin, 1978), p. 10.

38 See Richard Reid, 'Aspects of Irish assisted emigration to New South Wales, 1848–1870, , 2 vols, PhD Thesis, Australian National University, Canberra).

39 Reid, *Farewell my Children*, pp. 117–39.

40 'Agent's Immigrant List', *Chance*, arrived Sydney 13 July 1860 (State Records of New South Wales, 4/4796).

41 For the baptisms of the Dwyer children see the Clonoulty Parish register, Cashel Diocesan Archives, Thurles, County Tipperary; 'Agent's Immigrant List'. The *Queen Bee*, arrived Sydney 31 March 1861 (State Records of New South Wales, 4/4796). Nine of the children were born in Ballagh.

42 Entry for Edmund Dwyer (spelt Edmond in valuation), office, yards and forge, 'House Book', 'Town of Ballagh' valued by William Ryan on 31 May 1848, 'House Book' Parish of Clonoulty, County Tipperary (National Archives of Ireland).

43 The last of the family, Mary, born in Ballagh in 1857, died in Goulburn in 1938, aged 85. See *The Burrowa News*, 13 May 1938.

44 Entry for Margaret Kane 'House Book', 'Townland of Ballagh', valued by James Johnstone on 11 February 1848 (National Archives of Ireland).

45 See http://landedestates.nuigalway.ie/LandedEstates [accessed 14 October 2015].

46 See www.templehouse.ie/history [accessed 14 October 2015].

47 *Freeman's Journal*, 22 August 1850.

48 James S. Donnelly Jnr, 'Landlords and Tenants' in W.E. Vaughan (ed.), *A New History of Ireland: Ireland Under the Union, 1801-1870*, vol. 5 (Oxford, 2001), p. 338.

49 *Burrowa News*, 11 March 1876.

50 Ibid., 13 July 1906.

51 'Board's Immigrant List', *Switzerland*, arrived Sydney, 20 June 1854 (State Records of New South Wales, 4/4942).

52 Quoted in Kevin Whelan 'The Famine and Post Famine Adjustment' in

William Nolan (ed.), *The Shaping of Ireland: The Geographical Perspective* (Cork, 1986), p.164.

CHAPTER 11

1 See Ciarán Reilly, *Strokestown and the Great Irish Famine* (Dublin, 2014) and Stephen J. Campbell, *The Great Irish Famine: Words and Images from the Famine Museum Strokestown Park, County Roscommon* (Strokestown, 1994).

2 A comprehensive account of Famine memorials compiled by Emily Mark-Fitzgerald can be seen at http://irishfaminememorials.com/about [accessed 1 November 2015]. For a more in-depth analysis of these memorials see Fitzgerald, *Commemorating the Irish Famine: Monument and Memory* (Liverpool, 2013).

3 Other workhouses were demolished or re-invented as county hospitals, healthcare facilities or readapted as business premises, such as at Celbridge, County Kildare, which is occupied by a paint manufacturing company. Other workhouses which survive, such as Birr, have local historical societies and individuals working to save them from demolition.

4 See for example Michael O'Gorman, *A Pride of Paper Tigers: A History of the Great Hunger in the Scariff Workhouse Union from 1839 to 1853* (Clare, 1994); Danny Cusack (ed.), *The Great Famine in County Meath* (Navan, 1996); Brege McCusker, *Lowtherstown Workhouse* (Irvinestown, 1997) and Daniel Grace, *The Great Famine in Nenagh Poor Law Union Co. Tipperary* (Nenagh, 2000).

5 See for example two of the more recent studies: Anthony Begley, *From Ballyshannon to Australia: Memories of Famine Orphan Girls* (Ballyshannon, 2014) and Kay Maloney Caball, *The Kerry Girls: Emigration and the Earl Grey Scheme* (Dublin, 2014).

6 Trevor McClaughlin, *Barefoot and Pregnant? Irish Famine Orphans in Australia* (Melbourne, 1991); Richard Reid & Cheryl Mongan, *'A Decent Set of Girls': The Irish Famine Orphans of the 'Thomas Arbuthnot' 1849-1859* (Yass, 1996).

7 For example see biographies of first and second convict fleet convicts, crew and military in Molly Gillen, *The Founders of Australia: A Biographical Dictionary of the First Fleet* (Sydney, 1989) and Michael Flynn, *The Second Fleet: Britain's Grim Convict Armada of 1790* (Sydney, 1993).

8 For more see Peter Mayberry, 'Irish Convicts to New South Wales, 1788–1849' see www.members.pcug.org.au/~ppmay/cgi-bin/irish/irish.cgi [accessed 15 October 2015]. It is worth noting that these Irish convicts were tried in all parts of England, Ireland, Scotland and Wales as well as India, Ceylon, South Africa, Gibraltar and Canada, places where many Irishmen served in the army.

9 'Papers connected with the appropriation of the fifty free girls by the *Palambam*, July 1831' (SRNSW, 4/211.2).

10 Perry McIntyre, *Free Passage: The Reunion of Irish Convicts and their families in Australia, 1788-1852* (Dublin, 2010) p. 9, 74 & 115.

11 Elizabeth Rushen & Perry McIntyre, *Fair Game: Australia's First Immigrant Women* (Melbourne, 2010).

12 Elizabeth Rushen, *Single & Free: Female Migration to Australia, 1833-1837* (Melbourne, 2003) & *Colonial Duchesses: The Migration of Irish Women to New South Wales before the Great Famine* (Melbourne, 2014).

13 Richard Reid, *Farewell my Children: Irish Assisted Emigration to Australia 1848-1870* (Australia, 2011), pp. 140–1.

14 Cashel Poor Law Guardian Minutes, 8 February 1849 (Tipperary County Library, BG/52/A9).

15 Reid, *Farwell my Children*, p.42. All the CLEC emigrants to Sydney from Ireland between 1848 and 1870 had to cross the Irish Sea on steamers and did so as deck passengers since the ships dispatched to the colony sailed only from Plymouth, Liverpool, Southampton or London.

16 For more on the *Arbuthnot* see Reid & Mongan, *'A Decent Set of Girls'*.

17 'Certificate of Final Departure, *Elgin* which sailed from Plymouth on 31 May 1849' (South Australian Archives, 49/17).

18 McClaughlin, *Barefoot and Pregnant?* ii, pp. 397–402.

19 See www.irishfaminememorial.org [accessed 6 November 2015].

20 Shipping list *Inchinnan*, arrived Sydney, 13 February 1849 (SRNSW, 4/4909); Shipping list *Digby*, arrived Sydney, 2 April 1849 (SRNSW, 4/4908) and Convict Indent, *Eliza*, sailed from Cork, 10 May 1832 (SRNSW 4/4017).

21 Immigration Deposit Journals 1853 (SRNSW, 4/4576) and shipping list *Sabrina* (SRNSW 4/4940).

22 Trevor McClaughlin correspondence with Pat Astill, a descendant, 13 May 1986.

23 Immigration Board's list of *Thomas Arbuthnot* (SRNSW, 4/4786).

24 Governor FitzRoy's Despatch No. 127 of 1850 (Mitchell Library, Sydney, A1256 CY2056).

25 Poor Law Guardian Minute Book, Rathdrum, 13 October 1849 (Wicklow County Council Archives).

26 Ibid.

27 Immigration Board's list of *Lismoyne* (SRNSW, 4/4786). Aged 37, she was the daughter of Isaac and James Markes/Marks (both dead), while her husband, John Stephens, was living in Van Diemen's Land.

28 Convict Reference Files, CON/33/1-85/00191/S (Archives of Tasmania).

29 Eliza and John Stephens had a daughter, Hannah Eliza, born in Hobart in May 1851, indicating that Eliza and probably her daughters left Sydney for that

colony soon after the arrival of the *Thomas Arbuthnot* on 9 August 1849.

30 *Report from the Select Committee on Irish Female Immigrants, Proceedings of the Committee and Minutes of Evidence*, NSW Legislative Assembly, 2 February 1859, 'Return of Cases of Orphan Female Apprentices whose Indentures were cancelled by the Court of Petty Sessions at the Water Police Office', Appendix J [here after Appendix J].

31 South Dublin Workhouse registers (NAI, BG79/G/3); Appendix J; NSW Marriage Records, 1850 (NSW State Archives, Kingswood, 774/36); correspondence with descendants.

32 See Appendix J. See also *Sydney Commercial Directory for the year 1851*.

33 See NSW marriage & birth register, 1851–57 (NSW State Archives, Kingswood).

34 NSW Marriage Records, 1858 (NSW State Archives, Kingswood, 1264).

35 Darlinghurst Gaol Photographic Register (SRNSW, NRS 2138, 3/14030).

36 *Sydney Morning Herald*, 19 December 1887.

37 Wesleyan Methodist records, film 33, volume 305 (Mitchell Library, Sydney). This writer has consulted these records which were microfilmed by Society of Australian Genealogists and which can be viewed on Biographical Database of Australia, www.bda-online.org.au [accessed 6 March 2015].

38 *Souvenir Booklet to Mark the Unveiling of the Australian Monument to the Great Irish Famine 1845-1848*, 28 August 1999.

CHAPTER 12

1 Thomas Quinn, 'Une Voix d'Irlande', in *Premier Congrès de La Langue Français au Canada. Québec 24-30 June 1912* (Québec, 1913), pp. 227–232. All translations are my own.

2 Thomas Quinn, 'Une Voix d'Irlande', pp. 229–230.

3 Jason King, 'Remembering Famine Orphans: The Transmission of Famine Memory Between Ireland and Quebec' in Christian Noack, Lindsay Jannsen, and Vincent Comerford (eds), *Holodomor and Gorta Mór: Histories, Memories and Representations of Famine in Ukraine and Ireland* (London, 2012), pp. 115– 44.

4 'Speech by the Taoiseach, Mr. Enda Kenny, T.D. at the National Famine Commemoration, Strokestown, County Roscommon, 11 May 2014'. (www.ahg.gov.ie/en/NationalFamineCommemoration2014/Taoiseach's%20 Speech%20-%20NFC%202014.pdf) [accessed 31 July 2014].

5 *Irish Independent*, 22 July 2013.

6 Quinn, 'Une Voix d'Irlande', pp. 228–229.

7 *Emigration Vessels to Quebec, 1847*, No. 8, '*Return of passenger ships arrived at the Port of Quebec in the season of 1847*', *British Parliamentary Papers*, vol. 17, Sessions

1847–1848, pp. 471–7.

8 Marianna O'Gallagher, 'The Orphans of Grosse Île: Canada and the adoption of Irish Famine Orphans, 1847–48', in Patrick O'Sullivan (ed.), *The Irish World Wide: The Meaning of the Famine*, (5 vols, London and Washington, 1997), iv, 90.

9 Thomas Quinn, 'Une Voix d'Irlande', p. 229.

10 *Roscommon Herald*, 23 May 1931. I am grateful to Mike Lennon for this reference.

11 Marianna O'Gallagher, 'The Orphans of Grosse Île', p. 91.

12 Richmond County Historical Society, *The Tread of Pioneers: Annals of Richmond County and Vicinity* (2 vols, Richmond, Quebec, 1968), ii, 39.

13 Marianna O'Gallagher and Rose Masson Dompierre, *Eyewitness Grosse Isle 1847* (Ste. Foy, Quebec, 1995), p. 408.

14 'Second Parish Priest of Richmond 1864–1914', n.d. (Richmond County Historical Society, Melbourne, Quebec, Hayes Papers, 03-G-F- 26.62).

15 King, 'Remembering Famine Orphans', pp. 128–135.

16 'Second Parish Priest of Richmond 1864–1914', n.d. (Richmond County Historical Society, Melbourne, Quebec, Hayes Papers, 03-G-F- 26.62).

17 Garth Stevenson, *Parallel Paths: The development of Nationalism in Ireland and Quebec* (Montreal and Kingston, 2006), pp. 95–134.

18 *The Vindicator*, 20 March 1835.

19 *True Witness and Catholic Chronicle*, 17 August 1860.

20 Ibid.

21 'Monsieur L'abbé Thomas Quinn, 1841–1923', Soeurs Grises de Montréal, Prov. Nicolet, Québec, Archives, Métairie St. Joseph, Nicolet (Chroniques), 1895–1923, vol. 1, pp. 58–60.

22 Peter Southam, *Irish Settlement and National Identity in the Lower St. Francis Valley* (Quebec, 2012), pp. 94–5.

23 Ibid., p. 151.

24 *Richmond Times*, 12 March 1915.

25 Nick Fonda, *Roads to Richmond* (Montreal, 2010), ebook location 2278.

26 King, 'Remembering Famine Orphans', pp. 128–40.

27 *The Pilot*, 22. July 1847.

28 *True Witness and Catholic Chronicle*, 5 August 1859.

29 King, 'Remembering Famine Orphans', pp. 130–133. See also Jason King, 'L'historiographie irlando-québécoise: Conflits et conciliations entre Canadiens français et Irlandais' in *Bulletin d'histoire politique du Québec*, 18:3 (2010), pp. 13–36.

30 Pastoral Letter of November 21, 1866. Reprinted in Anon, *The Case of St. Patrick's Congregation as to the erection of a new canonical parish of St. Patrick's,*

Montreal, published by order of the committee of the congregation (Montreal, 1866), p. 12.

31 Patrick Dowd, *Objections and Remonstrances against the Dismemberment of the Ancient Parish of Montreal, and the Proposed Erections of the Parishes of St. James and St. Patricks, made at Meetings held in September and November, 1866* (Montreal, 1867), pp. 14–15.

32 J.J. Curran, *Golden Jubilee of St. Patrick's Orphan Asylum* (Montreal, 1902), pp. 41–3.

33 Garth Stevenson, *Parallel Paths*, p. 196.

34 Robert Choquette, *Language and Religion: A History of English-French Conflict in Ontario* (Ottawa, 1975), p. 254.

35 Mark McGowan, *The Waning of the Green: Catholics, the Irish, and identity in Toronto, 1887-1922* (Montreal and Kingston, 1999), p. 244.

36 Cited in Robert Choquette, *Language and Religion*, p. 164.

37 Cited in Yvan Lamonde, *The Social History of Ideas in Quebec, 1760-1896* (Montreal and Kingston, 2013), p. 394.

38 See Jason King, 'The Genealogy of *Famine Diary* in Ireland and Quebec: Ireland's Famine migration in historical fiction, historiography, and memory' in *Éire-Ireland: A Journal of Irish Studies*, 47: 1 & 2 (2012), pp. 45–69.

39 Robert Sellar, *The Tragedy of Quebec: The Expulsion of its Protestant Farmers* (Toronto, 1974), p. 304.

40 Choquette, *Language and Religion*, p. 219.

41 Quinn, 'Une Voix d'Irlande', pp. 227–8.

42 Ibid., pp. 229–30.

43 Thomas Quinn, 'Une Voix d'Irlande', p. 232.

44 See Ciarán Reilly, *Strokestown and the Great Irish Famine* (Dublin, 2014).

45 Colin McMahon, 'Recrimination and Reconciliation: Great Famine Memory in Liverpool and Montreal at the Turn of the Twentieth Century' in *Atlantic Studies: Global Currents*, 11:3 (2014), pp. 347–349.

46 *Irish Independent*, 22 July 2013.

47 'Second Parish Priest of Richmond 1864–1914', n.d. (Richmond County Historical Society, Melbourne, Quebec, Hayes Papers, 03-G-F- 26.62).

48 *Roscommon Herald*, 23 May 1931.

49 'Jacket once belonging to [Thomas] Quinn, a 6 year old Irish Famine orphan', 1847, Textile, Archives du Séminaire de Nicolet, 1990.21.226.1-32; 'Being Irish O'Quebec' (www.mccord-museum.qc.ca/pdf/exhibits/Texte_Irish_EN.pdf) [accessed 31 July 2014].

CHAPTER 13

1 The author thanks Pádraig Ó Siadhail, D'Arcy McGee Chair of Irish Studies, St Mary's University, Halifax, Nova Scotia for assistance with the Irish texts; Jerry White, Canada Research Chair in European Studies, Dalhousie University, Halifax, Nova Scotia, for the inspiration and Helen McDonald for editorial expertise.

2 J.A. Jordan, *The Grosse Île Tragedy and the Monument to the Irish Famine Victims 1847*, (Quebec, 1909), p. 12.

3 Ibid., p. 45.

4 Ibid., p. 13.

5 See Marianna O'Gallagher's speech, 'The Genesis of the Celtic Cross at Grosse Île', given at the AOH centenary celebration of the unveiling of the Celtic cross at Grosse Île, 15 August 2009 and available at www.irelandmonumentvancouver.com/side-3-the-100-names/the-100-names/jeremiah-gallagher [accessed 27 June 2012].

6 Marianna O'Gallagher, *Grosse Île: Gateway to Canada 1832-1937* (Quebec, 1984), p. 86.

7 D.C. Lyne and Peter M. Toner, 'Fenianism in Canada 1874-84' in *Studia Hibernica*, no. 12 (1972), p. 50.

8 O'Gallagher, 'Genesis', op. cit.

9 Ibid., p. 50.

10 Marianna O'Gallagher, 'The Irish in Quebec', in R. O'Driscoll & L. Reynolds (eds), *The Untold Story: The Irish in Canada* (Toronto, 1988), p. 260.

11 The lists were compiled from ibid., passim; from Peter M. Toner, 'The Home Rule League in Canada: Fortunes, Fenians and Failure' in *Canadian Journal of Irish Studies*, xv, 1 (1989); from Marianna O'Gallagher's recollections (personal communication, July 1995) and her notes on her grandfather and on the genesis of the Celtic cross.

12 Lyne & Toner, 'Fenianism in Canada', pp. 47-8.

13 Toner, 'The Home Rule League in Canada', p. 10.

14 Lyne & Toner, 'Fenianism in Canada', p. 50.

15 David A. Wilson, 'The Fenian World of Jeremiah Gallagher', paper delivered at the 'Marianna O'Gallagher Memorial Lecture', at the Canadian Association for Irish Studies, Halifax, NS, May 2015. The author thanks Professor Wilson for this reference.

16 O'Gallagher, 'Jeremiah Gallagher'.

17 Toner, 'The Home Rule League', p. 10.

18 O'Gallagher, 'Jeremiah Gallagher', op. cit.

19 W. O'Brien & D. Ryan (eds), *Devoy's Post Bag* (Dublin, nd), v. II, p. 358.

20 See www.aoh.com/aoh-history/ [accessed 12 January 2013].

21 O'Gallagher, 'Genesis'.

22 Jordan, *The Grosse Île Tragedy,* pp. 84–5.

23 Ibid., p. 89.

24 Ibid., p. 97 (Translation, with many thanks, by Pádraig Ó Siadhail).

25 O'Gallagher, 'Genesis'.

26 Ireland Fund of Canada, *Journal* (1992), p. 14.

27 'Address by the President of Ireland, Mary Robinson, at Grosse Île on 21st August, 1994', pp. 1–2. See (www.president.ie/en/media-library/speeches) [accessed 14 October 2015].

28 Ibid.

29 Ibid., p. 3.

30 Canadian Association for Irish Studies, *Newsletter* (Fall, 2010), p. 10.

31 Parks Canada, *Grosse Île: Proposed Development Concept* (March, 1992), p. 62.

32 See for example Michael Quigley, 'Grosse Île: Canada's Island Famine Memorial' in *History Ireland* (Summer 1997), pp. 22-26.

33 Cited by Brendan Landers, 'The Ghosts of Grosse Île' in *Irish America* (November-December 1994). See also www.brendanlanders.ie/index.php/journalism/tales-of-the-diaspora/the-ghosts-of-grosse-ile [accessed 14 October 2015].

34 Marianna O'Gallagher, '100th Anniversary of Celtic Cross at Grosse Île' in *Irish America* (October-November 2009).

Index